COMMUNITY IN THE AME S0-AVP-090

DATE DUE

EDITED BY STEPHEN TCHUDI

Community in the American West

PUBLISHED BY
THE NEVADA HUMANITIES COMMITTEE
RENO AND LAS VEGAS

A HALCYON IMPRINT

The Nevada Humanities Committee logo is derived from a petroglyph representing a human hand at Rattlesnake Well, Mineral County, Nevada, carved ca. AD 800-1200.

Community in the American West is published by the Nevada Humanities Committee, 1034 Sierra Street, Reno, Nevada 89503 U.S.A.

ISBN 1-890591-03-3

Cover design: Carrie Nelson House

Design and typography: Halcyon Imprints of Nevada

As the ancient bird,
the halcyon,
calmed the waters
in the face of winter gales,
so can the humanities
calm our fears and make safe
our voyage and our young.

The Halcyon series is published annually by the Nevada Humanities Committee through a grant from the National Endowment for the Humanities. *Community in the American West* is volume #21.

This volume is dedicated to the memory of Dr. Bill Abrams, September 16, 1932—February 12, 1998. His poem, "For Those Carrying On Their Business in Front of Supermarkets," appears on pages 79-80.

Halcyon
Volume #21
Community in the American West

Editor
Stephen Tchudi
University of Nevada, Reno

Associate Editors
Brad Lucas
Susanne Bentley
University of Nevada, Reno

Executive Director
Nevada Humanities Committee
Judith K. Winzeler

CONTENTS

Editor's Note, xi
Stephen Tchudi

RE–VISIONING COMMUNITY

Mending Babel's Walls, 3
Asao B. Inoue

Red River Valley, 29
Crag Hill

Reconstructing Memory
in the American West, 31
Thelma Shinn Richard

Wendover, 55
Shaun T. Griffin

Building and Subverting Community
in the New American West, 57
A. Chiaviello

For Those Carrying On Their Business
in Front of Supermarkets, 79
Bill Abrams

Walt Disney vs. Wallace Stegner:
Community Leadership and Masculine Myths, 81
Eric Bateman

DIVERSITY AND COMMUNITY

Community on the Comstock:
Cliché, Stereotype, and Reality, 93
Ronald M. James

American Canyon: A Chinese Village
David Valentine, 107

African American Communities on the Western Frontier, 131
Roger D. Hardaway

Nevada's Pioneer Portuguese Communities, 147
Donald Warrin

Between Feast and Famine:
Coal Communities in the American West, 175
Eric Margolis

Catholics in Nevada, 201
Kevin Rafferty

The Age of Institutions:
Basques in the U.S., 231
Carmelo Urza

EVOLVING WESTERN COMMUNITIES

Are You Sure You Belong?, 255
Kevin Hearle

Four Poems on Southwestern Cities, 265
Steven Schroder

"A Child Goes Forth," 269
The Unnamed Writers' Group

Night at the West Edge of
Grand Forks, North Dakota, 299
Bill Stobb

Prisons and Economic Diversification, 301
Marie Boutté

Watering Los Angeles, 321
I-5 at 3:30 PM
Marsha Rogers

Barthell Little Chief:
Kiowa Visionary Artist, 323
Michael Flanigan

The Strange Career
of the American Hobo, 337
Todd DePastino

Las Vegas: Community as
Real Life Virtual Reality, 359
Felicia Florine Campbell

At the Enchanted Palace, 369
Stephen Liu

Sim(ulacrum) City, 371
ShaunAnne Tangney

EDITOR'S NOTE

In the Introduction to his *Portable Western Reader*, writer/scholar William Kittredge argues that "Western lives, for a long time, as understood by outlanders, swirled by inside pretty much pure make-believe" (xvi). According to Kittredge, the major source of information about life in the West came through "'the Western,' a morality play about the invasion and conquest of the wilderness and native savagery which was taken to be the essence of North America" (xvi). The Western, he claims, is "a story which details the triumph of European people and their laws (read civility and community) in conflict with both wild indifferent nature and bad men . . . " (xvi). Kittredge calls for a demythologizing of the West, and that is precisely what this collection of essays and poems on *Community in the American West* aims to do.

Ironically, the selection of this theme as a book in the *Halcyon* series was prompted by the remarks, not of an outlander, but of an insider, one who has been instrumental in defining, understanding, and promoting the real West. In his essay, "A Sense of Place," Wallace Stegner declares flatly that because of its transient inhabitants, the West is lacking in community:

> Migratoriness has its dangers, unless it is the traditional, seasonal, social migratoriness of the shepherds, or of the academic tribes who every June leave Cambridge or New Haven for summer places in Vermont, and every September return to their winter range. Complete independence, absolute freedom of movement, are exhilarating for a time but may not wear well. That romantic atavist we sometimes dream of being, who lives alone in a western or artic wilderness, playing Natty Bumppo and listening to the loons

and living on moose meat and moving on if people
come within a hundred miles, is a very American figure but he is not a full human being. He is a wild man
of the woods, a Sasquatch. (200)

In calling for contributions to this volume, I invited writers to respond to Stegner, to refute or confirm him, but in the
process to look in depth at historical and contemporary views
of community in the American West.

Two writers in this collection directly assess Stegner's view
of western "migratoriness," and both weigh in on the negative
side, arguing that despite his own rootedness in western
America, Stegner tended to import stereotypical or "eastern"
views of what a "proper" community would look like (witness
his selection of New Haven and Cambridge in the passage
cited above). In "Walt Disney vs. Wallace Stegner," Eric
Bateman suggests that Stegner may have misconceived the
nature of western community and argues this point by analyzing community relations in a most unlikely of oevres, Walt
Disney's *Toy Story*, which "questions the West's cherished
myths and the actions people take based on them." Another
writer, Todd DePastino, finds community of the sort ignored
by Stegner in another apparently unlikely place as he explores "Masculinity, Myth, and Community" in western hobo
communities of the first half of the century.

The distance between the textual sites of those two rebut-
tal pieces gives the reader some indication of the depth and
complexity of the explorations of community in this volume.

In Part One of the book, writers explore and discuss the
concept of community itself, a "Re-Visioning Community" for
the late twentieth century. In addition to Bateman's piece on
Stegner and Disney, the section contains a powerful essay by
Asao B. Inoue on "Mending Babel's Walls," a reminiscence of
growing up as an identifiable minority child in Las Vegas.
Inoue questions humankind's propensity for raising walls—
physical, spiritual, racial, and linguistic—and describes the
human need to "protect"and "sustain" communities while recognizing that walls also "isolate" and "exclude." "Walls," he
concludes, "are ideology."

Further challenging traditional concepts of community,
Thelma Shinn Richard explores "Reconstructing Memory in
the American West." Richard objects to the stereotypes of

western women as *hausfraus*, citing as evidence the works of three women writers who "document in their autobiographical and fictive observations, so often dismissed as merely local color, the need to *re*-construct eastern memories by marrying them to the realities of western experience." Tony Chiavello then provides an insightful rhetorical analysis of the language of divisiveness and community in "Building and Subverting Community in the American West." Poets Crag Hill, Shaun Griffin, and Bill Abrams round out that section by looking anew at people and places in the west: hitchhikers, shoppers, apparently isolated folk who are, in fact, demonstrable members of our community.

In Part Two of the collection, "Diversity and Community," we look directly at historical communities of the nineteenth and early twentieth centuries, in particular at communities of ethnic and religious minorities. Writers note that values people might see as "European" exist in many places and in many ways, yet each community constructs its own unique, enduring, and valuable set of traditions. Thus we learn of the communities of Virginia City miners (Ronald James), African Americans (Roger Hardaway), the Portuguese in Nevada (Donald Warrin), Colorado coal communities (Eric Margolis), Catholics in Nevada (Kevin Rafferty), and Basques in the West (Carmelo Urza).

Our third and final section looks at "Evolving Western Communities." With other writers having established the viability of community as a concept applicable in the West, the writers in this section suggest some of the ways in which the concept of community itself is necessarily evolving in the urbanized-yet-rural contemporary American West. In an imaginative essay, "Are You Sure You Belong?" Kevin Hearle compares the concept of community in his time to that of his mother. In a group project, the Unnamed Writers' Group of Reno interviewed and photographed homeless children to show both highly conventional as well as newly constituted concepts of what creates "community" and "family." Anthropologist Marie Boutté examines community in a town that has become the site of a state prison as she examines myths and stereotypes about "Prisons and Economic Diversification." Michael Flanigan analyzes the work of Kiowa visionary artist Barthell Little Chief and reflects on Little Chief's views of community as a Native American. Poets Steven Shroder, Bill Stobb,

Marsha Rogers, and Stephen Liu subject a half dozen western towns and cities to poetic inspection, and our volume closes with imaginative nonfiction pieces about the two major city/communities of Nevada: Felicia Campbell describing Las Vegas as "Real Life Virtual Reality" and ShaunAnne Tangney offering a view of Reno as "Sim(ulacrum) City.

"Westerns," William Kittredge writes, " . . . are basically about reestablishing community," but he argues that community issues are not restricted to towns west of the hundredth meridian:

> Children kill other children, with handguns, settling scores, on playing fields in New Orleans. We have insane bombers getting even in Oklahoma. We try to forget Vietnam." (xvii)

Community in the American West, then, may be too narrowly titled. Although we begin by discussing problems and people situated in the western half of the country, clearly the message in each article, photograph, and poem in this collection is a broader one that links this book to our traditions in the humanities: This book is about the community of humankind.

REFERENCES

Kittredge, William, ed. "Introduction." *The Portable Western Reader.* New York: Viking, 1997. xv-xxi.

Stegner, Wallace. "A Sense of Place." *Where the Bluebird Sings to the Lemonade Springs: Living and Writing in the West.* New York: Random House, 1992. 199-206.

Stephen Tchudi
University of Nevada, Reno
January 1, 1999

Re-Visioning Community

Mending Babel's Walls

ASAO B. INOUE

Throughout my first, second, and third grade years, I lived in an apartment on Statz Street in North Las Vegas, the city's "ghetto." Now I live in a cozy three-bedroom home in the small college town of Monmouth, Oregon (population just over seven thousand). In my memory, I distinctly recall trees, grass, a small parking lot off the street. On one of those "Cops" shows a while back, I saw my old neighborhood, but on TV there was only dirt and the white brick walls of the apartment buildings I lived in. There was also a lone car, sitting on the street, gutted, the windows smashed in, spray paint up and down its sides. There was litter flooding the gutters, and no one was out, not one person, except two policemen, chasing down an elusive paint-sniffer.

It's funny how your mind can re-draw things, incidents, people, places, or how it can cling to a detail, a word your wife whispered to you at a party five years ago in a certain tone that was new then: "Let's go." Your brother's crooked smile in an old photograph that you just like to look at. Or brick walls. White brick walls. This is the detail of my youth, the detail most remembered from every community I've ever lived in. But it's not so unusual, not so unique. In fact, walls are a rather typical metaphor in our culture—maybe even typical to all cultures. There was the great quasi-mythical battle between the Greeks and the Trojans, a war that lasted years, killed thousands of soldiers, created heroes by death and triumph. It has become one of the best known markers

Asao Inoue is an essayist, adjunct English faculty member at Chemeketa Community College in Salem, Oregon, and a technical writer for Hewlett-Packard. He would like to acknowledge and thank, first, his wife, Kelly, and second, his colleague and good friend Chris Anderson at Oregon State University.

of time for Greek (even Western) civilization. We live after the fall of Troy's walls.

China has a great wall made of dirt, stone, and brick, erected in 204 B.C.E. by Shih Huang Ti of the Ch'in and Ts'in Dynasties to keep invaders and nomadic groups from attacking from the north. This "Great Wall of China" ranges from fifteen to thirty feet in height and is fifteen to twenty-five feet wide, stretching 1,500 miles east to west, dividing the country in half. Then there is an ideological wall made tangible by a great war, some say the greatest American war, because every casualty was an American. It was the American Civil War, a war fought for various reasons but almost always designated as the war between "the North and the South."

Of course, there is W.E.B. Du Bois's "color-line," another wall of ideology, defined by contrast, by light and dark skins. He writes in *The Souls of Black Folk*:

> Then it dawned upon me with a certain suddenness that I was different than the others; or like, mayhap, in heart and life and longing, but shut out from their world by a vast veil. . . . Why did God make me an outcast and a stranger in mine own house? The shades of the prison-house closed round about us all: walls straight and stubborn to the whitest, but relentlessly narrow, tall, and unscalable to sons of night who must plod darkly on in resignation, or beat unavailing palms against the stone, or steadily, half hopelessly, watch the streak of blue above. (2)

We can see this "vast veil" in Richard Wright's novel *Native Son*. By the end of the novel, Bigger Thomas sees a wall that has been built around him, one he himself helped erect, and he gives voice to it as he sits in jail for the murder of a white girl: "Was there any way to break down this wall of isolation? Distractedly, he gazed about the cell, trying to remember where he had heard words that would help him. He could recall none" (386).

And more recently, Kenneth McClane, an African-American poet, essayist, and Cornell University Professor, describes the walls of the Auburn Correctional Facility. In his autobiographical essay, "Walls: A Journey to Auburn," describing a visit as a participant of the Elmira Community College Inmate Higher Education Program, he writes: "[f]or whatever else prison does, it demands that one confront it. If you are a prisoner, it might take you a dozen years to realize that the life you hope to create requires, above all else, that it be lived within these walls, for *these walls do not go away*. Here, of all the world's places, there is everything to accept" (36). Shorn against my own feelings and the images on my TV, McClane's words suggest that I cannot escape those brick walls of Statz Street in North Las Vegas, that those walls, too, "do not go away"—that no walls can really ever go away. But why don't they go away? What is so special about walls?

Throughout history people have needed to define space, know boundaries, see where one thing ends and another begins. Solon's ancient Athenian building ordinance prescribing a clear space of one foot alongside each wall, two feet alongside each house, shows how Athens institutionalized space and boundaries, how it used walls. We do similar things now with our building ordinances; however, the sixteenth century French educator and rhetorician Pierre de la Ramée, or Ramus, applied this law (calling it "Solon's law") in more philosophical areas, extending its meaning and implications. Walter Ong nicely describes Ramus's intentions: "Ramus calls on this law when he cries haro at Cicero's and Quintilian's failure to keep dialectic and rhetoric distinct from one another. The quantitative basis of the cult of distinctness is only too evident; Ramus is saying that a 'place' is really a 'place,' and that it cannot be occupied by rhetoric and dialectic jointly" (280). Ramus wanted rhetoric, the art of persuasion (that is, elocution and pronunciation), and dialectic, the training and method of rhetoric (which includes the other traditional parts of rhetoric: invention, disposition, and memory), to be separate, because he understood them separately, saw them having distinctly different elements and characteristics.

Ramus wanted boundaries set between rhetoric and dialectic, in effect, departmentalizing his academic subjects. Today the modern university is a cumbersome colossus built and designed around this same notion of departmentalization. Oregon State University, for instance, has departments of History, Business, English, Sociology, Psychology, Physics, Engineering, Art, Ethnic Studies, Women's Studies, Philosophy, and the list continues. Modern discussions on language and thought, pioneered by scholars like Janet Emig, prove that the two elements Ramus attempted to separate aren't neatly separable. University programs that attempt to integrate studies like OSU's Bac Core requirements (which all students must complete) attempt to reassemble and synthesize the scattered knowledge attained in the university educational experience. These kinds of programs provide connections that get lost when students learn only one thing in one building and something else in another, never being asked to connect or given ways to link chemical engineering with ethics or psychology to computer design. The driving premise under all this is simple: Academic subjects and their corresponding departments don't neatly separate like oil and water.

I see this fundamental problem in a particular class I teach, Technical Writing, a course comprised of mostly juniors and seniors, designed around a final project in each student's field that must be presented to the class at the end of the term. Each student's project must incorporate the class as one of its audiences, providing ways for the class to enter the discussion and become interested during the oral presentation. And this is universally everyone's problem. There are always a hoard of interesting project topics chosen, but most lack ways a lay audience can connect to the project. I have students streaming into my office, unsure of how they can make their projects interesting for the class, how they can show that what they do in their fields has relevance to class members that aren't in those areas. One of my students, a chemical engineering student, told me that there would be no project she could come up with that would interest the class because of the nature of her field, because only those in her field would be interested in her work. Her response is very typical, and I can see how she might perceive this, but of course it can't be true. Otherwise what good is her field if it doesn't interest those outside it? My assumption is that every field of study touches, and so interests, all. This problem stems from departmentalization. Students lose connections because they either forget how to make them or aren't taught how to see them—by default, they understand that calculus is only calculus, English only English, that our world can and should be divided up into neat little squares.

Mike Rose, a UCLA writing instructor, describes in *Possible Lives* a team-taught elementary school classroom dubbed the "Brown Cow classroom," named after its two teachers. This class contained three grades: kindergarten, first, and second. The vignettes that Rose provides (42-46) illustrate the success of pedagogies that use the fundamental differences inherent in students (and people), like age and experience. Older more experienced children help younger ones with math problems. Simultaneously the children not only teach math to each other but learn a fundamental aspect of knowledge: the joy of sharing it. Sharing space and ideas, like the Brown Cow classroom, is the first step to making connections because it allows us constantly to confront people who are different and ideas that are new. It forces us to share.

Some will say that drawing boundaries is necessary, that it must be done in order to survive. Troy needed its walls in order to last so long against the Greeks. Shih Huang Ti needed to build that great wall, which still stands today, if he was to protect his civilization from slowly being eroded away by bandits and nomads. The simple geographics of the American Civil War show us that it was a war between the North and the South, a war between a northern way of life and a southern one, that one could chalk a line on a map of the U.S., showing the division between one ideology and another. So in many ways walls identify and protect; walls defend; walls unify and stabilize a common geographic place. We could also talk about walls and homes, about how walls function in the home, how they create homes and environments, expectations and ideology.

In *Design of Cities*, Edmund Bacon says, "in all the cultures of the world, architectural form is an expression of the philosophical interaction of the forces of mass and space, which, in turn, reflects the relationship between man and nature and man and the universe" (16). Bacon suggests that the physical structures around us, our houses, office buildings, and streets, all spring from the interaction between people and their environments. Our cities are a reflection of our philosophical notions about ourselves and our relations in the world. The architectural structures around us possess meaning as well as function. One could place a Freudian interpretation on all this. A house could be a womb-like structure that protects, sustains, provides, and comforts. The best examples of structures whose meanings tend to overshadow their functions are ones like the Eiffel Tower, the Statue of

Liberty, Mount Rushmore. They are tourist attractions because what they symbolize is more important to us than how
they function as structures in their environments; but what
they are is a combination of these two factors.

Is it possible that the physical walls around us, our neighborhoods, our streets, the imaginary lines between states and
countries, are not built simply because there are differences
or things to identify, but instead could these boundaries be
built because they themselves mirror some meaning about
ourselves and our world? Is it possible that those white walls
in North Las Vegas have meaning, that they aren't simply an
apartment building? Amos Rapoport from the Department of
Architecture at the University of Wisconsin-Milwaukee says:
"[i]f architecture encloses behavior tightly [if "built environments are created to support desired behavior"], then activities will tend to shape architecture" (11). So walls and structures of division are more than manifestations of pre-existing
ideas and relationships in our minds but also support and
reaffirm behavior, solidify ideology. Walls are ideology.

In an article from *Domestic Architecture and The Use of
Space*, Donald Sanders affirms this conclusion, saying, "[a]
building is a cultural unit of meaning before it is an object of
practical function" (45). He summarizes the current semiotic
approach in architectural analysis: "architecture, like language, is comprised of a system of signs for the communication of information. . . . Buildings, like writing or speech, can
be correctly read or understood only if the coded meanings
can be accurately interpreted by the users" (46). This becomes
more complicated if you insert modern notions of thought
and language as a communal act, reading and writing as a
collaboration toward meaning. "Signs" and "coded meanings"
then tend to shift and change as time and circumstances
progress. The Statue of Liberty can then mean something
completely different in another fifty or one hundred years.
Yet the essence of Sanders's idea can still be used: The walls
we've constructed, whether physical or metaphoric, were produced not from a functional need but from a need to express
meaning.

To the Greeks, the wall of Troy also excluded and separated Paris from his wife, Helen. In China, the great wall also
separated the south from the north, just as that invisible
chalked line of ideology also separated the north and south

in America. W. E. B. Du Bois also labels his racial separation as a "vast veil," as "the color-line," and as "white walls." Richard Wright, writing almost a half century later, describes the relationship between Bigger Thomas, his novel's protagonist, and everyone else as a "wall of isolation." Functionally all of these "walls" separate people, but their meanings are more significant because they shape our behavior. They provide points of reference by their geographic location, which in turn influences our ideology, informing the way we live and think and act toward each other. In our Trojan example, this dynamic might be stated as: I live inside the walls of Troy (geographic/functional reference); therefore, I am Trojan (symbolic/ideological reference).

The Walls of Babel

My wife and I recently moved into her grandmother's vacant house here in Oregon. It has an extra lot on the east side that we used this year to plant vegetables: corn, beans, carrots, lettuce, peppers, and tomatoes. The lot separates the property our house sits on from our neighbor's. Our neighbor is a friendly, chatty lady in her seventies named Silvia. A few weeks back she came by to "confess" that she'd taken grapes off our vines on the extra lot. She said that grandma and she always had an agreement about the grapes since grandma didn't do much with them. The agreement was: "Whatever I can grab." We didn't mind. "Don't worry. Take as many as you like— take them all," we kept saying between her apologies.

The year before Silvia took grapes from the same vines but didn't come over and confess to grandma. Things were different then. Grandma lived in the red house on the other side of the lot. This year we do. And this one element in the equation changed the nature of Silvia's behavior. It demanded that she come over and ask for the grapes located on our side of the lot. The lot had not changed, only its meaning had.

As a child living on Statz, I remember a story my mom would read to me, one about differences—the origin of differences. It came from the first real book I owned, a thick Bible storybook that contained Old and New Testament stories written for kids. I never read it myself. I just looked at the pictures. They were the typical kind for Bible storybooks. The artist used lots of dark colors: deep reds, oranges, and muddy yellows. The men were all bearded and somewhat ugly, like stocky dwarves. One particular picture I remember distinctly—because it had such a profound effect on me, even as an eight or nine year old child—was the one attached to the story of the tower of Babel.

It was a full page picture of a crumbling girthy tower that looked more like a stump. Dark clouds ringed its middle section, light flashing in some of its cracks. It was night, or dusk, and fire was falling from the sky. There were hundreds of men all over the tower, disturbed right in the act of construction, many falling off at different spots. Some were running away from the base with their hands in their hair. I remember that the picture was obviously apocalyptic (of course, I couldn't have labeled it as such then). It was a dark and ominous picture, looking suspiciously like images described in Revelation. But most of all, I remember what it suggested about the story of Babel. The story told by the picture was that of the destruction of the tower, emphasizing it as the most important act of the story.

My mom read the story to me first from the Bible then from that storybook. In Genesis, it can hardly be called a story. It is only a few verses long, maybe ten. It's not even its own chapter (it only begins the eleventh chapter). Structurally, it acts and looks like a prelude or prologue, heading the Abram (later to become Abraham) and Lot section after it and following the Semite lineage section. It could be seen as a segue between two epochs: that of Noah and that of the people after Noah, his descendants—a story showing the transition from an age in which the world was unified to one that became scattered and fragmented, a world of sameness crumbling into one of differences.

The story from Genesis goes something like this (I have adapted it from the *NIV Study Bible* version of Genesis, Chapter 11):

> The descendants of the great flood (those of Noah and his sons) all spoke the same language. As they moved eastward, they found a plain called Shinar (or Babylonia). They began to build a city and a great ziggurat, or tower, made of mud brick and tar that would reach from the earth to the heavens. All of this was in the hopes to make a name for themselves and be united forever with this one great accomplishment.

When God came down to the city, he said, "If as one people speaking the same language, they have begun to do this, then nothing they plan to do will be impossible for them." So God scattered them across the world and confused their language.

The story of the tower of Babel is really only a beginning, not a story that has an end itself. Even though it was the end of one era, it seems more like the beginning of another, the one we live in now. I am a descendent of those vain Babylonians (either figuratively or literally, it doesn't matter; both are significant). I am living the end of that story. My brother, Tad, a Biblical and theology graduate student at Wesley Seminary in Washington, D.C., says that one must take the stories written in the Bible as religious mythology, or parables, which are not necessarily intended to be read as historical accounts, but were written instead as accounts that explain or give insight into God's divine power and mystery, accounts that describe the universal human need to touch the divine. The story of Babel explains the world's fragmentation: the reason why cultures and ethnicities across the globe have differences, and why those differences are meaningful and important. It also graphically illustrates the human need to reach the divine as well as our inevitable failure to do so by fusing together meaning and function. The tower meant unification and was built to unify. It symbolized humanity's greatness and commonality through a misguided mission, to touch God.

The story does not explain God's reasons for erasing that commonality, for one Biblical theme is that we aren't to question God's motives, but it does give us an account of our world's apparent chaos. I understood what happened at that great ziggurat in Babylon as only the very beginning of our civilization, yet that picture suggested to me that the tower's destruction and the scattering of its people was the end. I don't remember the account of the story in my storybook, but I do recall my jolt of confusion when I first saw that picture and realized that this was not the way I'd seen the tower of Babel in my mind's eye as my mom read me the story from the Bible. And I think the reason I was so jolted was because throughout my entire life—and even then at eight years old living on Statz in North Las Vegas—I felt that fragmentation.

On Statz I had two neighbors: Lester who lived next door in
"B" and Lashawn who lived in "A" on the other side of Lester.
Lester was a skinny kid who always wore multi-colored striped
shirts and pants. I can barely remember what he looked like,
but I still recall what it felt like when we played together,
when I shook his hand for the first time late one summer
evening as we moved our things in the apartment, smelling
for the first time what I thought was an odor coming off his
skin but was really coming from his hair. I felt different from
him. I was a thin boy, only sixty pounds in the second grade,
but Lester was even thinner. I could feel the bone in his arm
when I grabbed him, could see all of his ribs and his sternum
clearly and the triangle shape his solar plexus made through
his dark skin. I was one year older than both Lester and
Lashawn. Despite my being older, Lashawn never followed
me around like Lester. Lashawn was also constantly looking
for ways to outdo me and Tad. Yes, Lashawn was a bully.

Once we were all hanging out in the grass courtyard, just
talking. Lashawn and I started to argue, shouting at each
other. He called me "Honky." We were all gathered in a circle:
him, Lester, Lateesha (Lester's little sister), Tad, me, and
maybe one or two others (everyone was black except Tad and
me). We were about to play a game of tag or something. Tad
happened to have his cowboy cap gun in his hand. Lashawn
told me he didn't really care if I liked being called honky or
not. That was what he said, and he wasn't going to take it
back. It seemed like everyone agreed with Lashawn. They all
stood next to him, shaking their heads at me. I said, "How
would you like it if I called you black boy?" He hit me with a
slapping motion across the cheek. It didn't really hurt, but I
spit a little blood and that scared me and I cried. He just
looked at me, and as I turned to go into our apartment, I saw
Tad strike Lashawn with his cap gun, making Lashawn cry.

Even at seven years old, I can remember thinking how
wrong Lashawn was, how he didn't see or care to see his
mistake, and how happy I was that Tad had "gotten him back"
for his injustice. It was instances like this one that fueled a
hate in me for blacks. I hadn't done anything to Lashawn. I
was willing to be his friend for the afternoon, to play a game
of tag. I wanted so much to make him understand, to make
him see me differently, but Lashawn, and even Lester,

wouldn't. I'm sure Lashawn knew that I disliked him. Maybe that's why he called me that name and hit me, and maybe he too felt I was doing him injustice by disliking him for simply being black. Maybe he felt misunderstood too.

There in our little grass courtyard under our tree, Lester, Lashawn, Tad, and I experienced the fall of Babel's walls all over again. There was, even in our little group of eight and seven year old kids, a fundamental chasm splitting us—a chasm that divided Lester and Lashawn from Tad and me. We all went to the same school, played in the same courtyard, lived in the same roach-infested apartments, and yet we didn't see things the same way. We couldn't agree. Lashawn had drawn a line on the dirt and Lester had quickly jumped to his side. By some cosmic default, Tad and I were occupying the other side. And strange as it sounds (or maybe not so strange), we all knew deep inside that this was the way things were meant to be, that that division was "right" at some level. Lines had to be drawn in order for us to know who we were and how we were to act toward one another. Now, I wonder where we got those assumptions and why we all clung to them so desperately.

It wasn't until years later that I began to process my experiences at Statz, realizing how much they still were a part of me. After graduation I joined the Oregon Army National Guard to get money for college. At Basic Training on the base at Fort Dix, New Jersey, my company, consisting of platoons A, B, C, and D (we were B), stayed in large brick barracks. We were a divided group of privates. Nobody was anybody's friend that first week, but no one was any more emphatic about it than I was. I tried very hard to keep to myself. I wasn't interested in making friends. My platoon was mostly African-American and white. Out of the forty or so privates in Bravo platoon, maybe twenty-five were African-American, ten white, three Hispanic, and then there was me. Each platoon had a section of the building. Ours was the third floor, north side.

The building was always cold. The floor was cold; the walls were cold; your pants were cold when you put them on in the morning; the toilets were cold when you sat on them at night; the faucet water was cold when you brushed your teeth; and sometimes if you didn't get an early enough shower, your shower was cold, too. But the one thing that seemed strangely familiar was the walls. They reminded me of the walls of our apartment building on Statz. They were made from the same kind of big square brick. I hadn't thought of Statz for a long time, but looking at that wall as I lay in my bunk at night, it almost seemed like the wall next to my bed in my bedroom at Statz with that thick coat of white paint, my sometimes friend Lester just on the other side. My stomach sickened because I realized that it seemed I'd never gotten out from behind those walls.

In my room, shared by seven other privates, there was another person very much like me: Private Alvarez. Both of us kept to ourselves most of the time, doing our chores at night and quickly getting into bed and reading or listening to headphones. We didn't make friends or sneak out to the PX like many of the others. But Private Alvarez was a pariah. He was always by himself. At the time, I failed to see his position as similar to mine, because I saw mine as a decision to separate and his as a result of others' decisions to exclude. He was a tall kid and, like me, only eighteen. He was usually quiet. Mostly he thumbed through car and truck magazines, bragging about his own truck, how it was better or had similar rims and tires. He said his family was rich and owned a large three-story house in California. He constantly talked about his Nissan, how he'd had it professionally lowered ("slammed" is what he called it). He was just there "because." He had no real goals, and he didn't care whether he graduated Basic Training or not. He didn't care about much of anything, except for his car magazines. I wasn't sure what to make of him. He'd failed every physical training test and most of the weapon ranges. His presence there made no sense to me. On top of all this, he looked ethnically ambiguous. He looked Hispanic or Native American, maybe African-American, but at other times he didn't look like any of these nationalities, just tanned.

One night he was reading his truck magazine, and I was sweeping under his bunk. He asked me, "What are you?" I just looked at him. At first, I didn't know what he meant, or if he was even talking to me. Then he said, "Are you Mexican, Puerto Rican, Mulatto?" No one had ever confronted me like this. It was as if he was upset at me because my ethnicity wasn't apparent to him. I wasn't sure what to say. I had been asked frequently what "nationality" I was and what "country I was from." People had always understood me as "ethnic," labeled as a "minority," but it didn't feel like Alvarez was thinking in those terms. To complicate this, I realized I had the same question about him but was afraid to ask.

"Why?" I asked him.

"I just want to know where you fit in around here. Who do you hang out with? I mean, I'm Mulatto." He'd said the word so nonchalantly, as if he were telling me the color of his truck. We both paused for a second, looking at each other.

"Oh, I'm Japanese-Hawaiian." He squinted at me. I could tell I'd caught him off guard.

"You look black, maybe even like me."

I couldn't see it then, but Alvarez was simply being honest and straight-forward about the groups that our platoon naturally fell into. He could see clearly the way the social networks formed after chores were done and couldn't tell where I fit in. My hair was shaved off. My skin was a dark olive color. I didn't talk much, and since everyone wore the same clothes, there was no way for him to tell where I came from or who I was. He saw me talk to Angel, my Puerto Rican bunkmate and "Ranger Buddy," the one I had to depend on out in the field, but we didn't talk all that much during our free time. I think he probably saw me the way I saw him: estranged and usually alone either reading or listening to headphones. I thought it kind of funny that he had mistaken me for black. I thought I'd lightened up since I'd moved away from Las Vegas, but I was still dark. In the army, skin color was just about the only physically distinguishable feature anyone could use as a marker of identity, of inclusion and commonality. And that is what Alvarez was trying to do: identify me and place me into a group, or maybe include me into his very limited group of one. He simply wanted to know how to act around me by knowing who I was.

The assumption Alvarez made about my appearance is one we all tend to make about differences and the divisions that form because of them. For those that build them, walls are divisions that both separate and include, defend and protect. In a way, the walls of ethnicity are walls of prejudice that seem both necessary and obsolete, unavoidable and easily discarded. The army taught me that we use racism and divisions to survive and live.

I have never been innocent of racist stereotyping or prejudice. I grew up around African-Americans and Hispanics, as
well as white middle class. I know them all intimately. I preferred the latter throughout my childhood because it was a
step up economically. I found bigots at all levels—maybe none
more bigoted than myself for a time. And maybe the army's
impossible assumption that I could escape all those ethnic
assumptions and stereotypes attracted me, that I could be in
an environment where the color of my skin and the economic
strata I came from didn't matter anymore—where I was just a
private like everyone else. The idea is attractive: "Come live in
a community of equals" would be the advertisement poster.
Yet this very democratic notion puts us back behind the walls
of Troy, keeping the Greeks at bay. For if the army did anything, it forced everyone—especially those like me who already saw absolutely nothing in common with anyone else—
to look deep inside himself and find the differences he could
use to construct his own protective walls, and those walls of
separation were stronger than any cold brick barracks walls
could ever be.

Walking Atop

Statz and the army also pull against the notion of walls as
definitive markers. In both experiences, I was mistaken for
someone else, or some other ethnicity, suggesting that walls
do not constitute the space they necessarily define. In *People
Space: The Making and Breaking of Human Boundaries*,
Norman Ashcraft, an anthropologist, and Albert E. Scheflen,
a psychiatrist, communication theorist and urbanologist,
agree: "[a] territory is not its boundary, just as a cell is not its
membrane. But boundaries catch our attention and this is
what they are designed for" (5). And the thing that has caught
the most attention about me—and caused the most anguish—
is my decieving appearance. I do not look Japanese-Hawaiian or Cherokee Indian.

The *Dictionary of Race and Ethnic Relations* defines
"ethnicity" as follows:

The actual term derives from the Greek *ethnikos*, the
adjective of *ethnos*. This refers to a people or nation.

In its contemporary form, ethnic still retains this basic meaning in the sense that it describes a group possessing some degree of coherence and solidarity composed of people who are, at least latently, aware of having common origins and interests. So an ethnic group is not a mere aggregate of people or a sector of a population, but a self-conscious collection of people united, or closely related, by shared experiences. (102)

Terms like "self-conscious collection" and "shared experiences" allow me to conclude that I am not ethnic in any way, even though my father is Japanese-Hawaiian and my mother is Cherokee Indian. I do not feel (even though I've always desperately wanted to) a conscious relation—neither close nor far—to Japanese-Hawaiians or Cherokee Indians. I have no shared experiences with these groups of Americans. It is also not the same definition that I've found working in the communities I've lived. It definitely wasn't the assumption those in Bravo platoon worked under. Otherwise Alvarez may have had a better time of it and I a worse time.

But "ethnic groups" are not so easily chalked off into neat squares; nor are those who find themselves in them, as well as those who find themselves forced into them by others, so neatly a part of those groups. I find myself realizing that if I choose to adopt the definition of the *Dictionary of Race and Ethnic Relations*, then I am guilty of the same thing I've found Solon and Ramus guilty of. Instead of geographic or topical boundaries, this definition of "ethnic" places other kinds of boundaries on my identity. It suggests I not only *must* "possess some degree of coherence and solidarity" with Japanese-Americans, *must* have "shared experiences" with other Cherokee Indians, in order to be Japanese and Cherokee, but also that those things define me as a person—which, at this point in my life, I have a hard time swallowing. And it completely skips the most important factor in any discussion of ethnicity or race: other's perceptions and assumptions.

In Mr. Hicks's third grade class, we had an assignment to do at home (virtually the only "homework" I remember from that class) which asked us to describe the color of our skin. Mr. Hicks had always liked me. He offered me a "tester" of the Halloween party candy before the party, saying to me: "Ty, shhhh, what do you say we test some of this candy?" And

before the Christmas party: "Ty, come here, let's try some of
this Christmas candy just to make sure it's safe for the rest of
the class." I liked him, too. He seemed parental and fatherly.

I went home that day, consulted with my mom and studied my skin very carefully. When he asked me to share my
conclusions the next day, I said: "My skin is dark red, a little
orange, some yellow, and white." I saw dark red from the
Cherokee Indian in me, giving my skin a tan which seemed a
"dark red" and not a brown. I saw "a little orange" from the
mixture of Indian and Hawaiian, the blend of the two genes. I
saw "yellow" from the heritage that I identified myself as, Japanese. My skin, especially around my palms and joints, seemed
more yellow, or olive color, blending from the darker color of
my arms. And I saw white in my finger nails and scalp. I
didn't pretend to see these colors. I remember actually seeing
them. As I put my arm and hand up just an inch or two from
my face, I could see specks, dots on the surface of my skin.
Some were dark red, some yellow, some orange, and some
white. When I spoke these words, I got to yellow and the entire class erupted into laughter, including Mr. Hicks. He said,
"Yellow?" through his bursting. I could only look at him, his
stomach burping up laughs intermittently, the rest of the
class, all around me, laughing. I could hear kids repeating
my words in mocking tones: "red," "orange," "yellow"?

My first reaction was to cry, to feel ashamed, to run out of
that room full of laughter. What was so funny about being
those colors, I thought, looking around the room at a sea of
brown and white children, none of whom were even close to
my complexion—all were either African-American or Cauca-
sian. Mr. Hicks said, "Don't you mean *light-brown* or something like that?" raising his eyebrows on the words "light-
brown" and smiling. I couldn't say anything; the wall of laugher
was slamming into my face. I just looked at him, and he moved
on to the next student. I don't think Mr. Hicks meant to make
me feel inferior or ridiculed or ugly, but he did. Looking back
now, I know that his assignment was meant to help all of us
see the differences in each other's appearance, to acknowledge them; however, his and my classmates' laughter only
made it all too apparent that it didn't matter what I saw in my
skin, didn't matter how I identified myself, only what
they saw.

A few years later when we were living in a single-wide trailer on Pecos Street across town on the east side, an all white, blue-collar neighborhood, Jon Copsey, the trailer park manager's grandson, was over at our trailer talking to us. It was early, about nine o'clock, and we were planning something to do. Somehow we began drawing on our paved porch with the charcoal briquettes that were left in the barbecue. As Jon was leaving, he took his briquette and threw it across our lawn right into the neighbor's fiberglass awning. It hit with a very loud bang and left a good size black stain on its cream-colored surface. Tad and I quickly scurried inside. Jon ran home. The next week we got a notice that our neighbors, an elderly couple, had filed a complaint against Tad and me for throwing rocks at their trailer. We said we didn't do it. Of course, they didn't believe us, and when we tried to appeal to Fred Copsey, the manager, he didn't want to discuss it. That was our first warning (three meant eviction). Mom suggested that Tad and I go next door and apologize, but we argued that we didn't do it. Apologizing would only incriminate us, and we felt stupid apologizing for something we didn't even do. Mom said that it was in the best interest for our relations with our neighbors. We had to live next to them, and it would be better in the long run if we tried to put this experience behind us. No sense in anyone carrying grudges. Our neighbors accepted our apology but never talked to us afterwards. In fact, that same year, just a month or so later, they erected a chain link fence between their carport and our lawn. Whenever our neighbor got a chance, he'd stand on his side and tell us to be careful and not hit his fence.

My neighbor wasn't interested in patching things up between us or burying grudges. Just like our park manager, he, too, didn't want to hear what we had to say. We weren't intending to blame Jon for it, though we thought about it, only to get things straight about us, let everyone know we didn't do it. You see in our trailer park, we were considered the trouble makers from the first day we entered the front gates—Pecos Trailer park was completely enclosed by a six foot brick wall. We were constantly being blamed for something, some mishap, chalk marks on sidewalks, rocks at trailers, the broken Coke machine at the office. Even during the two summers we left to visit Oregon and our grandma, we returned to find a list of complaints against us, things we couldn't have done because we weren't even there. It wasn't until years later living in Oregon that mom told me the story behind the trailer park. They originally wouldn't let us in because Tad and I looked "Mexican." They said in so many words that Tad and I weren't the right "kind" of people for the park. Mom got a lawyer and they quickly backed down, but it set a precedent for veiled prejudice against us. During the entire five years we were there, Fred always had a complaint against us. Thinking back now, I know that neither Fred nor my neighbors could have even imagined Jon, Fred's own grandson, a cleancut, blond haired kid, to have thrown that briquette because he didn't look like a "bad kid."

In many ways everyone in my childhood memories, Lester, Lashawn, those at Pecos, even my fellow privates in Basic Training, have mistaken my identity somehow. They've seen me and translated my appearance wrongly. David Mura, a Japanese-American writer asks White Americans: "Why can't I be who I am? Why can't you think of me as a Japanese-American *and* as an individual?" (138). He says this is his response to people who say "I think of you just as a white person," or "I think of you as an individual." The statements that Mura recalls for us identify what many Americans, including myself growing up, have seen as the "typical American": a white person. It shows why we have chosen Chuck Norris instead of Jackie Chan or even Bruce Lee as a cultural superhero. Mura also illustrates how important, even all-consuming, others' perceptions become when ethnicity is the issue—when one is "ethnic." Mura wants people to "see" him in a certain way, one that reflects his own understanding of himself. Regardless of ethnicity, everyone feels this same way. We want those around us to understand us the way we understand ourselves: from the inside out.

In "How I Started to Write," Carlos Fuentes remarks about rhetoric's relation to his own identity. He says, "My passage from English to Spanish determined the concrete expression of what, before, in Washington, had been the revelation of an identity. I wanted to write and I wanted to write in order to show myself that my identity and my country were real" (93). But this identity is not simply one distinct and separate from an English or American one; instead it is simply one that is, as Fuentes himself calls it, an "enigma." He ends his essay saying, "[D]on't classify me, read me. I'm a writer, not a genre"

(110). Language has been Fuentes' way of identifying himself as a duality, as American and Mexican. However, by saying "don't classify me, read me," Fuentes asks us not to taxonomize but to understand him on his own terms, to see him as he secs himself. This is the way I have come to understand my own identity, not as Japanese or Hawaiian or Cherokee, but as all of these and yet, unfortunately (here is where I differ from Fuentes), none of them. At Statz, Pecos, Corvallis, and Fort Dix, I've constantly had others attempt to tell me who I was. You are "Mexican," a "beaner," a "Jap," a "mulatto," a trouble maker. Most times I accepted it, knowing that others misunderstood who I was, feeling solace in the fact that at least I knew who I really was, at least I dwelt within the walls of my identity. Yet how does this matter? What does it matter that I was the only one in Bravo platoon that knew I was not Mexican or mulatto, the only one in Mr. Hick's class that was willing to understand my own ethnic complexity, the only one at Pecos who didn't see me as a trouble maker and a beaner? How do we get around the walls others construct for us, the walls that cage us in like Bigger Thomas' "wall of isolation" or exclude and separate us like Du Bois' "vast veil of race"? And if we did, what would we do then?

Michael Omi and Howard Winant suggest that the political engines—right, left, and center—of America since the early 1970's have one tendency in common: to "diminish the significance of race, to treat it as a mere manifestation of some other, supposedly more important, social relationship" (viii). They continue, suggesting that the ethnicity-based paradigm, the "mainstream of the modern sociology of race," states that "race was a social category," a key determinant of an ethnic group's identity "based on [its] culture and descent" (15). They offer this theory not as one to adopt, but as one that has been adopted in America since the African-American movement in the late 1960s. It is this ethnicity-based paradigm that I see Mura, Fuentes, and myself struggling against because we don't fit into its parameters neatly. For the assumption is that "ethnic groups" simply exist, that we all fit somewhere on a landscape, that we have an ethnic place and call it home, and that everyone can find and know where he or she belongs—and even that everyone is easily identifiable by others—that perception and assumptions don't matter. It seems that most understand ethnicity as a constant, that the gap between one's own self-understanding and other's perceptions doesn't exist. Japanese-Americans become, in this paradigm, not simply an ethnic group but a thing that can be seen, examined, and finally reduced to its lowest common denominator: a common set of "cultural experiences."

Too many times during my life, I've found myself placed behind the wrong walls. Things have just always been confusing for me. The boundaries have always been fuzzy and elusive to trace. At Pecos I remember jumping the trailer park wall occasionally when I was late for the bus (in sixth grade I was bussed back to North Las Vegas to Madison Sixth Grade Center because of non-segregation laws). I'd jump that wall because the bus stop was in a cul-du-sac just on the other side of our park's south wall. The cul du sac was a part of a neighborhood that was predominantly Mexican. They were modest houses, owned by working class people just like us in the park. I remember times standing on that wall between my neighborhood and that other one, thinking how different and scary *those* people seemed, even their Hispanic accent sounded menacing to me, always questioning, always on the edge of frenzy. For a long time my memory of that neighborhood was one cloaked by the dark shade of trees (I remember lots of trees over there), like a jungle, dangerous, and off limits to us. Sometimes I'd even walk the narrow edge of the wall, balancing myself atop to catch a glimpse of a place I knew I didn't belong, allowing that feeling of exhilaration and fright to surge through my blood. It was a common saying with us kids, "Don't go over there; the Mexicans will beat you up." And we never did, never made friends with the kids living there. We stayed in our park and they stayed over there. Now I wonder: What really stoped us from crossing over that wall and meeting those other kids?

Mending the Babel

Mura, Fuentes, and I have resisted a tendency to see a unified quality in Americans, and even in any one ethnicity. It is a quality that J. Hector St. John de Crèvecoeur applauds in his epistolary novel *Letters From An American Farmer*, one that his narrator James calls "new." At one point James says: "*He* is an American, who, leaving behind him all his ancient prejudices and manners, receives new ones from the new mode of life he has embraced, the new government he obeys, and the new rank he holds . . . Here individuals of all nations are melted into a new race of men" (70). Crèvecoeur is defining a new citizen, an American, one who is radically different from his European counterpart because he is a conglomerate. He establishes here a philosophy that will get well used in future generations of Americans to identify themselves: the "melting pot." Crèvecoeur also establishes an idea that many Americans today fight against: that all Americans are the same, that we are all on equal footing, that we can be considered one unified "kind" of people. But this isn't really possible in America—never has been. The walls America was built behind suggest that a people, united and indivisible, under God, can in fact be one kind of people—we have "melted into a new race of men," and yet these same walls divide us, square us off into smaller groups, which is the process of walling. Can we even escape the nature of the walling process, one that is both productive and counter-productive, necessary and destructive? Finally, is it possible to see what the walls around us mean, what they represent, instead of always seeing what they do?

Robert Frost's poem "Mending Wall" illustrates this dialectical relationship between a wall's function and its meaning. Frost declares there is "something . . . that doesn't love a wall," for the winter ground swell "spills the upper boulders: and "makes gaps even two can pass abreast."

It is these "gaps" that I want at the same time to acknowledge and destroy. On the one hand, I want to celebrate the differences that exist between me and many white Americans. I want people to understand who I am, what being me means and is like, that just because I look Mexican, or even Japanese, doesn't allow anyone to assume I share a certain cultural background or traits. On the other hand, the gaps in the walls that separate me from my neighbors are also points of entry, places of commonality.

Close to the end of Frost's poem, the narrator reiterates and extends his opening line by pondering his neighbor's words, "Good fences make good neighbors." "Why," Frost asks, "*Why* do they make good neighbors?" He wonders, "Isn't it / Where there are cows?." Yet, "here there are no cows." Frost

concludes that before building a wall, "I'd ask to know/what
I was walling in or out . . . "

I can't say that the differences in my life, between me and
my neighbors, have made us "good neighbors," that the fences
we built made us any more friendlier to one another, but then
just as in the poem, it depends on which neighbor you ask.
The extension that Frost puts on his initial line is the phrase,
that something "wants [the wall] down." This is the difference
the poem elicits; this is the relationship that the wall forces
onto these neighbors. The narrator, after understanding that
there are no cows, that one needs something to "wall in" or
"wall out," ponders the different effects that the same wall
has on two neighbors and which neighbor might want the
wall down first. The narrator knows that the wall serves only
to separate because his (or her) neighbor only sees it serving
that function. Yet Frost suggests much more here. He suggests that the wall could *mean* something much more significant than a division. It could be a symbol of their mutual
mending, of their search for commonality in an area that both
share. And yet ironically Frost lets us understand that neighbors, and here we may insert ethnicities or communities or
academia or America, feel a need to hold up their own walls—
just as I have as well as my neighbors at Pecos and Statz and
in the army. At the same time, we attempt to tear down others' walls because no one likes to be excluded or labelled so
neatly. But what happens when the walls come down completely? Is it like Jericho or Troy—annihilation, destruction,
plunder? Is it like before Babel—unity?

Unfortunately we cannot simply insert ethnicities into this
equation so easily. Orchards and people are different things
altogether. While Frost acknowledges the relationship inherent in walls, that their functions are often to separate while
their meanings are more complicated because they shape
behavior and are created by it, he doesn't acknowledge the
real problem—and maybe he can't with the analogy he is using here, or the one I'm placing on his poem about simply two
neighbors. The real problem is that among people, especially
in America, there are racial and ethnic differences, walls that
cannot be broken because they are the differences that must
always be in every cultural equation. The walls that create
identity are always being mended, not because we are ignorant or prejudiced, necessarily, but because those walls are

what make us who we are. We need them. I can no more be a Japanese-American like Mura than he can be one like me. We share only a small part of the walls of identity, sharing those unmended places "Two can pass abreast." Yet the wall we do share *means* something more; it is significant more so by what it represents and not what it does. Just as in Frost's poem, the Japanese-American wall means that there is a common ground, a place of mutual respect, a part of America Mura and I happen to share by luck of birth, an inheritance I've yet to collect. It doesn't mean that we are the same, that we think alike, that we talk similarly, or even that we share some common experience. It only means that we share a mending wall, and that is the beginning.

The Babel story is another kind of beginning, the beginning of our present predicament. In Babylon, the people saw their tower, their great wall, as a unifying structure, one that took everyone to build and symbolized their solidarity. The destruction of it meant fragmentation and the creation of many smaller walls that identified their differences. Those walls were built of stone and prejudice, complexion and language. Frost hints at the power of smaller walls, showing that walls must have entryways, places where each side can meet and "pass abreast" and their meanings over simple functions, yet those gaps aren't that easily negotiated because, just as Frost's wall illustrates, the borders between and among differing ideologies and ethnicities are constantly being rebuilt in new ways and from different sources. As Solon and my army experiences have suggested, we do need divisions to identify ourselves and keep things straight. The problem is that with our divisions also comes separation. We think that a wall means we can't pass through it or over it, that gaps don't exist. We think that they only serve us in a functional way. We don't realize how powerfully physical and ideological structures shape and reshape our interactions and attitudes, our lives. The solution must be in finding ways to see divisions without being overcome by separations. We must leave gates open for passage, walk atop the walls between us, glimpsing the other side. Yes, logical and seemingly impossible, but then so was a wall to heaven, a wall that kept Achilles at bay for so many years, and a 2,500 year old wall that still divides China today.

There's a wall that was recently torn down, the Berlin Wall. Constructed in 1961, it was literally pulled apart in 1990. At the time, its destruction seemed impossible and wonderful, not because of the barbed wire or electrified fences, the guard posts, or its imposing twelve foot stature, but because it had always been there for those of my generation. It was taken for granted, was an earthen fixture like Mount Everest. And when it was torn down, destroyed, everyone realized what that meant because it was so obvious, so apparent—there was no more wall! It didn't just erase a separation between East and West Germany—that wall goes much deeper, is more ubiquitous—it made everyone re-evaluate the Germans' relationships with each other and the rest of the world. That wall was not there to inform and shape behavior anymore, yet its shadow remains just as Babel's silhouette lingers in our hearts.

One More Fall

There is one story in my life, a story about me and the first time I came to my identity face to face, that is indicative of my whole life's struggle with this issue:

There is a boy, four years old, living in Dallas, Oregon. His name is Ty Inoue. He and his mom, Dixie Garrett (after the divorce, she has chosen to keep her maiden name) are sitting on their couch, a long golden couch. The boy practices writing his name on a piece of paper as Dixie reads.

"Mom, how do you spell it again? Is it 'YT' or 'TY'?"

"'TY' son. And what does that spell?"

"Ty."

Three years pass. Ty is seven now and living in Las Vegas. He attends Fay Heron Elementary school. It is report card time. He accidentally leaves his card in the school cafeteria during breakfast and comes back in a rush after school. He finds a report card there with a strange name on it, one he's never seen before: ASAO B. INOUE. He thinks it may be the girl's that was sitting across from him during breakfast that morning, but takes it home because he has to give some report card to his mother. She might get suspicious. That night he gives the card to his mother, but she acts as if nothing is wrong.

"Mom, it's not mine."

"What do you mean? This is your report card."

"No mom, it's the girl's that I sat with at breakfast. I forgot mine and she left hers. I picked it up instead. See," pointing to the foreign and feminine, vowel-laden name on the front cover. "See, it's a girl's name."

"No Ty, this is yours. That is your real birth name. Ty is your nick-name. That's what we call you."

The boy is confused. He feels as if everything is collapsing around him. He has nothing solid to hold on to. If he isn't Ty, then who is he? Why isn't he called by that funny name on the report card? Why does he need two names? What does that second name mean? For the rest of his life, the boy will grow up with two names: one he will have to put on applications, school documents, his driver's license; the other he'll use and know himself by, his friends and family will call him it, he may write it on a note or a letter to a friend but never sign it on a document because it doesn't belong there. The first name will often sound clumsy or awkward when he tells it to others. Most will mispronounce it. Even more will misspell it. In high school, he will laugh at a Korean boy whose family changed his name to "Huey," after the Walt Disney duck, so that he would be "more American," but he won't realize that his name has also been Americanized. And just like Huey, it won't erase others' notions of him. Very late, the boy, now a man, will realize that underneath the first name is a whole culture, a whole nationality, a group of Americans that have built walls and have had walls built around them, some with barbed wire, because of assumptions and perceptions, prejudice and fear. He will realize that he has never understood or lived within the community of this identity that is supposedly his. Many tell him it is significant to his life's story. While he is unsure about this, he will constantly feel his lungs burn from exclaiming: "I am not a Beaner. I am not a Chink. I am not a trouble maker. I am not-I am not-I am not! I am Japanese! I am Cherokee! I am American! I am-I am-I am!"

REFERENCES

Ashcraft, Norman, and Albert E. Scheflen. *People Space: The Making and Breaking of Human Boundaries*. Garden City: Anchor,

1976.

Bacon, Edmund. *Design of Cities*. New York: Viking, 1969.

De Crèvecoeur, J. Hector St. John. *Letters From An American Farmer*. 1782. New York: Penguin, 1986.

Dictionary of Race and Ethnic Relations. London: Routledge, 1994.

Du Bois, W.E.B. *The Souls of Black Folk*. 1903. New York: Bantam, 1989.

Frost, Robert. "Mending Wall." *American Literature Volume 2*. Ed. Emory Elliott. Englewood Cliffs: Prentice Hall, 1991. 932-33.

Fuentes, Carlos. "How I Started to Write." *Multi-Cultural Literacy*. Ed. Rick Simonson and Scott Walker. Saint Paul: Graywolf, 1988. 83-111.

McClane, Kenneth. "Walls: A Journey to Auburn." *Walls: Essays 1985-1990*. Detroit: Wayne State UP, 1991.

Mura, David. "Strangers in the Village." *Multi-Cultural Literacy*. Ed. Rick Simonson and Scott Walker. Saint Paul: Graywolf, 1988. 135-53.

The NIV Study Bible. Grand Rapids: Zondervan, 1985.

Omi, Michael and Howard Winant. *Racial Formation in the United States*. 2nd ed. New York: Routledge, 1994.

Ong, Walter J. *Ramus, Method, and the Decay of Dilaogue*. 1958, 1983.

Rapoport, Amos. "Systems of Activities and Systems of Settings." *Domestic Architecture and The Use of Space*. Ed. Susan Kent. London: Cambridge UP, 1990. 9-20.

Rose, Mike. *Possible Lives*. New York: Penguin, 1995.

Sanders, Donald. "Behavioral Conventions and Archeology: Methods for the Analysisof Ancient Architecture." *Domestic Architecture and The Use of Space*. Ed. Susan Kent. London: Cambridge UP, 1990. 43-72.

Wright, Richard. *Notes of a Native Son*. 1940. New York: Harper and Row, 1989.

Red River Valley

CRAG HILL

Surrounded by flat
            rounded by flatness
    lone man, dressed in black

    long black hair
walks I-29's shoulder
            outside of Fargo

            too proud to hitchhike
    how far will we go
as a civilization

before we know
            how far we've driven him
    from his way of life?

    as he gets smaller
in the rearview mirror
    the answer swells

Crag Hill teaches at Moscow High School in Moscow, Idaho, and is editor of newsletter of the Inland Nortwest Council of Teachers of English.

Reconstructing Memory in the American West

THELMA SHINN RICHARD

Mary Austin, Mary Hallock Foote, and Caroline Kirkland are representative of the women who treated relocation to the American West as an opportunity to construct, both in their writings and in their lives, a new home predicated on their memories of a more civilized past. True to the didactic tradition of nineteenth century American women's narrative, their writings constitute teaching stories for the female community they left behind. Their sketches and fiction reveal that the shape those memories gave to western life widened the gender gap even as it seemed to lessen the space between their past and present lives. While the necessities of western life often led to dissolution of gender roles, the memories of eastern values and social expectations often kept individuals from enjoying the greater freedom and potential equality the evolving lifestyle promised. These women document in their autobiographical and fictive observations, so often dismissed as merely local color, the need to *re*-construct eastern memories by marrying them to the realities of western experience. Such reconstruction of memory enables their characters and their readers to share in the preservation and the transformation of the ideals of community and individual female possibilities in order to create a new home in the American West.

The title of Caroline Kirkland's book of sketches, *A New Home, Who'll Follow?*, indicates that she will discuss domestic concerns and that she is addressing an audience of those

Thelma Shinn Richard is Associate Chair of English and Professor of English and Women's Studies at Arizona State University. Her most recent book is Women Shapeshifters: Transforming the Contemporary Novel *(1996). She acknowledges the contributions of Jennifer Parra and other students, her husband, Jon, their ten children and twelve grandchildren.*

who "will follow" her to the West. A second reading of this final phrase also reminds us that women were the followers, rather than the leaders, in the westward expansion of America. As Nancy Woloch asserts,

> [W]omen moved west as members of families, not of their own volition. . . . Women migrants lost their friends and relatives, churches and homes; comfort, companionship, and community vanished. They also lost the benefits of eastern society, where women were held in higher esteem, enjoyed one another's company and had more influence within the family." (143)

If the West was to become truly a new home, it would be women who would establish that home, because, as Annette Kolodny quotes a popular novelist of 1838, "'Home was her true sphere'" (*The Land* 110). As Woloch has further observed: "Within their self-contained female world—noncompetitive, empathetic, and supportive—women valued one another and thereby gained a sense of security and self-esteem" (119). Thus both the domestic establishment and the sense of community fell under the authority of women, despite their lack of power in "the larger world of male concerns" (Woloch 120), so much so that when they followed their husbands westward, "[w]omen migrants were often left with the sense that they had lost the benefits of civilization itself" (Woloch 143).

Yet it is precisely these benefits that woman could bring to the West, Kirkland will remind her readers through her sketches. Certainly her sketches would reveal the "uncivilized" surprises she would encounter when she moved with her husband to Michigan in 1837, but those graphic details would be accompanied by the insightful observations of Kirkland's narrator, Mrs. Clavers, herself an easterner who has journeyed West. Thus, as Sandra A. Zagarell notes, she "embodies an eastern sensibility that must adjust to western life" (Kirkland xxix). As the vehicle through which Kirkland shares her autobiographical experiences, Mrs. Clavers allows the eastern reader both to identify with her in her initial discomfiture and later to share with her the experiences and individuals who effect her transformation into a "denizen of the wild woods—in my view, 'no mean city' to own as one's home. . . " (186). In this way, Kirkland creates what she describes as "a veritable history; an unimpeachable transcript of reality; a rough picture, in detached parts, but pentagraphed from life; a sort of 'Emigrant's Guide'" (1). This "Emigrant's Guide" begins and ends with Kirkland's memories of home, but by the end that home is reconstructed on the western frontier, not only the individual's home but a new home for the female community she thought she had left behind and finds even in the "wild woods" of Michigan to be "'no mean city.'" As Zagarell has said elsewhere, the purposes of sketch writers often "included presenting—and preserving—the patterns, customs, and activities through which, in their eyes, traditional communities maintained and perpetuated themselves, and nurturing a commitment to community in readers" ("Narratives" 500).

However, Kirkland is careful to differentiate her "Emigrant's Guide" from the travel narratives of the period. Even Americans moving westward carried the European imperialistic attitudes that Edward Said tags as the "Orientalizing" of other cultures; also, as Sara Mills observes, "most travel writers portray members of the other nation through a conceptual and textual grid constituted by travel books" (74). Kirkland quickly announces the inadequacy of such books in preparing her for her move westward as she ironically echoes the language and descriptions offered by her sources:

> When I first "penetrated the interior" (to use an indigenous phrase) all I knew of the wilds was from Hoffman's tour or Captain Hall's "graphic" delineations: I had some floating idea of "driving a barouche-and-four anywhere through the oak-openings"—and seeing "the murdered Banquos of the forest" haunting the scenes of their departed strength and beauty. But I confess, these pictures, touched by the glowing pencil of fancy, gave me but incorrect notions of a real journey through Michigan. (6)

As Kolodny notes, in Kirkland's sketches "the male tradition of high romantic western adventure had been challenged at its very core. . . . In the view of her female contemporaries, Kirkland had provided the kind of details that would enable them now to locate their plots of domestic piety in a log cabin on a far frontier" (*The Land Before Her* 157).

Kirkland's readers begin to learn how romantic and inadequate other "baggage" from the East proves to be when Mrs. Clavers encounters her first "Michigan Mudhole." Rather than the carriages which her memory calls up from the travel books, Mrs. Clavers follows her description of the mud-hole experience with more realistic advice: "I seriously advise any of my friends who are about flitting to Wisconsin or Oregon, to prefer a heavy lumber-wagon. . ." (6). Similarly, she will laugh at her own request to see the hotel when she discovers that "[m]y Hotel was a log-house of diminutive size. . . . I was then new in Michigan" (8).

Memory does not serve her well in anticipating western alternatives to eastern experiences, but it will serve her far better in terms of values and attitudes than landscape and things. By her second night's lodging she has learned to appreciate what those who have preceded her to the West have been able to accomplish, as "Mrs. Danforth's breakfast table, which had appeared in the morning frugal and homely enough, was filling my mind's eye as the very acme of comfort. Everything is relative" (15). Mrs. Clavers, then, recognizes that she too is one who has followed previous settlers to find a new home in the West. Even in this earliest sketch she begins to revise her eastern expectations. She listens to Mrs. Danforth's "homely recital with a good deal of pleasure" (17), and she passes on what she learns to her reader. The sketches provide both Mrs. Clavers's observations of her new neighbors and her recording of their own stories, illustrating Zagarell's definition of the sketch as "highlighting individuals' separate stories yet conjoining them" ("America" 147), in order to reconstruct the community she remembers in terms of the community in which she finds herself.

As she views the things she brought from the East, Mrs. Clavers soon recognizes that "myriads of articles which crammed the boxes, many of which though ranked when they were put in as absolutely essential, seemed ridiculously superfluous when they came out" (42). She does not, however, dispose of the "home" and "community" values lodged in her memory. "In this newly-formed world, the earlier settler has a feeling of hostess-ship toward the new comer" (64), she explains in a later sketch. When she arrives, Mrs. Rivers too must learn the relativity of the "things" she might encounter: "Mrs. Rivers, who was fresh from 'the settlements,' often curled her pretty lip at the deficiencies in her little mansion, but we had learned to prize anything which was even a shade above the wigwam, and dreamed not of two parlours or a piazza" (65). Now Mrs. Clavers must carry out her communal duty of teaching the new arrival: "I assumed the part of Mentor on this and many similar occasions; considering myself by this time quite an old resident, and of right entitled to speak for the natives" (66).

While seeing oneself as "entitled to speak for the natives" sounds suspiciously Orientalist, Mills has addressed the difference in terms of travel writing by women and that by men; women's texts, she observes,

> display an alignment with other nations. . . . [T]heir accounts demand a recognition of the importance of interaction with members of other nations, not as representatives of the race, as in male-authored accounts, but as individuals. This alternative, more personalized form of writing by women, this "going native" by women, constitutes both a challenge to male Orientalism and a different form of knowledge about other countries. (99)

Women traveling to the American West, even when that "west" is Michigan and seems more eastern to us today, were really going to another country as surely as British women who ventured away from their island home. They too were aware that they would need to interact with the individuals who best knew their new home. Aligned now with the West, Mrs. Clavers offers its realities as the stuff of which community must be made. Notably, however, Kirkland's alignment does not extend to the native American cultures that already inhabit the region; of the works we are considering here, only Mary Austin's stories reflect the heritage of those indigenous communities. However, American women's nineteenth century novels from Catherine Maria Sedgwick's *Hope Leslie* to Helen Hunt Jackson's *Ramona* will further this alignment through the literary convention of intermarriage, positing a commitment to a larger human community. As we shall see in the Austin's sketches, that alignment will lead even further to the sense of a universal community, in which humans can learn the real meaning of community from the western landscape itself. However, all of these writers willingly give up misconceptions rooted in the memories of an imperialist, patriarchal past while preserving and transforming the memories of home and community, memories which "civilize" the West in quite different terms than is found in male adventure texts.

Yet, as Sandra L. Myres notes, "The frontier, like the trail, tended to blur sex roles. Everyone was expected to 'lend a hand'" (160). Kirkland's Mrs. Clavers makes a similar observation: "[E]very man, whatever his circumstances or resources, must be qualified to play groom, teamster, or boot-black, as the case may be; besides 'tending the baby' at odd times, and cutting wood to cook his dinner with" (72). This new equality is threatened by memory of power, however, and Mrs. Clavers adds that "If he is too proud or too indolent to submit to such infringements upon his dignity and ease, most essential deductions from the daily comfort of his family will be the mortifying and vexatious result of his obstinate adherence to early habits" (73). Such habits defeat Mr. B—, for instance, who attempts to maintain a "gentlemanly residence" (77) without working at all. Memories of eastern luxury alter the appearance of their log-house with "tasteful drapery of French chintz" and "vases of flowers, books, pictures, and music" (73); but Mrs. Clavers notes that, because "Mr. B—'s character had by no means changed with his place of residence" (77), the family is "growing poorer and poorer" (78) and "persuade themselves that all who thrive, do so by dishonest gains, or by mean sacrifices, and they are teaching their children, by the irresistible power of daily example, to despise plodding industry, and to indulge in repining and feverish longings after unearned enjoyments" (78).

On the other hand, Mrs. Clavers suggests as she tells the story of Mr. and Mrs. Beckworth that being able to change with one's "place of residence" by learning new, more egalitarian social attitudes can result in preserving rather than abandoning the home we remember. Mr. Beckworth is described as "a man of deeds, not words" (96), and his wife's "cheerful and ungrudging industry" (90) enables them to create "not a Michigan farm-house, but a great, noble, yankee 'palace of pine boards,' looking like a cantle of Massachusetts or western New-York dropped *par hazard*, in these remote wilds" (87).

Overall, Mrs. Clavers has shown the reader her evolution from a fanciful eastern tourist to a western settler. Although she worries that "I have already been adventurous, far beyond the bounds of prudence. . . that in acknowledging even a leaning toward the 'vulgar' [western] side, I place myself forever beyond its [eastern society's] pale" (186), she has indeed taught the reader the value and the dangers of memory. Domestic memories of home and communal values richly take root in the new land, but neither social restrictions nor eastern things necessarily transplant well to the western garden. By perceiving the realities of western life within her memories of domestic and communal ideals, Kirkland has married East and West and delineated a new home for her readers. Gender and social limitations originating in "the larger world of male concerns" can be left behind as the demands of western life blur such distinctions. As Kolodny argues, "women claimed the frontiers as a potential sanctuary for an idealized domesticity. . . . They dreamed, more modestly, of locating a home and a familial human community within a cultivated garden" (*The Land Before Her* xiii).

The concept of "a cultivated garden" does not immediately spring to mind either in Kirkland's Michigan mud-holes or "in a lofty valley of Colorado, not far from the summit of that great 'divide' which parts the waters of the Continent . . . where the tough fir forests bend, and fail, and finally give up altogether the ascent of those bare slopes, ever whitening" (9-10), which provides the opening setting for Mary Hallock Foote's first novel, *The Led-Horse Claim*. Yet these seemingly wild settings do constitute "a home and a familial human community" for the central female character in each work. Foote, as had Kirkland, moved West with her husband, and the novel is set in the town of Leadville, Colorado, where he was "offered the management of the Adelaide Consolidated Silver Mining Company, which comprised four mines in Leadville" (Johnson 44). Cecil, the novel's heroine, is yet another "follower." She has left her family in the East to follow her brother Conrath, who manages the Shoshone mine in a western Colorado mining town. Dependent upon him for financial and emotional support, she soon discovers that he is an alcoholic. Later she must return east because he is killed in a battle between two mines. Appearances to the contrary, however, Cecil does achieve both independence and community in her western home; as in Kirkland, it is not the things but the community and lifestyle that promise a "cultivated garden" in the wilderness of the New World.

Foote achieves her contrast of East and West dramatically in this fiction by reversing the pattern we have seen in Kirkland's sketches of an eastern tourist slowly evolving into a western settler. Her novel, assuming that the reader's memory already supplies the eastern formulas, begins with only the contrasting western portrait of Cecil: "She wore no habit; the plaited skirt of her cloth walking-dress permitted her stirrup-foot to show, and a wide-brimmed straw hat shaded the heightened bloom in her cheek" (16). Cecil rides without an escort, relying solely on her own abilities, and when she visits the mine she talks with a man, Hilgard, without being formally introduced to him. Her "hot blush" at this situation reflects that she is still a lady even if she has departed from eastern rules of decorum, and although she "could not help smiling at her own discomfiture, when it had reached this point" (20), she conducts herself as his equal.

Next, at the Younger Sons' Ball, we learn that her brother Conrath does not fulfill his social roles to her. For a chaperone, he provides her with Mrs. Denny, a woman for whom "his admiration . . . was no secret in the camp, but that he should expect his younger sister to share it seemed incredible. It was more probable that he had sacrificed his sister's tastes to his own" (51). Still Cecil thrives in the freedom of this western environment, making responsible choices for her own best interests. For instance, she rejects the offer of Hilgard's friend the Doctor to be her social guardian. "Here, there is no classification," he warns her. "You have to pick your way among all the people who are crowding you, elbow to elbow. What is a young girl to do? You are no judge of character, Miss Conrath" (91). Perceiving that he has Hilgard's rather than her best interests at heart, she replies, "I must ask you to excuse me from any more discussion of your friend" and then because "[s]he felt that her discourtesy had been well deserved, . . . without further apology, she left the room" (95).

The independence we see in young Cecil does not come from the guides her eastern expectations would teach her to accept—Mrs. Denny or the Doctor or even her brother. Still, her memories of home, as would be shared by her readers, demand a female community to support her. Earlier settlers are conscious of this need, sharing Kirkland's awareness of the duties of "hostess-ship," but the western landscape is not supportive of their efforts:

> Cecil's life at the mine was a lonely one. Even the ladies who lived in the populous parts of the camp struggled vainly to fulfill duly that important feminine rite, the exchange of calls. . . . Cecil, two miles from the post-office, at an isolated mine, was out of reach of all but the most persevering of her new friends. In truth, there were not many of them." (131)

Ultimately, however, Cecil discovers her supportive community free of social limitations in, as is indicated by the title of Chapter 8, "The Shoshone Kitchen." In this domestic, nurturing space which is the heart of a woman's home, she can overcome the isolation she would otherwise experience in the widespread western setting by her friendship with the maid, Molly, a friendship the hierarchical values of the East would have found distasteful at best. In the West, Foote again informs her reader, necessity helps transform social prejudices: "Mistress and maid, living so near together, and being of nearly the same age, did not pretend to a very formal relation" (132). The kitchen welcomes Cecil, while the formal parlor depresses her: "Cecil, alone in the silent parlor, heard the burst of boyish laughter that followed this sally, and said to herself, rather wistfully, that the Shoshone kitchen was much the most cheerful room in the house" (134).

While her brother would keep her in the parlor, in her traditional role as the protected female, even he admits that "it is a dull cage for such a petty bird!"(136). However, he lies to her of his economic manipulations because "[g]irls ought not to know what is going on in a place like this" (137), revealing his own lack of adaptation to his new environment that underlies his willingness to exploit it for financial gain. Molly, on the other hand, does tell Cecil the truth: "On the days after these evening visits, Molly was unusually communicative, and had a great deal of information to give on the progress of the dispute between the mines" (135). In this way, Foote suggests that gender limitations are inextricably intertwined with class barriers. Molly, the working class woman, does know what goes on "in the larger world of male concerns," and expanded definitions of the female community make that information available to Cecil as well.

Cecil uses her expanded knowledge to try to effect change in that "larger world": she meets Hilgard in the woods and tries to persuade him to leave before the conflict escalates. Although he promises to do so in hopes that she will be his, a telegram changes his mind and he is still there and involved when Conrath is killed. Because of this, Cecil chooses to break with him completely, sounding a chord similar to Nora's remark as she leaves Torvald in Ibsen's *The Doll's House*: "'There is an instinct that forbids me,—I must follow that! . . . You have done your duty, in spite of the cost,' she said. 'But you cannot judge for me. A woman's duty is different'" (186).

A "woman's duty" had been carefully defined in nineteenth century literature, and choosing the right path is mapped out in what Nina Baym in her analysis of women's fiction has called the "heroine's tale." Foote's novel can be seen both in these terms and in the terms of Susan K. Harris' description of the "exploratory novel." Baym describes "the story of a young girl who is deprived of the supports she had rightly or wrongly depended on to sustain her throughout life and is faced with the necessity of winning her own way in the world" (11) and yet who still achieves the "happy ending" of marriage, which Baym explains as the reward for a "successful negotiation of the undifferentiated child through the trials of adolescence into the individuation of sound adulthood" (12).

Foote's novel, however, ironically reverses this pattern. Cecil leaves her supportive family in the East, not to win "her own way in the world" but to seek support from her less dependable brother. She finds independence in the West despite Conrath and independent of the marriage offered by Hilgard. When she is duly deprived of male support there, she is returned by her father to the East and the familial fold. Her marriage to Hilgard is negotiated despite her, and Foote's, objections. While there is some evidence that Cecil might have chosen Hilgard on her own at one time, after his involvement in the death of her brother she quite clearly states that "We must keep apart, because that is the only way to bear it" (183). Lee Ann Johnson, Foote's biographer, quotes Foote as describing her preferred ending for the novel as follows: "the young pair would, in the order of things as they were, never have seen each other again. But my publisher wouldn't hear of that! I had to make a happy ending" (50).

The female community which best supports Cecil is, therefore, in the West, because the eastern community is still completely under the domination of patriarchal demands. Foote's presentation of the wedding, for instance, belies any conventional "happy ending." Cecil's father chooses not to attend, and while her grandmother gives her away, "[i]t was with a stern reluctance in her heart that she fulfilled this duty of relationship" (267). Furthermore, "[t]he two women who represented the family of the bride, wore their dull, black mourning robes" (267), ostensibly because of her brother Conrath's death, but obviously their appearance reinforces the irony of this wedding, as does Cecil's grandmother's question to the other woman, Miss Esther: "Why is n't [sic] it respectable for a woman, now and then, to stay at home and keep things together for those who go and make a shipwreck of it? Why could n't [sic] she [Cecil] have been to you what you have been to me?" (272). Later, these two women "spoke of Cecil as if she were already in the past, in which their thoughts habitually dwelt" (274).

Harris has argued that women's novels evolved over the century into "exploratory novels" which "effected a change in readers' horizons of expectations" (33). "On the one hand," she explains, "the writings show an intense, almost paranoid awareness of the needs, and censures of 'the public,' an entity conceived of as easily influenced by the written word. On the other hand, they are equally intensely aware of other possibilities for female protagonists than the ones they publicly espouse" (19). When we acknowledge this possibly subversive element and read Foote's novel ironically, the individuation process of the heroine's story is reversed despite the "happy ending." Rather, it records Cecil's temporary blossoming and subsequent failed initiation as she returns to a childlike role in the East. Foote confirms this pattern when she describes Cecil's homecoming. "Everything is just as it used to be—only then I did not know how lovely it was!" (242), Cecil exclaims on her homecoming, and the narrator states ironically that "Her childhood seemed waiting, with gentle, appealing touches of memory, to heal the wounds that womanhood had given her" (244).

A final irony contrasts Cecil's return to the East with the impression she had left in the West of her hopes for independence. The novel ends when the current superintendent of the "Consolidated Led-Horse and Shoshone mine" (275) finds Cecil's ring and comments that "he had not found it easy to believe in the existence of a young girl, such as Miss Conrath had been described, in such a place, under such circumstances. It had been his experience that women generally fitted the places they were found, and the men who were their companions"; yet he concludes that the ring "was presumptive proof of civilized feminine occupation at an early period of the Shoshone history" (277). This ending underlines the ironic reversal of the novel. By moving its heroine from West to East, from independence to dependence, from an expanded female community in a wilderness home to a dying female community in her grandmother's childhood home, Foote accesses her readers' memory to contrast shrinking eastern possibilities for home and female community with the alternative of western potential.   As Baym argues, the heroine's tale "also fits the pattern of the comic hero, whose displacement indicates social corruption and whose triumph ensures the reconstruction of a beneficent social order" (11-12). Cecil's evolution in the West reveals the "social corruption" of the empty forms provided by her brother Conrath and reconstructs her memory of home and female community in the warmth of the Shoshone kitchen and her friendship with the maid Molly. In the West, therefore, Foote posits that "beneficent social order," still evolving out of women's memories of home and the female community but expanding to embrace the democratic ideal that guides America. As Louis Auchincloss argues in *Pioneers and Caretakers* about the nine women writers he chose to discuss, "They have a sharper sense of their stake in the national heritage, and they are always at work to preserve it" (3).

Finally, Mary Hunter Austin also found herself translated from East to West in the late nineteenth century and used this experience to pass on to her readers the ways in which the western landscape itself transformed eastern memory into western community and offered her a new home. Moving with her family in her late teens from Illinois to California, she survived malnutrition by acquainting herself with the desert.

Marrying Stanford Wallace Austin in 1891, she developed her sketches from that experience and published *Land of Little Rain* in 1903 and *Lost Borders* in 1906, both of which have been collected in the text used for this essay, Marjorie Pryse's 1987 edition of *Stories from the Country of Lost Borders*.

Even more than Foote's Cecil in a Colorado mine, Austin found herself isolated from her eastern memories of home and female community in the desert. Nor would she find long-term male protection as eastern memories claimed to promise her: Her brother's homestead had soon faltered, and her marriage virtually ended in a 1906 separation. Consequently, "[i]nto her writing she poured not only her love of the land but also the aching loneliness and frustration she had known in her twelve years of wandering in the Country of Lost Borders" (Fink 104). Her search for a female community led her back to the universal community of nature, in which she found models for transformation of the eastern human community she remembered into a western community in tune with its environment and egalitarian in its social possibilities.

To convey what she has learned to her readers, Austin creates a narrator/mentor similar to Kirkland's Mrs. Clavers. However, when we meet her in *Land of Little Rain*, this narrator has already evolved into a western settler. Therefore, her observations directly link her eastern memories to her new western perspective. Unlike Kirkland, however, Austin begins with the landscape itself rather than the stories of earlier settlers. "The region must enter constructively into the story, as another character, as the instigator of plot," Austin has explained while defining herself as a regionalist ("Regionalism" 105). In the sketch "Little Rain" which opens the collection of the same title, the narrator is quick to personify the desert into a female guide: "One hopes the land may breed like qualities in her human offspring" (11).

Both Kolodny in her study *The Lay of the Land* and Mills have discussed ways in which male texts define the land in female terms, as virgin territory, in order to claim domination over it. Austin's metaphor, however, images the desert as the powerful Creatrix/Destroyer, transforming the romantic male fantasy into an almost scientific study of the environment, which her editor, Marjorie Pryse, has noted "places her in a tradition of other American nature writers, especially Henry David Thoreau and John Muir" (xiv). Pryse also argues that

THE CHILDREN SING
IN THE FAR WEST

BY
MARY AUSTIN

WITH DRAWINGS BY
GERALD CASSIDY

BOSTON AND NEW YORK
HOUGHTON MIFFLIN COMPANY
The Riverside Press Cambridge
1928

Facing pages. From Mary Austin, The Children Sing in the Far West. *Drawings by Gerald Cassidy. Boston: Houghton Mifflin, 1928.*

the protective color of his surroundings."
Austin, The Pocket Hunter

PREFACE

THESE songs began to be made nearly forty years ago, when the author was young and the West so new that there were no songs about it that children could have for their own. Partly because I was teaching school and felt obliged to have something for my pupils about the land they lived in, and partly because I loved the land so much I couldn't bear not having grown up in it, I made most of the poems in this collection with the help of the children in my school. We had a wonderful time doing it, they because children always love poetry if it has a good rhythm tune and is about something they can understand, and I because I was in this manner let into the secret of how the great Southwest feels to those who have never known any other country. So I have gone on adding to this list from time to time, hoping that I was still keeping the child's approach and the child's feeling for the movement proper to his thought. All this time I have been waiting for a poet to come along and do for all Western children what I tried to do for those

vii

"Austin 'defines the path' of human emotional and spiritual experience by focusing on the geological, biological, and botanical details of the desert" (xx). It is this 'path' that Austin offers in order to transform eastern memories of home and community—"of human emotional and spiritual experience" — into western possibilities. "The regionally interpretive book must not only be about the country, it must be of it, flower of its stalk and root," Austin reminds us ("Regionalism" 106).

"The desert floras shame us with their cheerful adaptations to the seasonal limitations," Austin's narrator reports on the first "members" she introduces in her desert community. "Their whole duty is to flower and fruit" (11). Their ability to adapt to necessity in order better to fulfill their "whole duty" will be the first lesson Austin offers her readers. "There are hints to be had here of the way in which a land forces new habits on its dwellers" (15), the narrator asserts as she describes a pair of blackbirds who have learned to overcome gender roles in order to survive in the desert: "The quick increase of suns at the end of spring sometimes overtakes the birds in their nesting and effects a reversal of the ordinary manner of incubation" (15). Two more sketches, "Water Trails of the Ceriso" and "The Scavengers," will teach her readers of communal alternatives before Austin introduces a human character in "The Pocket Hunter." Yet he too is presented as simply one more member of this natural community: "He was a small, bowed man, with a face and manner and speech of no character at all, as if he had that faculty of small hunted things of taking on the protective color of his surroundings" (43). The Pocket Hunter survives and succeeds in his endeavors precisely because he does *not* try to dominate the land; rather, "the land tolerated him as it might a gopher or a badger. Of all its inhabitants it has the least concern for man" (45). This reversal of male domination fantasies is reinforced when he survives a storm by seeking natural shelter while another man, Bill Gerry, takes cover in a house he has built and is killed: "It went on against the cabin of Bill Gerry and laid Bill stripped and broken on a sand bar at the mouth of the Grape-vine, seven miles away" (47). The Pocket Hunter has found the desert to be a supportive community, as the narrator explains: "I suppose he never knew how much he depended for the necessary sense of home and companionship on the beasts and trees, meeting and finding them in their wonted places" (47).

We arc one of the land's inhabitants, not its owner, Austin makes clear in the next sketch, "My Neighbor's Field." The narrator traces the field's human owners from "the Paiutes, mesne lords of the soil" to her current neighbor and observes that "all this human occupancy of greed and mischief left no mark on the field, but the Indians did, and the unthinking sheep" (75–76). The natural community in this sketch serves as a model for what Pryse has called "a utopian vision of a community" (xxviii) in the final sketch of *Land of Little Rain*, "The Little Town of the Grapevines."

Austin's second book of sketches, *Lost Borders*, focuses on the relationship between the desert and the human community. "Regionalism," Austin argues in her essay of the same title, "since it is of the very nature and constitution of the planet, becomes at last part of the nature and constitution of the men who live on it" (98). Continuing her metaphor of the desert as female in *Lost Borders*, the narrator explains in the first sketch, "The Land," its fascination for men in particular and its effect on human character:

> [S]uch a countenance as should make men serve without desiring her, such a largeness to her mind as should make their sins of no account, passionate, but not necessitous, patient—and you could not move her, no, not if you had all the earth to give, so much as one tawny hair's-breadth beyond her own desires. If you cut very deeply into any soul that has the mark of the land upon it, you find such qualities as these. (160)

This land in which borders are lost, in which "the boundaries which should logically have been continued until they met the cañon of the Colorado ran out in foolish wastes of sand and inextricable disordered ranges" (155), offers freedom from social restrictions as long as the individual respects the demands of nature, "[f]or the laws run with the boundary, not beyond it" (155). "I am convinced most men make law for the comfortable feel of it, defining them to themselves," the narrator muses; "Out there, then, where the law and the landmarks fail together, the souls of little men fade out at the edges" (156).

FURRYHIDE AND GLITTERSKIN

Round about the choyital
Where the blue-throat lizards run,
Hoots the elf-owl from his burrow,
Squats the horned toad in the sun;

Where the glossy greasewood twinkles
And the mesquite dunes begin,
They have made their summer dwelling,
Furryhide and Glitterskin.

It has dark and winding hallways
And a chamber low and wide,

20

Facing pages. From Mary Austin, The Children Sing in the Far West. *Drawings by Gerald Cassidy. Boston: Houghton Mifflin, 1928.*

sense of home and companionship on the beasts and trees."
Austin, The Pocket Hunter

Walls and floors all smoothly patted
By the feet of Furryhide.
It has seven doors of exit
And not one the rain comes in,
But no doorway in that dwelling
Is too small for Glitterskin.

Dark those doorways and deserted
In the blinding desert noon,
But when night-jars chirr and hurtle,
When up comes the mesa moon,
Furryhide goes whisking, frisking,
Dancing with his fairy kin,
Gathering mesquite, nibbling grass seeds; —
Not a stroke does Glitterskin.

When the morning sun has warmed him,
And the kin of Furryhide
Sound are sleeping, he comes creeping,
Wicked jaws distended wide. —
Stoop you to the ruined dwelling,
Oh, so cautiously look in,
Red eyed in the dusky doorway,
There is only Glitterskin.

Such a little man is found in another sketch, "The Return of Mr. Wills." To the narrator, Mr. Wills is a man who "should never have moved West. Back East I suppose they breed such men because they need them, but they ought really to keep them there" (181). She remembers the East in terms of restrictions and argues that "[t]here is a sort of man bred up in close communities, like a cask, to whom the church, public opinion, the social note, are a sort of hoop to hold him in serviceable shape" (181-82). She equates Mr. Wills with the dominant male romantics of adventures:

> And of all he heard, the most fascinating to Mr. Wills, who was troubled with an imagination, was of the lost mines. . . . Out there beyond the towns the long Wilderness lies brooding, imperturbable; she puts out to adventurous minds glittering fragments of fortune or romance, like the lures men use to catch antelopes — clip! then she has them. (182)

Mr. Wills is enticed into the desert by his fantasies until his mind "faded out at the edges like the desert horizon that melts in mists and mirages, and finally he went on an expedition from which he did not come back" (184).

Unsuited to the freedom of western life, Mr. Wills needed borders within which the world fit the definitions he remembered; for Austin's narrator, however, his "lost mine was the baldest of excuses merely to be out and away from everything that savored of definiteness and responsibility" (184). It is Mrs. Wills who assumes that responsibility, who preserves home and community by adapting to the demands of her new environment. Not only does she begin working, but one day she makes "the remarkable discovery that after the family bills were paid at the end of the month, there was a little left over. A very little" (184). The narrator sees a parallel of Mrs. Wills in the regional community of nature: "All up and down the wash of Salt Creek there were lean coyote mothers, and wild folk of every sort could have taught her that nature never makes the mistake of neglecting to make the child-bearer competent to provide" (184). Nature validates Mrs. Wills's adaptation and predicates a new human community in which gender and other social limitations are as superfluous as Kirkland's Mrs. Clavers had found the things she brought from the East to Michigan. Yet Mrs. Wills could not enjoy her new independence because of her memories of eastern roles: "She had most of her notions of it from the church and her parents, and all under the new sense of independence and power she had an ache of forlornness and neglect" (184). The narrator's ironic comment should teach Austin's readers to overcome such remembered "notions."

A more successful adaptation to this new environment is achieved by two other women characters in these sketches: the narrator herself and the title character of "The Walking Woman." The narrator has indeed become a western settler, as she recognizes herself on her return: "The sky was alight and saffron-tinted, the mountains bloomed with violet shadows; as we came whirling by the point of Dead-Man, we saw the wickiups of the Paiutes and the little hearth-fires all awink among the sage. They had the look of home" (197). This should remind us of Mills's comments on women's texts that recognize "the importance of interaction with members of other nations, not as representatives of the race, as in male-authored texts, but as individuals" (99); however, Austin addresses this idea somewhat differently, arguing that "what is race but a pattern of response common to a group of people who have lived together under a given environment long enough to take a recognizable pattern?" ("Regionalism" 97). Thus, her narrator is representative of the *human* race as it has been defined in her region of the West: "It is not in the nature of mankind to be all of one pattern in these things any more than it is in the nature of the earth to be all plain, all seashore, or all mountains" ("Regionalism" 98).

This narrator shares the storytelling with Walking Woman, of whom even "men speak respectfully" (255), although the woman who has earned this title clearly breaks all the remembered rules for female behavior by her independent wanderings and lifestyle. "But you could not think of these things pertaining to the Walking Woman," our narrator comments; "and if there were ever any truth in the exemption from offense residing in a frame of behavior called ladylike, it should have been inoperative here" (256).

Walking Woman had begun her unconventional life "by walking off an illness" (257). What that illness was even the narrator does not know, but she speculates that "it might very well have been an unsoundness of mind which drove her

to the open, sobered and healed at last by the large soundness of nature" (257). So, too, Austin seems to teach us, can
the human community itself be healed; so too can we learn
as does Walking Woman that what is important in life is "[t]o
work together, to love together" (261).

Lost borders can be a blessing, as Austin's sketches re-
late. As America expanded westward, the loss of eastern limitations, especially those of gender and class, allowed the values of home and community to expand and blossom, become
more and more inclusive not only of the human community
but of the universal community which has always surrounded
us. Women brought their memories of an ordered domestic
sphere and a female community to this new land, but they
were not satisfied to live in the past of memory. To these memories, therefore, they added their direct experience of the new
human and physical environments in which they found themselves, until they were ready to return to their eastern female
community the lessons they had learned in the sketches and
novels they created. They did not forget from whence they
came, nor did they ignore the new home which it was their
duty to furnish with a supportive community. Reconstructing their memories by marrying them to western experience
allowed them to envision a more inclusive and egalitarian
society whose borders were lost in the shifting sands of the
desert so that they could be easily crossed by other living
inhabitants in an ever-expanding natural community.

REFERENCES

Auchincloss, Louis. *Pioneers and Caretakers: A Study of Nine Ameri-
can Women Novelists*. Minneapolis: U of Minnesota P, 1961.
Austin, Mary. "Regionalism in American Fiction." *English Journal*
21 (February 1932): 97-107.
———. *Stories from the Country of Lost Borders* [includes *Land of
Little Rain* (1903) and *Lost Borders* (1906)]. Ed. Marjorie Pryse.
New Brunswick: Rutgers UP, 1987.
Baym, Nina. *Women's Fiction: A Guide to Novels by and About Women
in America, 1820-1870*. Ithaca: Cornell UP, 1978.
Fink, Augusta. *I—Mary: A Biography of Mary Austin*. Tucson: U of
Arizona P, 1983.
Foote, Mary Hallock. *The Led-Horse Claim: A Romance of a Mining
Camp*. 1882; rpt. New Jersey: Gregg Press, 1968.
Harris, Susan K. *Nineteenth-Century American Women's Novels: In-
terpretative Strategies*. Cambridge: Cambridge UP, 1990.

Jackson, Helen Hunt. *Ramona: A Story.* 1884; Boston: Roberts Brothers, 1887.

Johnson, Lee Ann. *Mary Hallock Foote.* Boston: Twayne, 1980.

Kirkland, Caroline M. *A New Home: Who'll Follow? Or Glimpses of Western Life.* Ed. Sandra A. Zagarell. New Brunswick: Rutgers UP, 1990.

Kolodny, Annette. *The Land Before Her: Fantasy and Experience of the American Frontiers, 1630-1860.* Chapel Hill: U of North Carolina P, 1984.

———. *The Lay of the Land.* Chapel Hill, U of North Carolina P, 1975.

Mills, Sara. *Discourses of Difference: An Analysis of Women's Travel Writing and Colonialism.* New York: Routledge, 1992.

Myres, Sandra L. *Westering Women and the Frontier Experience 1800-1915.* Albuquerque: U of New Mexico P, 1982.

Pryse, Marjorie. Introduction. *Stories from the Country of Lost Borders.* By Mary Austin. New Brunswick: Rutgers UP, 1987.

Said, Edward W. *Orientalism.* New York: Pantheon, 1978.

Sedgwick, Catherine Maria. *Hope Leslie, or Early Times in Massachusetts.* New York: White, Gallaher and White, 1827.

Woloch, Nancy. *Women and the American Experience.* New York: McGraw-Hill, 1994.

Zagarell, Sandra A. "'America' as Community in Three Ante-bellum Sketches." *The (Other) American Traditions: Nineteenth-Century Women Writers.* Ed. Joyce W. Warren. New Brunswick: Rutgers UP, 1993. 143-63.

———. Introduction to *A New Home: Who'll Follow? Or Glimpses of Western Life.* By Caroline M. Kirkland. New Brunswick: Rutgers UP, 1990.

———. "Narratives of Community: The Identification of a Genre." *Signs: Journal of Women in Culture and Society* (1988): 498-527.

Wendover

SHAUN T. GRIFFIN

The bus driver from Ibapah
wakes at four to drive the sixty
miles of morning stars.
The pupils have no recollection
of stories laced with coyote.
They squirm to learn
the Wendover ways: beached
on the salt flats, this town
born under Ike's umbrella,
and now the sinful outpost
for jack Mormons.

But to children on the bus
it is school in the dark flanks
of winter, the failing
plumage of casino light,
a beacon on the desert
where no child is sheltered
from the wind and when the driver
cranks the yellow rocket,
they go with him
to ride the road home
festering with obligation.

Shaun Griffin is an educator and poet from Virginia City. He is editor and compiler of Desert Wood, *an anthology of Nevada poets. He also serves as a poetry editor for the Halcyon series.*

Building and Subverting Community in the New American West

Fantasy Themes and Metaphors in the Rhetoric of Division

A. CHIAVIELLO

The Courier was a weekly newspaper (defunct as of January 1997), published in Hatch, New Mexico, whose banner head proclaimed it, "Your Regional Independent Newspaper." It circulated by subscription and in selected retail outlets throughout the West, particularly in cattle-ranching regions of the Southwest, Nevada, and Oregon. Its self-image as a voice of the "Cowboy Custom & Culture" movement of the rural West was expressed in each issue in the form of rancher profiles, opinion columns, and "exposés" of the latest outrages of intrusive Federal bureaucracies: the Bureau of Land Management (BLM), the U.S. Fish and Wildlife Service (USFWS), and the US Forest Service (USFS).

My project for this critical appraisal of rhetoric in *The Courier* is to show that the appeals created in its pages serve both to build the ranching subcommunity in the West while simultaneously subverting the larger community of the "New West." I have selected a particularly exemplary text because of its broad rhetorical strokes and striking, if clichéd, metaphors.

My critique focuses on the fantasy themes that one example of such rhetoric "chains out" (Bormann 1984), and on the metaphors of division which it uses to establish and rein-

A. Chiaviello was born and raised in New Jersey, escaping to Arizona in 1968. He was an Army journalist in Vietnam and graduated from Oberlin College in 1976. After twenty years in journalism and public relations, he took up college teaching in 1987 and now lives in La Mesa, New Mexico.

force the self-image of the ranching community. The example I use here is rather typical in its tone and content of the sort of rhetoric that has lately emerged from various factions of the so-called "Wise Use" movement, but most especially in *The Courier*. An exhaustive empirical study would be required to track the themes of this rhetorical community's texts across a number of discourse situations (Hart), in order to defini- tively characterize and evaluate its "bifurcated rhetoric."

The bylined column I have selected to critique is entitled "National Notice of New Mexico," authored by Beth Tietjen, and published in April 1995. (It is reprinted in facsimile on pages 60-61). Its form constitutes a "script" or implicit sto- ryline. While a single such case may not equal the inductive evidentiary force of a statistical survey, I do feel it offers an engaging and revealing way of appraising the evidence. Fan- tasy themes implicitly dramatize the past: This is an impor- tant dimension for the present text. For group members, fan- tasy "participation . . . builds cohesiveness . . . and creates a group culture through expression of cherished attitudes and beliefs" (Porter 272). This participation—here in the form of writing and reading the sort of bombastic language that has given rhetoric its unsavory popular image—constitutes the chaining-out process, motivating individuals and resulting in action, as when the born-again Christian accepts Christ as her personal savior, or when a scientist accepts a new para- digm of research, or when a reader of *The Courier* makes a commitment to the "Cowboy Custom & Culture" political movement. After analyzing the fantasy themes of this arti- fact, I will go on to isolate its metaphors—noting the presence of their "focus" and "frame"—and to assess its metaphorical system.

For this analysis and critique, I will adapt two procedures outlined by rhetorical scholar and critic, Sonja Foss. Each method involves five steps. For fantasy-theme criticism, they are: 1) finding evidence of shared fantasies, 2) coding for fan- tasy-themes, 3) constructing the rhetorical vision, 4) naming the underlying motives, and 5) assessing the rhetorical vi- sion. For metaphoric criticism there is a similar process: 1) examining the artifact as a whole, 2) isolating the metaphors; then, 3) sorting, 4) analyzing, and 5) assessing the metaphoric system (Foss "Fantasy Theme"). I have adapted these critical approaches in order to provide a deeper analysis. First I will examine the artifact's dimensions and context, identifying its possible fantasy themes, and seeking evidence of their sharing; then I will proceed to a reconstruction of its rhetorical vision and a naming of the underlying motives for this vision. Moving on to metaphor, I will abridge the text to a version that highlights its major metaphors, then use this to analyze how these metaphors "create a particular reality" (Foss 191); this is accomplished by isolating, sorting, and classifying the artifact's metaphors into groups according to their vehicles, or topics. To conclude, I will analyze the metaphors' function, assess the overall metaphoric system for its effectiveness in constructing the intended reality, and assess the "rhetorical vision of the sharing community" (Foss 293-94), finally venturing my own interpretation and evaluation.

Dimensions and Context

The "complete experience" (Foss 191) of this text requires a comment on its layout. It runs fifteen paragraphs, continuing in sections B and C of the newspaper. This fragmenting scheme goes beyond the typical newspaper custom of continuing front-page articles elsewhere in the issue, normally to support advertising that appears on later pages. Continuing the article across three sections is an extreme example of this marketing device, particularly as there is very little advertising to justify it. Instead of drawing the reader into the publication, it becomes an inconvenience and may work against the image of solidarity cultivated both in the overall editorial voice and in the text under analysis here. Comparing the artifact to other contemporaneous examples of similar rhetoric, both in *The Courier* and in other Wise-use movement publications, I conclude that this story may represent a possible genre of polemic-posing-as-news. It is not, technically, an editorial column, though its boxed headline and tone make it seem like one.

Following pages: facsimile of the original Courier *story. Beth Tietjen, "National Notice of New Mexico."* (The Courier *March 7, 1995: A3ff.) Paragraph numbers have been added. Spelling and punctuation are as per the original. As noted, the original story was broken into three parts, indicated in the facsimile. Reprinted by permission.*

National Notice Of New Mexico
By Beth Tietjen

(1) Come Alive in '95. New Mexico!

(2) The New Year has produced a national review of the individualistic attitudes of some New Mexico residents, mostly from Catron County. *The Wall Street Journal* of Jan. 3, 1995, featured a front page article about Catron County and the Diamond Bar Ranch vs. "the greens."

(3) The thing that is apparently lost on eastern writers and a few western residents is that there is no "war" against intelligent planning. The "war" is against terrorists who have a corporate bankroll of over ten billion dollars to finance their "eco-warriors." Their mission is to harass, intimidate, and spew forth "eco" papers of absolute unfounded lies or well-doctored disinformation. For years now they have been testing the water to see how far they can push the American people. Well, push has come to shove. Somewhere along the way the government of the people and by the people shifted to government (with a capital G) against the people.

(4) Our Founding Fathers never envisioned a godless society with dictatorial powers granted by the (G) government allowing the destruction of personal freedom. Therein lies the struggle, not only of Catron County and the Diamond Bar Ranch but of all the United States.

(5) One quote from *The Wall Street Journal* reads thus "Indeed throughout the Diamond Bar, as on much Western rangeland, the damaging legacy of cattle is apparent. The banks of Main Diamond Creek, one of several Gila River tributaries weaving through the Diamond Bar, are bare and crumbling, mainly because creekside willows and cottonwoods that once checked erosion were long ago devoured or trampled by cows. Though the Main Diamond once brimmed with fish and bird life, the creek is now a muddy, cowpatty littered trickle much of the year. It's current condition, say biologists, helps explain why every native fish species existing in the Gila River 50 years ago is now either extinct, endangered, or under consideration for federal protection."

(5) Cattle had nothing to do with the introduction of rainbow or brown trout into Gila trout waters. People, well meaning, enlightened, college degree carrying, improvement oriented, biologists, did. As things turned out, the rainbows crossed with Gila's and the browns

See NOTICE pg. 8B

****

NOTICE from pg. 5A
ate them, hence the endangerment.

(7) Wilderness patrolmen for the Forest Service in the 70's helped pack in 50,000 pounds of cement, many mule trips from Willow Creek to upper Iron Creek. The Forest Service biologist supervised the building of a fish barrier to contain the Gila Trout in upper Iron Creek. Joe has a framed commendation from the Forest Service for his efforts that "saved" the Gila Trout from extinction. The fish barrier silted in the next snow melt which resulted in a man-made waterfall.

(8) To prepare Iron Creek for the salvaging of Gila Trout, the biologists killed out all the existing trout. Zapped out were many nice, healthy browns, rainbows, Gila's and crosses thereof. After barrier construction the Gila trout were considered saved. One problem with that premise was also man-made. One of the disillusioned ex-environmentalist fishermen who were so infuriated by the "official" destruction of the trout in Iron

Creek, carried several brown trout up the creek and released them behind the fish barrier. No cow was involved in any of this activity as they have been kept out of the creek for over 50 years.

(9) Back to Main Diamond Creek. A deadly forest fire, several years ago roared up over the top of the mountain, killing all the trees, shrubs and underbrush. The Aftermath of that fire, mud and ash, killed the fish in Main Diamond, not cows. We all know what killed the fish, as do the pseudo-environmentalists who continue with their anti-cattle

See NOTICE pg. 6C

****

NOTICE from pg., 8B

diatribe hoping to sway public opinion to help them achieve their goal of the unlawful takeover of the West.

(10) As for the Main Diamond water supply, it has always been muddy during spring snow melt, after which it runs clear and cold. We carried water for our camp out of it, drank it, washed dishes and ourselves with no ill effects whatsoever. The water quality guys from New Mexico State University were our only constant visitors all summer. They did periodic checks to measure water flow and the algae growth necessary to sustain the Gila trout, when they should be reintroduced to Main Diamond.

(11) Kit Laney, who is described as "an amiable, broad-chested cowboy" in the *W.S.J.* (no physical descriptions of "greens" were given in the article, only ranchers) purchased the Diamond Bar Ranch because of the Memorandum of Understanding (MOU) authored by the Forest Service. It INSISTED on dirt water tanks in the uplands, built at the RANCHERS EXPENSE. The Laney's accomplished the construction of two tanks the first year, both of which are used by elk and deer as well as cattle. It was the terrorists who came from other places and stopped all tank building and fence repair. They made sure the cattle remained on the creek bottoms and now are screaming in print and in person about the results.

(12) I have been unable to find anyone, in any agency, state or federal, who can tell how these "greens" gained total power over government agencies. Nor can anyone tell me what good has come from their lengthy challenges to federal, state, and county laws. Talk about muddy water and erosion of law, try to find anything about the background of the "greens."

(13) I have printed my name, address and phone number with the articles on the Diamond Bar. With one (1) notable exception of a "green" hiker from Silver City who gave me his name and phone number, all of my mail from the "greens" has been unsigned and no return address. What does that tell you? Other readers have questioned my motives, my sources, my knowledge and my ancestry. Good! People are beginning to wake up and look around.

(14) If anyone comes to see, hear and learn, you'll be welcome in Catron County and the rest of New Mexico. If you come with the attitude we are all a bunch of ignorant, back-woods land rapists; that you alone have revelation written in stone on how to "save the west", you'll probably meet your match behind every broken promise and under every stack of lies fostered by government (G) agencies. When the hardest working people on earth see themselves described as "welfare ranchers" by people with no need of work, funded by deep corporate pockets and many times drawing state welfare checks, it tends to incite ranchers to fight back.

(15) I can be contacted at [author's address]. It's going to be an interesting year.

Audience reactions among students in a graduate class in rhetorical criticism indicated that, at first, they perceived it to be an argument. After further consideration, however, we concluded that it is not persuasion, but rather reinforcement and articulation of opinions already held by its intended readers, i.e., an articulation of an existing fantasy theme.

The tone of this article is casual and aspires to an intimacy with its readers, the writer, as I have already suggested, assuming that most of them already agree with her expressed opinions. Its initial metaphor, "Come Alive in '95, New Mexico" (paragraph 1), is an exhortation to action, implying that New Mexicans have been dead (-asleep?) and need to arise, to "wake up and look around" (paragraph 13).

Shared Fantasy Themes

The sharing of fantasy themes is first evident in the tone of the piece, addressing its audience as friends who share the same outlook on life, implicit in the phrase, "individualistic attitudes of some New Mexico residents" (paragraph 2). As Jack Turner notes, "Almost everyone agrees that the use of public and private resources is out of kilter, but here the agreement ends. This absence of agreement is the key to our difficulties, not, for instance, the cost of grazing fees" (52). In the third paragraph, the author claims that "there is no war against intelligent planning," a concept that may be "lost on eastern writers and a few western residents," implying that those people are not part of her rhetorical community. In fact, the author seems to assume that her community is at one with "Our Founding Fathers." Here, we might safely conclude that she shares a certain Lockean fantasy-theme with her readers, a theme that could be fleshed out more fully in a wider sample of texts. It's pertinent to quote Turner here, to the effect that,

> A civil society is marked by a barely conscious consensus of beliefs, values, and ideals—of what constitutes legitimate authority, on what symbols are important, on what problems need resolution, and on limits to the permissible. . . . a shared vision of the good. . . . In the West, these sharings have vanished. (52)

Evidence for the existence of shared fantasy themes in this text is implicit or explicit in the following examples:

• "Catron County and the Diamond Bar Ranch vs.'the greens'" implies a contest or confrontation. The statement that, "The 'war' is against terrorists who have a corporate bankroll of over ten billion dollars to finance their 'eco-warriors'," explicitly characterizes the conflict as war. "Their mission is to harass, intimidate, and spew forth 'eco' papers of absolute unfounded lies or well-doctored disinformation. . . . to see how far they can push the American people." This assertion extends the military metaphor (mission, harass), adding the dimension of covert counter-intelligence (disinformation).

• "Our Founding Fathers never envisioned a godless society with dictatorial powers granted by the (G) government allowing destruction of our personal freedom." This theme identifies the rhetor with foundationalist, God-fearing values, by implication assigning to her opponents the opposite values of dictatorship and opposition to freedom; the parenthetical uppercase G seems to qualify "government" as "big." "When the hardest working people on earth see themselves described as 'welfare ranchers' by people with no need of work, funded by deep corporate pockets and many times drawing state welfare checks, it tends to incite ranchers to fight back." This theme emphasizes both the Protestant work ethic and arrays itself against a corporate-patronized or welfare supported opposition, while glibly avoiding the implications both of the expression "welfare ranchers," and of the well-documented fact of broad corporate funding of the Wise-use movement (Helvarg, Echeverria and Eby). To her enemies Tietjen ascribes the aggressive, unlawful motives that accompany an effort to achieve an "unlawful takeover of the West." All these examples share the fantasy theme of an embattled community, facing up to a totalitarian threat in the form of "Government" and corporate–supported environmentalists.

• Finally, there are those themes that have to do with vilification of the opposition by characterizing it as phony, preoccupied with power, unlawful, foreign, and cowardly. They are "pseudo-environmentalists," with an unlawful goal of achieving unwarranted power. Unlawfulness is emphasized and buttressed by a xenophobia toward strangers, evident in the phrase, "terrorists who came from other places. . . ." Finally, Tietjen implies that her opposition lacks the courage of their convictions because, with one exception, "all of my mail from the 'greens' has been unsigned and no return address [sic]."

Rhetorical Vision and Underlying Motives

What we see emerging from these fantasy themes is a self-image of the rhetor (and her group) as occupying the last stronghold of rugged individualism and the pioneer spirit, fighting to preserve sacred and traditional "American" values in the face of an onslaught of secularists (and immigrants?), who have no appreciation of God's will or the customs and (sub)culture of the American Cowboy. Government, freedom, and the intentions of the Founding Fathers have all been subverted by godless eco-terrorists, and only the Bible and the Constitution remain as sources of authority. What is central to this rhetorical vision is the apparent need to vilify the opposition, to create division rather than to build bridges, and this is a key to a Burkean detection of its underlying motives.

A passing familiarity with the political and environmental issues confronting the "New West" enables us to see beneath the stated motives of American values and preservation of a traditional "custom and culture," to the underlying motives of self-interest in maintaining the right to continue in a way of life that has perhaps outlived its economic viability and now relies on government subsidies for its continued existence.

Yet the cachet of the cowboy subculture still holds sway in the imaginations of many Easterners who see the ranching way of life as embodying the myths of the American Frontier, as depicted in film and TV Westerns and manifest in the Shane legend.

Ironically, the rhetoric here explicitly excludes from the community these potentially important, if largely passive, supporters of the Cowboy Vision. This key rhetorical exclusion of a potentially large financial and political power base weakens the center of this rhetorical community, at the same time demonstrating both its political naïveté and its rustically provincial world view.

The text must be considered as an example of divisive rhetoric, chiefly because of its unrelenting vilification of those whom the author identifies as her opponents or "enemies." I believe that its harsh tone, and the wounding intent of its language, come from its concept of "the world conceived of as a collection of resources" (Turner 52), as well as from a very real sense of persecution, both by agencies of the Federal Government and in the rhetoric of environmentalism. Overall, the text is an effort to reawaken and reinforce an appropriate response in its readers, to recruit them into militant participation in "The War for the West," or the fifth and latest Sagebrush Rebellion (Graf), what I have elsewhere called "Range War 2000" (Chiaviello).

What is further revealed is an at least rhetorical attachment to the traditional Protestant work ethic ("the hardest working people on earth"), and an enshrinement of a life style whose intact preservation will assure the continuing flow of government subsidies and thus the continued ability to play cowboy without having to turn a profit at ranching.

Thus are revealed the ultimate hidden motives, what can be interpreted as greed embedded in the self-regarding fantasy theme of an unfettered personal "freedom" to continue behaving as if this is still the 1880s, not the 1990s, and to do so at the taxpayers' expense. Couched in an atavistic commitment to "tradition," the rhetoric here supports the luxury of ignoring economic reality, and continuing, to paraphrase Porter, literally to live in a dream world (273).

The Metaphoric Text

In this section, I first reduce the text to an abridged version, consisting of metaphors and their descriptions, identifying the major metaphors (in boldface) and their context. I then proceed to specify relevant frame and focus, terms that refer to the metaphoric language (frame) and that which is represented by the metaphor (focus).

The author opens with a call for New Mexicans to **come alive**, to join the contest **vs. "the greens,"** in a **war** against **eco-warriors,** whose military **mission** includes producing **unfounded lies** or **well-doctored disinformation,** while **testing the water to see how far they can push** the real Americans. Now push **has come to shove,** to a struggle with **government (with a capital G),** which, unlike that envisioned by **Our Founding Fathers,** is on the side of the environmentalists, as are **degree carrying . . . biologists and Wilderness patrolmen** who **Zapped out** the exotic brown trout in the Gila.

Overgrazing did not kill fish, it was a **forest fire . . .** [that] **roared,** as those who aspire to sway public opinion, to execute **a takeover of the West,** will know, though they refuse to acknowledge it. Unlike the friendly, **New Mexico State University water quality guys,** who are the only constant visitors to the Main Diamond Creek watershed, the **terrorists . . .** [are] **screaming in print,** and **muddy water and erosion of law** prevents us from finding out who they are.

But **people are beginning to wake up and look around,** to recognize that **ranchers are not backwoods land rapists.** If you think you have **revelation written in stone,** you will **meet your match** under a **stack of lies.** When **the hardest working people on earth** are called "welfare ranchers" by people **funded by deep corporate pockets,** they are incited to **fight back.**

Sound like a lot of clichés? Right. Clichés are simply the metaphors we know best. The presumptions reflected in these common expressions construct a familiar reality. Tietjen uses them because her intended audience already knows and shares the meanings that these clichés represent. Many of them are god-terms (Burke), ideographs (McGee), or fantasy-types (Bormann): value-terms that have been elevated to unquestioned (and unquestionable) status in this community's hierarchy of motives. These metaphors "encourage the adoption of a particular perspective by the audience" (Foss 193). Those who share the meanings and motives entailed already know who they are, and the use and repetition of these familiar metaphors function as a reinforcing mechanism for their sense of community and not as an argument intended to convince the unbelievers.

Coding Themes and Sorting Metaphors

The coding process highlights the setting of "the Old West" as one key theme, equaled if not surpassed by themes that characterize participants as rugged individualists, literally (grand)sons of the pioneers: hard-working and god-fearing ranchers clinging to a rich though brief, traditional but vanished, frontier subculture. Action themes are more veiled: "push has come to shove," but the form this shove might take remains unspecified.

The action theme of "struggle" is evident in the war metaphors; but beyond "waking up [to] look around," further action is left to the readers' imaginations, as in the last substantial paragraph, in which visitors to cattle country who disagree with this rhetorical vision can expect to "meet [their] match." What this match might comprise, hidden behind "every broken promise" and Government "lies," also remains unspecified, leaving the probative reader to fill in possible consequences appropriate to the vision: showdowns, standoffs, shootouts, ambushes, and holdups?

I have sorted out seven groups of associated frames (see following page), all revolving around one topic. Some metaphors might fit into more than one group, and perhaps an argument can be made for the creation of additional categories, but these groupings seem plausible to me. All of them seem more or less "major," though I relegate the frames *Alertness* and *Nature* to "minor" status. At first glance, this might seem ironic; one might easily be excused for supposing that Nature and Alertness are the key themes (environment and the wake-up call) of this text. In reality, however, Tietjen's text is more concerned with *Opposition* and *Force* than with

Metaphors and their Frames

ALERTNESS (minor): Come Alive, screaming in print, People are beginning to wake up and look around

OPPOSITION (major): "the greens," "eco-warriors," degree carrying . . . biologists, Wilderness patrolmen, terrorists. . . . screaming in print, revelation written in stone, (use of the term:) "welfare ranchers," deep corporate pockets

WAR/BATTLE (major): war, terrorists, "eco-warriors, struggle, Wilderness patrolmen, Zapped out, mission, takeover of the West, meet your match, fight back

UNTRUTHFULNESS (major): unfounded lies, well-doc-tored disinformation, terrorists . . . . screaming in print, muddy water and erosion of law, revelation written in stone

NATURE (minor): testing the water, forest fire . . . [that] roared, water quality guys, revelation written in stone, back-woods land rapists, the hardest working people on earth, [not] "welfare ranchers"

FORCE (major): how far they can push, push has come to shove, struggle, sway public opinion, meet your match, fight back

AUTHORITY (major): Our Founding Fathers, government (with a capital G), Wilderness patrolmen

any serious consideration of *Nature* or an actual conscious-ness of the multiple dimensions of the issues she raises.

Analysis of Metaphors

Analysis of the tabulated groups of metaphors reveals the system of metaphorical concepts and what effects the uses of the various metaphors might have on the audience: how metaphors function to argue for an attitude, and how they both limit and facilitate the adoption of certain perspectives (Foss 193). The metaphoric frames I have listed and demonstrated in the figure above to create a reality that preempts the opposition and precludes any compromise, resulting in a metaphoric rhetoric of war. The only strictly mixed metaphor, "testing the water to see how far they can push," is incidental and probably unintended. Again, the *Nature* category turns out to be the least central in what purports to be a text on an environmental issue. The author is remarkably consistent in her restricted use of the metaphoric categories of *Opposition, War/Battle, Force,* and *Authority*. The categories of *Alertness* and *Untruthfulness* are closely related in the need to be wary of lies. All of these are archetypal metaphors "that suggest basic, unchanging patterns of experience and function across situations and over time" (Foss 193), tying in to this community's identification with its mythical past.

The preponderance of war metaphors suggests that the rhetor intends to whip up war fever, projecting a leader's relationship with the audience. Directed against a foreign enemy in wartime, its author would be characterized as a propagandist. The metaphoric voice is prominent in the introduction and dominates the conclusion, a pattern that reinforces the pathos of the appeal and signifies that this is a classic example of wartime propaganda. The irate tone and vivid images enhance the capacity of the metaphors to resonate with and reinforce beliefs that the intended audience already hold. But they have the additional, unintended function of restraining a more sophisticated audience from responding as desired to the claims. From this, we can again conclude that the text's purpose is reinforcement, not persuasion, and is aimed at a less sophisticated, more rustic audience.

The monolithic imagery of these metaphors varies little throughout the text's development and constructs a (sub)culture of narrow horizons. Absent are any metaphors suggesting confidence in self or others, a desire to negotiate with the opponent, or an attempt to discuss or resolve the issues raised; such absences reinforce a view of the rhetor as divisive cheerleader. Proceeding from her opening call for dead-asleep (focus) New Mexicans to "come alive" (frame), Tietjen unstintingly urges joining the battle "vs." [versus] "'the greens'" (paragraph 2). Here she uses a well-worn cliché for environmentalists, evolved from their self-acknowledged concern for the greening of vegetative life.

In paragraph three, the claim that, "there is no 'war' against intelligent planning . . . , [that] The 'war' is against terrorists . . . " specifically identifies this contest (focus) as war (frame), the writer promptly assuming an adversarial stance for both herself and her opposition and then framing her foes as "terrorists" and "'eco-warriors'" (unstated focus: environmental activists). Another well-worn metaphor, the term "eco-warrior," connotes the primitive, as in an Indian or "native" warrior: an uncivilized EarthFirst!er and the opposite of the modern soldier. But the frame "terrorists"—applied to the same people—extends the image from hit-and-run guerrillas to fanatical, murderous zealots who might detonate bombs that they've strapped to their chests, killing people indiscriminately. "Their mission is to harass, intimidate" somewhat tempers that image, but completes the military metaphor. All of these are metaphors for battle, overt or covert, and fully establish the nature of the conflict, in the eyes of the author, as all-out war.

In the same paragraph, the expression, "spew forth" (frame) for the production (focus) of "'eco-papers'" (frame) or ecological literature (focus) assigns the negative connotation of vomitus to this kind of work. Somewhat aligned is the frame, "well doctored" for the same activity, which presents a metaphor of touch-up artists, witch doctors, or quacks, who harm rather than help the patient. In this case, the patient is accurate ecological information (focus), resulting in the frame, "unfounded lies." "Testing the water," however, is a gentle, tentative-sounding metaphor, and frames the focus of environmentalists' activism. It is quite out of place here, seemingly a literary lapse on the part of the author, calling up the image of *September Morn*. Tietjen quickly follows up with "how far they can push . . . ," which mixes in a more aggressive frame for the same focus. Now "push has come to shove," another cliché that frames the focus of escalating contention. The frame, "government (with a capital G)" uses the upper case to imply great size and power, remoteness, and hostility, as opposed to government in lower case, which is quite small, friendly, and close by, reflecting the values of the local electorate and county supervisors. Remaining unspecified is exactly who has been granted "dictatorial powers" in a "godless society" by this Government (paragraph 4). It seems we must infer that "eco-warrior terrorists" are the beneficiaries of this governmental largesse, as they are the only explicit opponents in this "struggle." Yet this is counterintuitive and dissonant, inasmuch as environmentalists are always complaining about the BLM favoring ranchers, the USFS favoring loggers; upon reflection, it's almost another cliché that the contemporary image of the concerned environmentalist is of someone continually preoccupied with raising money, and continually unable to raise enough of it.

In paragraph 6, college-degree "carrying" biologists are blamed for introducing exotic species to streams in the Gila. The metaphor, "degree-carrying" (frame) for educated (focus), puts a negative spin on education, making qualified biologists vaguely resemble the old card-carrying communist. That biologists have "Zapped out" (frame for "killed") the "existing [introduced, exotic, brown] trout" implies electrocution, though it is unclear how this has been accomplished (paragraph 8). At any rate, the metaphor links biologists to the military mission, certainly a dangerous potentiality. Likewise, framing forest rangers as "Wilderness patrolmen" (paragraph 7) characterizes them as nature cops, agents of a police state, participants in the militarist conspiracy against "personal freedom." In contrast, "the water quality guys" from NMSU (paragraph 10) are apparently friendly scientists (focus) framed in a minor metaphor as regular guys; yet, as "constant visitors," they remain outsiders, their sheepskins rendering them forever ineligible to become full-fledged members of this fantasy-sharing group.

Minor metaphors, like the forest fire that "roared"—and the militarist metaphor of "takeover" for the activities of environmentalists (paragraph 9)—are supplemented with the xenophobia about "terrorists who came from other places. . . . screaming in print" (paragraph 11). They lead up to the "muddy water and erosion of law" that make it difficult to "find out anything about the background of the 'greens'" (paragraph 12), implying that legal hurdles (focus) are comparable to muddy water caused by erosion (frame), in this case, ironically, of the law, not of the stream banks in question. The metaphor is appropriate for an article on the issue of cattle in riparian areas, but has the potential to work against this rhetor's message, inasmuch as the literal erosion to which environmentalists object is directly caused by the grazing of cattle belonging to Tietjen's constituency.

It's "Good!" that "People are beginning to wake up and look around," a frame for the unstated focus of increased awareness in the desired direction by the intended audience. Now, in a more sophisticated move, the author turns her adversaries' clichés ("welfare ranchers") around, with "the hardest working people on earth" functioning both as an ironic focus for "a bunch of ignorant, back-woods land rapists" and as a frame for the ranching community. She makes another deft move with "revelation written in stone," a Biblical allusion to the mosaic decalogue that serves to frame the focus of environmental activists as phony prophets.

This brings us to the final major metaphor, in which arrogant outsiders, the unstated focus for the extended frame, "people with no need of work [frame for elitists], funded by deep corporate pockets [frame for corporate contributions to environmental groups?] and many times drawing state welfare checks [frame for EarthFirst! freeloaders]," will "meet [their] match," another frame for some unstated power, hidden behind "every broken promise" and below a "stack of lies fostered by government (G) agencies," both of which are presumably frames for BLM and USFS actions and official decision documents considered to be unfavorable toward ranchers. What this "match" may entail also remains unstated, but we can assume, given the relative consistency of the metaphoric scheme, that this nonverbal metaphoric component involves violence, real or symbolic. That it is tied directly to the final assertion that "ranchers [will] fight back," leads to the inevitable conclusion that a battle is in the offing.

The Metaphorical System

Emerging from this analysis, we conclude without surprise that, in context, the metaphors are designed to inflame and divide, to reinforce existing animosities, and to begin drawing battle lines for an upcoming range war. This is "the nature of the reality that results" (Foss 194) from this rhetoric, and no matter how we might explicitly judge its implied ethos, we can only conclude sophistically that the metaphoric pattern has accomplished the rhetor's intended effect. In the long run, however, such a battle stance is likely to obstruct or problematize the realization of this rhetorical community's goals.

The tactic of warmongering has upstaged the strategy of retaining subsidies for ranching, and in a political arena that is much larger than this particular issue, little is to be gained from intransigence, unless it is rhetorical posturing: a ploy to set up the compromise card so as to trump the final trick in future negotiations.

It is a sign of desperation, I believe, that the rhetor and her community feel the apparent need to so woundingly malign their opposition. The West is no longer the Frontier, and the widely accepted reality of the now-urbanized "New West" mandates a political, not a military solution, as Tietjen must certainly be aware, no matter how eccentric her own vision of reality may be. Ultimately, the real value to whipping up Range War 2000 is pragmatically rhetorical: to intimidate and emasculate the political opposition. This is explicit in the "Bobbitt Babbitt" bumper stickers—invoking Lorena Bobbitt's emasculation of her husband, John Wayne Bobbitt, and suggesting the same fate befall Interior Secretary Bruce Babbitt—which have quickly sold out of stock in sympathetic Catron County retail outlets. Such an explicit, though unlikely, rhetorical threat is complemented by more tangible threats (Helvarg), as well as standoff language, such as that from Diamond Bar cattle operators Kit and Sherry Laney, who said they would meet attempted eviction from their formerly leased—then illegally grazed—USFS grazing allotment with "100 armed men." Yet it is worth noting that the confrontation ended in a whimper, when the Laneys docilely met the Forest Service's final deadline and sullenly moved their stock off the Diamond Bar in June, 1997.

Such bellicose posturing makes it too politically expensive for politicians to espouse environmental legislation that would alienate this faction. Because ranchers' political clout stems from the pioneers who were their fathers and grandfathers[1] most of whom are, or were, leaders of the local business community, as well as senators, congressmen, legislators, and governors of western states. Yet their now-anachronistic "grassroots" political position remains almost unassail-

able from a traditional patriotic perspective. Even in what
has been called a "post-Christian" era, what politician will
campaign against the Bible, Christianity, and private property? And who has more right to the "unclaimed lands" (the
BLM and USFS-administered public lands) than the spiritual
(if not actual) descendants of those who settled and claimed
the more desirable adjacent lands over 100 years ago? (It's
worth noting here that those spiritual ancestors declined to
claim these lands because the land lacked water.)

With national environmentalist legislative goals fading in
the neo-conservative gloaming, it is quite possibly the hope of
the wing-tip cowboys from the extractive industries to continue their support for the production of divisive rhetoric, in
order to prevent consensus, and to sabotage any precipitous
moves toward compromises that might dent their pocketbooks.
But by goading to action the relatively close-knit social environment of western ranching communities in a Burkean
scapegoating of the liberal environmentalist opposition, and
by failing to balance its verbal attack with overtures of compromise, this Cowboy Custom & Culture movement risks
marginalizing itself.

The risk must seem an acceptable one. Certainly it is the
traditional stance, the time-honored reaction over the past
one hundred years in a series of four Sagebrush Rebellions
(Graf). Response of pioneers and ranchers to the creation of
the forest reserves, to fees for use of the unclaimed lands, to
the legislation of wilderness, and to increased federal management of public lands has been consistent: after shouts of
outrage and appeals to tradition, there has been an eventual
acquiescence to government policy, a rolling-over or caving-
in, when the government promises to guarantee the continu-
ation of subsidies. Now, however, the stakes have been raised,
and the number of options on the table has shrunk. Subsidies themselves have become not the payoffs, but the major
issues, in an era of federal debt and deficit.

The Rhetorical Vision

We can conclude that there is a strong force for the creation
of a certain kind of community in this rhetoric, though we
might have no fondness for its nature. While this rhetorical
vision is weakest in its approximation of the "reality" of the

now-urbanized New West, events of the past few years show that it does function to bestow and affirm an outsize political power to this exceedingly tiny rhetorical community (at last count, less than 23,000 ranchers in eleven western states). The vision does seem closely adapted to the currently divisive national political climate as well as the (at least until recently) far more close-knit social environment of western ranching communities. But evidence of the past 100 years has demonstrated that continued ranching-as-usual is disastrous for much of the arid West. Certainly, community social norms of a conventional, Puritanical interpretation of Christianity are expressly supported in the rhetoric, but the remarkable divisiveness and Burkean_scapegoating fantasies belie the expected Christlike virtues of tolerance, charity, and generosity. Instead, themes of violence saturate the fabric of the text, possible excessive exploitation of natural resources is ignored, a struggle for dominance is expressed, and a resentment of perceived injustice remains unbalanced by a willingness to extend charity to those who disagree with this vision.

While perhaps most successful in creating, in Foss's words, "a panoramic vision that gives meaning" to this community, the vision fails utterly in its inability to interact meaningfully and productively with other rhetorical visions. In this failure lies the more important dimension of this rhetorical vision: the subversion of community by divisive language. As long as no option of compromise or dialogue is foregrounded, the possibility of consensus—of a "meeting of the minds" in Bormann's words—is precluded. As Turner observes, "decline in consensus erodes trust, and when trust erodes, personal relations, the family, communities and nations delaminate" (53). Meanwhile,

> These new forces have occupied the borders of our minds—strange figures claiming high moral ground, like Sioux along the ridges of the Missouri. It's unsettling. Folks employed in the traditional economies are circling the wagons of old values and beliefs. Their tone and posture is defensive, as it must be for those who, hurled into the future, adamantly cling to the past. (Turner 54)

Sadly, the evaluation of the community that emerges from this rhetorical analysis must conclude that whatever strength

this community gains from its coherent vision of itself is sacrificed in its aggressive pursuit of the status quo and its refusal to "build bridges" or accept compromise. Thus the stage is set for Range War 2000. Early, inconclusive skirmishes have taken place at the Diamond Bar Ranch in the Gila Wilderness, and at other isolated outposts in Arizona, Nevada, and Colorado. Battle lines are forming, with other Wise-use rhetors recruiting urban and suburban neo-conservative babyboomers to reinforce the traditional landed gentry of the rural West, even signing them up to ride herd on twenty-acre ranchettes, the subdivided remains of dysfunctional livestock operations. Shock troops of "Wise-users," property-rightists, county-power advocates, and cowboy culture have already been pressed into service, in an army supported by the financial power of East-Coast extractive industries, Japanese off-road vehicle makers, and Moonies (Helvarg). And the propaganda machine designed to dehumanize the enemy is shifting into higher gear, evident in the metaphors deployed here.
The battle may soon be joined.

NOTE

[1]A perhaps unusual instance comes from Catron County, NM, birthplace of the "County Supremacy Movement" (a "Wise-use" effort to interpret the Constitution to find that counties have preferential land-use planning rights over Federal lands within the said county). The county attorney for Catron County is James Catron, eponymous and at least a spiritual descendent of the nineteenth century James Catron: member of the "Santa Fe Ring."

REFERENCES

Bormann, Edwin G. "Symbolic Convergence Theory: A Communication Formulation." *Journal of Communication* 35.4 (Autumn 1984): 128-138.

————. "Fetching Good Out of Evil: A Rhetorical Use of Calamity." *Quarterly Journal of Speech* 63 (April 1977): 130-39.

Burke, Kenneth. *A Rhetoric of Motives.* 1950. Berkeley: U of California P, 1969.

Chiaviello, A. "Fantasy-Themes and Ideograms in the Cowboy Custom & Culture Movement." Paper delivered at the New Directions in Critical Theory Conference, University of Arizona, Tucson, AZ. April 1995.

Echeverria, John D., and Raymond Booth Eby, eds. *Let the People*

Judge: Wise Use and the Private Property Movement. Washington, DC: Island, 1995.

Foss, Sonja K. "Fantasy-Theme Criticism." *Rhetorical Criticism: Exploration & Practice.* Prospect Heights, IL: Waveland, 1989. 289-298.

———. "Metaphoric Criticism." *Rhetorical Criticism: Exploration & Practice.* Prospect Heights, IL: Waveland, 1989: 187-227.

Graf, William L. *Wilderness Preservation and the Sagebrush Rebellions.* Savage, MD: Rowman & Littlefield, 1990.

Hart, R. P. *Modern Rhetorical Criticism.* New York: HarperCollins, 1990. 329-338.

Helvarg, David. *The War Against the Greens: The "Wise-Use " Movement, the New Right, and Anti-Environmental Violence.* San Francisco: Sierra Club Books, 1994.

Lucas, S.E. "Review of Bormann's *The Force of Fantasy.*" *Rhetoric Society Quarterly* 16.2 (1986):199-205.

McGee, Michael C. "The 'Ideograph': A Link Between Rhetoric and Ideology." *Quarterly Journal of Speech* 66.1 (1980): 1.

Porter, L.W. "The White House Transcripts: Group Fantasy Events Concerning the Mass Media." *Central States Speech Journal* 27.2 (Winter 1976): 272-79.

Tietjen, Beth. "National Notice of New Mexico." *The Courier* 7 Mar., 1995: A3ff.

Turner, Jack. *The Abstract Wild.* Tucson: U of Arizona P, 1996.

For Those Carrying On Their Business in Front of Supermarkets

BILL ABRAMS

The man in grease-stained overalls,
maybe in his forties, maybe older.
His face, rutted deep, says he's been around.
He sets down a stack of quarters,
folds the want ads down the middle.

The young woman, cigarette and note paper
in hand, tries one phone, then the other,
finally steps back, arms folded tight,
as if trying not to let some important thing
escape. Tears begin to smudge mascara
under her darkened eyes.

Before she can make her call,
the mother has to arrange her brood of girls.
The two youngest stay put, sit next to each
other on a bumper curb. She tells them
to hold hands. An older sister steadies the stroller
where a slumped-over infant sleeps and another

Bill Abrams (1932-1998) served as English Consultant for the Nevada Department of Education for two decades and was revered by members of the English teaching profession. He was a member of the Ash Canyon Poets of Carson City, Nevada. This volume in the Halcyon series is dedicated to his memory.

secures the shopping cart so their seven bags
don't roll away.
The mother moves closer
to the phone, covers it with her arms and body,
showing her girls and anyone else
that whatever she has to say is not for them.

The thirty-year old, his muscles
bulge, escape from a strategically torn T-shirt.
He puts two six packs on the ground and dials.
With pounding gestures he spits out loud,
staccato words. He stomps through all the space
the cord allows. Finally he yells *Fuck you!*
and throws the phone against the wall.

The sad-faced man staring
out over the rows of cars while he talks
for fifteen minutes. He says there may be
better prospects East, hangs up, and limps
across the street against traffic.

The sharp-faced young woman, dark lines
under her eyes, gets out of a rusted-out
pickup crammed with boxes, bags
and Salvation Army furniture, scowls,
hurries to the phone, puts in her quarter.
A young man runs up to her, yanks
the phone out of her hand and yells
into it *You can take the bitch!* Inside
a bag boy stops and turns around.

They all carry on their business
in full view of those who go in and out
or wait outside in cars and give them
easy glances or none at all. Years ago
at least they would have been sitting
in phone booths with doors.

Walt Disney vs. Wallace Stegner
Community Leadership and Masculine Myths

ERIC BATEMAN

> Useful stories, I think, are radical in that they help us see freshly. They are like mirrors, in which we see ourselves reflected. That's what stories are for, to help us see for ourselves as we go about the continual business of reimagining ourselves.
>
> William Kittredge
> *Who Owns the West?* (158-59)

Wallace Stegner has written valuable and thoughtful books about the West, and we owe as much to him as any other writer for our understanding of and appreciation for its turbulent history; however, he overstates his case in *Where the Bluebird Sings to the Lemonade Springs* when he claims:

> transience in most of the West has hampered the development of stable, rooted communities and aborted the kind of communal effort that takes in everything from kindergarten to graveyard and involves all kinds and grades and ages of people in a shared past and a promise of continuance. (xvi)

This premise, varied and reiterated throughout his book, is doubly flawed.

Eric Bateman teaches English at the Great Basin College Educational Center in Winnemucca, Nevada. His two children are prime targets for Magic Kingdom demographers, but he tries to make the best of it.

First of all, Stegner repeatedly disqualifies "communities" he dislikes: the farming, ranching, mining, and timber industries in particular. In doing so, he defines "community" restrictively, overlooking that when a group of people with shared economic or other interests inhabit a particular region, that group qualifies as a community, regardless of whether someone considers the traditions, customs, actions, or beliefs of those people backward, barbaric, distasteful, or just plain strange. If people don't approve of cannibalism, it doesn't follow that a particular group of cannibals has no "community" or even "culture" or "society." What they have, instead, is something that is different from what people are used to and even to what they approve of. Regardless, one can't change behavior with imperialistic semantics.

The second flaw with Stegner's reasoning is that he implies that "community" on his terms exists elsewhere, presumably in the eastern United States, or Europe, directions to which he repeatedly points. It's difficult to see on what grounds he can do this. In the least, his reasoning requires a double standard, since for every western imprudence, there are eastern equivalents: We have Butte, Montana, and the Glen Canyon Dam; easterners have strip-mined ranges in Kentucky and Three Mile Island. If recklessness with natural resources has, like transience, hindered the development of community in the American West, it must have done the same in the American East, but Stegner recognizes no such parallel. The truth is not as simple as he explains it: Many problems of westerners and of western communities are also problems of easterners and eastern communities. We are all cut from the same bolt of rough, sloppy cloth.

Where the Bluebird Sings to the Lemonade Springs is a book determined to explain what is wrong with the West. And there are plenty of things that are wrong. Yes, transience is part of the western way of life, and that transience is relevant to any discussion of community in the West. Yes, westerners continue to try to make the land support more people than it will support. Yes, westerners continue to waste and exploit valuable resources for the benefit of a well-oiled industrial oligarchy. Yes, westerners have trouble distinguishing between the Myth of the West and actually living here. But to make the leap, as Stegner does, that because of these things the West lacks community is to make a blind leap indeed. Of course there is community in the West. To deny this is to disregard the millions of people who live here. There is more to gain, rather, by examining the dynamics of these communities. Even the Walt Disney Corporation knows that.

Yes, the Walt Disney Corporation. The same outfit that sold us *Pocahontas* and other historical and cultural travesties. The same people bent on sugar-coating and oversimplifying every reality of living. Yes, the Walt Disney Corporation and lackey Pixar, with *Toy Story*, which, underneath the technical innovation that dazzled audiences and critics, offers an evocative study of a struggle for community leadership that takes its cues from real struggles in the modern West. *Toy Story* questions the West's cherished myths and the actions people take based on them.

For those unfamiliar with the 1995 blockbuster children's film, the plot revolves around the idea that when people aren't around, toys come to life and play games of their own, which explains why toys never seem to be where children leave them (the film fails to explain why furniture and household appliances don't come to life as well). The plot thickens when Buzz Lightyear, a birthday present for Andy, the benevolent owner of the toys, threatens to unseat Woody, the sheriff, as leader of the rest of Andy's toys.

In true Disney fashion, this struggle for leadership is purely patriarchal. The community of toys in Andy's room is made up of a variety of masculine types (Woody the sheriff, Slink his toady, Rex the wimp, Potatohead the bully, Sarge the soldier); Bo Peep is the only female character of note. This community is ostensibly western since Woody, "Andy's favorite," the sheriff in hat, spurs, and (Andy Griffith-like) empty holster, is the leader. This western hegemony is re-enforced by a cowboy poster on the wall, a covered wagon toy box, and by Andy's blanket and pillow, which have a lariat design. Furthermore, the first view of this community is explicitly western: Andy plays out a stock western bank robbery on a western street complete with bank and saloon.

The most dependable motif of the western is the arrival of a stranger, whose function is to disrupt the established order. So, into the essentially stable, middle-class western community of Andy's room comes Buzz Lightyear: The Wild, Wild West meets Brave New World, two places that, it turns out, are more similar than they appear.

Buzz Lightyear's arrival turns the community upside down. First of all, it is at a moment of great anxiety—Andy's birthday party—when all the toys are worried that they will be replaced by new ones and end up, as Hamm puts it, as "garage sale fodder." This anxiety is heightened by the imminent move of Andy's family to another house. The character that is the least worried about these issues, however, is Woody, who, brimming with confidence, considers his position as leader to be unassailable. Potatohead says that Woody doesn't worry because he's "been Andy's favorite since before kindergarten." Woody's eminence is also obvious because he arrests One-Eyed Bart and rescues Bo Peep's sheep, calls and directs "staff meetings," instructs the toys on how to prepare for "the move," and organizes the reconnaissance of Andy's birthday party. Woody is efficient and respected. Buzz, however, immediately challenges Woody's supremacy.

To Buzz Lightyear, Space Ranger (Universe Protection Unit), Woody is merely "local law enforcement," whose concerns are routine and unimportant when compared to the threat of the Evil Emperor Zurg and his weapon that can destroy an entire planet. The differences, and conflict, between Buzz and Woody is immediately apparent: The characters are as different as Arnold Schwarzenegger and Michael Richards. Woody is taller and lankier. A rag doll, he is also floppy and soft. Buzz, on the other hand, is short and tough, built like a twenty-first century linebacker, encased in a tough plastic spacesuit, complete with bubble helmet that protects him from toxic environments and isolates him in test-tube sterility.

The other toys immediately marvel at Lightyear's high-tech advantage compared to Woody and recognize his leadership potential. Hamm, Potatohead, and Slink comment on the superiority of his "copper wiring" voice to Woody's pull-string voice, which Potatohead says sounds like "a car ran over it." When they learn that Buzz has a laser, Potatohead teases Woody because he doesn't have one, and then comments to Hamm that Woody has "laser envy." Bo Peep remarks that Buzz has "more gadgets on him than a Swiss army knife." And, of course, the toys are most impressed when they discover that Buzz can "fly." This scene is surely the best known of the film, because it was used in the interminable *Toy Story* advertising: Lightyear, perched on Andy's bedpost, stretches his arms out in front of him, closes his eyes, proclaims "to infinity and beyond," and jumps. He lands headfirst on a ball on the floor, bounces into the air, lands on his feet on a toy car at the top of a race track, rides the car—skateboard style—down the track, through the loop-de-loop, and up to the ceiling, where his outstretched arm catches on a toy airplane suspended from the ceiling. After soaring in dizzying circles, Buzz detaches from the plane and lands perfectly on Andy's bed, to the cheers of Hamm, Rex, Potatohead, Slink, Bo Peep and the other toys. Bo Peep then says, in what must be the final blow to Woody's already abused and rejected leadership and masculinity, "I've found my moving buddy."

It soon becomes apparent that not only has Buzz challenged Woody's leadership of the toy community, but he has taken Woody's place as Andy's "favorite." Soon, Andy has Buzz defeating Woody in his playtime dramas; Woody ends up in the toy box while Buzz sleeps in bed with Andy; Andy writes his name on Lightyear's foot with "permanent ink"; the western poster and blanket on Andy's bed are replaced with a Buzz Lightyear poster and blanket; sketches of Buzz Lightyear cover Andy's bulletin board; and Andy decides he'd rather take Buzz than Woody to Pizza Planet. Furthermore, Buzz begins conducting exercise sessions with the toys, teaches Rex to roar, gets the toys to help repair his space ship, and even offers hair styling advice to a troll. All of this infuriates Woody.

This drama of challenged leadership involves what many consider a key conflict of the West: the clash between the comforts of traditional ways of life and the threats that are perceived to these comforts from "progress" or the "future." This is a real drama Westerners have seen over and over. Just recently, for example, the newspaper in the small Nevada town where I live ran two articles on the top half of the front page. The first (and longer of the two) was titled: "Ranchers: We're in Danger of Being Crowded Out." The second, an interview with a resource management consultant, was titled: "'Voodoo Science' Driving People Off the Land." Both articles present accounts of people who have laid claim to the West but now feel threatened by outside pressures (Bauman). Such examples are not hard to find. Articles and letters to the editor with similar themes appear regularly in newspapers across the West, as well as in radio and television programs, magazines, and books.

What *Toy Story* offers to this reality is a view that dramatically contrasts to Stegner's dire pronouncements about Western inadequacy. Stegner implies that the West, to solve its problems, must take lessons from the outside, since we're too caught up in our mythology to see ourselves clearly. Westerners, of course, are hyper-sensitive to the advice thrust upon us by foreigners and other undesirables. Westerners see such struggles with a mixture of anger, resentment, regret, suspicion, or complacency and barricade themselves into enclaves of denial (or join their local militia). However, it is in the face of such threats (real or perceived) that new communities are and will continue to be formed in the west. But *Toy Story* offers a way out of these stubborn stalemates being played out around us by questioning the competing versions of masculinity represented by Woody and Buzz Lightyear.

Woody reacts to Buzz like the good westerner that he is. First, he refuses to acknowledge that Lightyear is a threat and tries to dismiss everyone's fascination with the new member of the community as a passing fad. Gritting his teeth, he says, "in a couple of days everything will be just the way it was. They'll see." However, when everything does not return to "just the way it was," Woody confronts Buzz, and tells him to "stay away from Andy." When Woody is essentially ignored, he escalates the violence and knocks Buzz out of Andy's window. Of course, he meant to knock Buzz behind the desk rather than out the window, but, as in real life, violence has unexpected outcomes. When the violence escalates even further with the fistfight at the gas station (the Disney equivalent of a barroom brawl), the situation gets even worse: The two toys end up lost and alone.

Buzz, however, is unknowingly obsessed with his own brand of foolishness. His "flight," as well as everything else he holds dear, is a sham. Woody is the only character to recognize the flight for what it is: a leap of self-deception, an act of blind faith in the Buzz Lightyear mythology. Lightyear's problem is his naive, stubborn and earnest belief in his extra-terrestrial powers. Woody points out that the laser is just "a little light that blinks," but Buzz thinks it's a real laser. Woody says Buzz can't fly; Buzz says he "*can* fly, since he thinks he's the real Buzz Lightyear stranded on an unexplored planet and not a toy at all, an illusion Woody repeatedly attacks. In the end, however, Lightyear's view of his own superiority is as flawed as Woody's view of himself.

Both characters learn that their views of themselves are incomplete, but this process is particularly interesting for Buzz. It is his mistake (climbing into the rocket crane game at Pizza Planet because he thinks it's a real rocket) that puts Buzz and Woody in Sid's clutches. Sid (the mean neighbor kid who destroys toys "just for fun") represents on a basic level the hell we can find ourselves in when we refuse to get along. In other words, no matter how bad we think things are, they can get worse. It is while trying to escape from Sid's house that Buzz learns the reality of who he is. When he ducks into a room to hide from Scud (Sid's dog), Buzz sees a commercial on television for Buzz Lightyear action figures, and learns that he is "not a flying toy" and is "available at Al's Toy Barns." His epiphany is singular in Disney. Usually, the Disney hero or heroine learns that he or she is more than imagined: a king, a princess. Buzz Lightyear, however, slumping in front of the TV in Sid's house as all the pride runs out of him, learns that he is less than he imagined, which is crucial to his growth as a character.

Woody learns a similar lesson, but less dramatically: Unlike Buzz, Woody has no illusions that he is not a toy. But Woody learns to swallow his pride and, while trying to escape from a milk crate cage weighted down with a tool box on Sid's work bench, admits to Buzz that he "can't do this alone." And Buzz, after Woody's metaphysical pep talk on the virtues of being a toy, does help Woody escape.

When it's all boiled down, "cooperation" is not a novel idea: it's more like Disney meets *Sesame Street*. But the message of the film isn't this simple. Both characters, paradoxically, are no weaker in spite of the fact that they've recognized their limitations. Woody shows his leadership skills in the way he organizes the elaborate rescue of Buzz with the help of Sid's mutant toys. Later, it's Buzz who has the idea to use the rocket taped to his back to catch up to Andy. It is Buzz, too, who knows what to do to prevent them from being destroyed by the rocket when it explodes. And, most important, they recognize each other as equals. At the end of the film, as the toys fret about the Christmas presents that may replace them and wait eagerly for radio reports from the plastic soldiers hiding in the Christmas tree, Buzz and Woody sit together on Andy's bed. The Buzz Lightyear blanket is on the bed, but Andy's pillow has a western pillowcase; similarly, both a Buzz Lightyear poster and a western poster hang on Andy's wall—clear indicators that this community now benefits from Buzz and Woody's shared leadership. But most importantly, Lightyear's helmet bubble is down, a significant symbol of how he has opened up to the community. Opening his helmet is no small accomplishment for a character who earlier worried about his eyeballs being "sucked from their sockets" if his helmet were opened.

Thus, *Toy Story* questions masculine myths underlying competing leadership philosophies that we see in the West. There is, however, relevance in this portrayal that transcends the western context. How often, for example, do political debates play themselves out largely in a Woody/Buzz Lightyear dichotomy? How often do conservatives, wary of rapid change, describe ways to regain the prosperity or stability of the good-old-days? How often do liberals, wary of past injustices, warn that we must prepare for the future? The 1996 presidential election, for example, revolved around this rhetoric.

But there is even more at stake here. Our sense of "community" is largely based on how we perceive the realities of existence to correspond with the myths we cherish. Because they are intertwined, we don't respond well to challenges to our myths or the realities of our existence. Likewise, getting people to abandon their myths is like convincing laid-off loggers that they need to find different careers—it's easier to blame it all on owls and environmentalists. Nevertheless, we must start to see past myths to recognize their limitations and understand how they hinder conversation between communities. William Kittredge has had a lot to say about this process. In *Who Owns the West?* he urges us "to talk things out, searching for accord, however difficult and long-winded the undertaking. We need to recognize that adversarial, winner-take-all, showdown political decision-making is a way we defeat ourselves." To this he adds: "We need a story in which the process of communality and mutual responsibility are fundamental. We need to figure out how many populations we have, try to name their dreams, and begin resolving those dreams into a societal agenda for the future" (142). To its credit, *Toy Story* shows such possibilities for resolving the deadlock and pointlessness that have been part of the West for so long.

REFERENCES

Baumann, Lorrie. "Ranchers: We're in Danger of Being Crowded Out." *Humboldt Sun* 10 Feb. 1997: 1, 2.
———. "'Voodoo Science' Driving People Off the Land." *Humboldt Sun* 10 Feb. 1997: 1.
Kittredge, William. *Who Owns the West?* San Francisco: Mercury House, 1996.
Stegner, Wallace. *Where the Bluebird Sings to the Lemonade Springs: Living and Writing in the West.* New York: Random House, 1992.
Toy Story. Dir. John Lasseter. Perf. Tom Hanks, Tim Allen, Don Rickles, Jim Varney, Annie Potts, Wallace Shawn, John Ratzenberger, and R. Lee Ermey. Walt Disney, 1995.

Diversity
and Community

Community on the Comstock
Cliché, Stereotype, and Reality in the Mining West

RONALD M. JAMES

One of the clichés of the nineteenth-century mining West is that it lacked a sense of community. Its transient nature, its lawlessness, its lack of families and churches, and its preoccupation with monetary gain are all aspects of a stereotypical mining boom town. These are the threads of myth people often use to understand and pass judgment on a period of western history that relied heavily on mineral exploration and exploitation. Reality, however, can deviate from folklore. Nevada's famed Comstock Lode, for example, had characteristics that both reinforced and contradicted popular perception. My examination of primary sources reveals a place that strived to build a community from its beginning in the 1850s.

Perhaps an evaluation of clichés and stereotypes of the mining West as a society should begin with an equally fanciful definition of "community." The word brings to mind order, longevity, respectability, families, churches, and government; in short, characteristics we normally attribute to "civilization." Such a definition may or may not be fair, but the popular perception of the word leads some to assume that the nineteenth-century mining West lacked community. Again, popular perception would have the place as too transient, lawless, irreligious, and male to be anything but uncivilized. Clearly such a definition is exceedingly rigorous and ethnocentric,

Ronald M. James is the Nevada State Historic Preservation Officer and a member of the Comstock Historic District Commission. He is co-editor of Comstock Women: The Making of a Mining Community *and author of* The Roar and the Silence: A History of Virginia City.

leaving it vulnerable to debate. Nonetheless, it is useful to start a discussion about community and the early mining boom town with the most difficult standard to attain.

A close analysis of the 1860, 8th U.S. manuscript census of the Comstock reveals a place different from the mining boom town of myth. The enumerators recorded Virginia City and Gold Hill thirteen months after the big strike started the rush to Washoe, transforming a local population of dozens into one of thousands. Most of the people living there were men, reinforcing what one might expect. There had been, however, sufficient time for women to begin arriving. Intuition has told historians of the West for over a century that these were prostitutes come to exploit an obvious business opportunity and to contribute to the care-free existence of life without civilization (Lord). Respectable women, according to this scenario, would arrive later to ruin all the fun and attempt to establish the first signs of law, order, religion, and prohibitions against all the vices that men would endlessly enjoy if they could. In short, these women who arrived on the frontier late in the game would attempt to nurture community in a place where the dark side of humanity threatened to kill the vine.

The problem with looking at primary sources carefully is that they often get in the way of a good story. Every indication is that the first Comstock women were almost all respectable by the standards of the day. Most were married, living with husbands and children. They were not the dance hall girls and soiled doves of western legend (James, "Women"). These were average people who arrived, like everyone else, to combine hard work and opportunity to win a fortune. What is more important for the discussion here is that these first women, by virtue of their families instead of their vices, support the cliché of community rather than that of boom-town chaos.

Yet another unexpected characteristic of these women was that many were Spanish speaking (James, "Women"). Again, cliché would have the tamers of the wild West as Euroamericans, but clearly the first seeds of community, as conventionally defined, were sown early, largely due to women from Mexico.

What had been a few dozen families in the summer of 1860 blossomed into hundreds and then thousands of households over the next twenty years. Still, it is reasonable to ask how this place exhibited the other characteristics of community, according to this most strict definition. In short, what evidence is there of law and order, organized religion, longevity, and respectability? When evaluated closely, it is clear that each of these aspects of society had a clear manifestation in early Virginia City, forming a foundation for later substantial development.

Establishing good government preoccupied the earliest settlers of the western Great Basin. Utah Territory administered the region from Salt Lake City, but the distance between the earliest settlements along the eastern foothills of the Sierra and the center of government was immense and largely unpopulated. The increasingly non-Mormon local population established a provisional territorial government in 1859. The local community leaders petitioned Congress to ratify what they saw as an inevitable division of the eastern and western halves of the Great Basin. Washington did not create the Nevada Territory until 1861, after the discovery of the Comstock Lode created international headlines, but clearly many felt the need to have some sense of law and order for the region, early in its development (James, *Temples*).

Two years after the 1859 strike and the famous "Rush to Washoe," the newly founded town of Virginia won the right from Utah Territorial government to organize as a city. With such authority in hand, the community elected officials and set to the task of establishing law and order. A few months later, in July 1861, President Lincoln's appointees to the new Nevada Territorial government arrived. They immediately began creating order at yet another level (Del Papa, Elliott).

The earliest period of settlement saw its share of lynchings and ad hoc committees that tried to impose imperfect brands of order on a young society. Nonetheless, those who would establish good government with legal authority from Utah Territory and then from Washington succeeded within months of the area's substantial development. The criminal and untamed aspects of humanity continued to be a factor in Comstock society, but government established itself early to hold these forces in check. Nearly from its beginning, this was a community that strived for law and order.

In the same way, many who first arrived on the Comstock sought religion and to establish churches. The Reverend Jesse

L. Bennett began administering to a Methodist congregation as early as 1859. According to tradition, those who heard his sermons answered with heaps of gold and silver. By 1861, his successor had built a church. Similarly, Father Hugh Gallagher came to the Comstock in 1860 where he built a small Catholic church. Within two years, the structure collapsed under the famed heavy winds known locally as Washoe Zephyrs, but another soon took its place (Angel, Shade, Lapomarda). All this happened before women arrived in significant numbers.

Eventually, however, families became an important part of Comstock society. The birth of Virginia Tilton, April 1, 1860, the first Euroamerican newborn in the new town, signaled a beginning for a place that sought to establish roots. For decades, residents of Virginia City took pride as this first citizen grew into a young woman, providing vivid evidence of the

Miss Virginia Tilton. From DeQulle, The Big Bonanza. *Courtesy of the Nevada Historical Society*

community's longevity and of the importance of family to its society (Wright).

The Irish immigrants of Virginia City also provide an opportunity to see how at least one group of people appreciated what aspects of community they could find in the mining West. By the 1870s, the Irish and Irish-Americans accounted for approximately one third of Virginia City. Unlike most ethnic groups, these sons and daughters of Erin settled in distinct neighborhoods. The largest of these areas used St. Mary in the Mountains Catholic Church and the Daughters of Charity orphanage and school as anchors. There is also evidence that Irish ethnicity formed a trade barrier of sorts against the labor of other ethnic groups. For example, they hired only Irish servants, avoiding the Chinese cooks who frequently found employment elsewhere. There were also no Chinese laundries, a ubiquitous institution throughout most of the Comstock, in their neighborhoods. Instead, Irish women provided this service to their fellow immigrants (James, Adkins, and Hartigan).

Of greater importance than their neighborhoods, however, is that the Irish stayed longer than many other groups. An analysis of the ages of the oldest Nevada born child of Irish couples shows that their Nevada sojourn lasted much longer than that of the English immigrants. In addition, they were most inclined to marry other immigrants from Ireland and to have more children. The ratio of Irish men to Irish-American children was three to one, while the same statistic for Cornish men was thirteen to one. The Cornish contrasted with the Irish by sending fewer of its daughters to North America. Even so, they appear to have pursued marriage, whether inside or outside their ethnic group, less vigorously than the Irish. All of this suggests that the Irish lingered as long as possible in Virginia City. When other immigrants found it prudent to move on, to look for better opportunities, the Irish tended to stay, perhaps feeling that the ethnic solidarity of their neighborhoods was sufficient reward (James, "Defining the Group").

While the Comstock quickly satisfied the stereotypical definition of community, it did so only by way of apology for those parts of its society that did not clearly meet the strictest criteria. After all, much of the mining district, like the West in general, was transient, male, and irreligious. It had the potential of being a rough-and-tumble, violent, lawless place. Nonetheless, while aspects of the Comstock fulfilled the popular image of a mining boom town, the Virginia City and Gold Hill metropolitan area was also struggling to become a community.

The stereotypical definition of a community ultimately revolves around respectability and desirability, highly subjective terms. Invariably, this means that a place attains the title of community when it meets the standards of acceptability as the social and economic elite define it. Rather than asking if the Comstock became a community in its earliest inception, it is perhaps more valid to ask what is the nature of those who would say it was not. Such a question is not unlike the debate that has recently involved family values. Some of our contemporaries seem to agree that if the government could effectively reinforce proper societal standards, it should, but there appears to be little consensus on what desirable family values are. For some, family means a married heterosexual couple with children. Others counter that the institution comes in all forms, defying the cookie cutter: families include those with single parents, surrogate relatives, grandparents raising grandchildren, and an occasional gay couple thrown in to demonstrate the full range of possibilities.

Thus, those who propose that the early western towns did not qualify as communities ignore the diversity that has always been a hallmark of humanity. There is also a hint of anti-western, anti-mining prejudice in such an assertion. True, the West lacks deep roots and has quickly shifting populations; mining accentuates this characteristic as it exploits nonrenewable resources, repeatedly moving the center of attention from one place to the next. Yet, to use a conventional definition of community, better suited to places founded on agriculture or longer-lasting industry, is to stack the deck against the West and one of its most important occupations.

It is easy enough to show that the Comstock attained a sense of community even using a conventional definition of the term. It is equally appropriate, however, to demonstrate

Facing page. Chinese Quarters, Virginia City, Nevada. Drawn by W. A. Rogers from Sketches by C. L. Sears. Harper's Weekly, *December 29, 1877: 1025. Courtesy of the Nevada Historical Society.*

CHOP AND SAUSAGE HOUSE

BULL RUN ALLEY

A STREET COBBLER

that the mining district had a depth of community that extended throughout its society and history, particularly when applying more flexible criteria.

For example, Virginia City's Chinatown lacked many of the stereotypical features of a community, yet it was a stable place of mutual support. The first Asian immigrants arrived in the western Great Basin in the late 1850s to assist in digging ditches and to help with other undertakings that required heavy labor. Consistent with the pattern common throughout the West, the earliest to arrive were all men. Women only rarely followed. While many Euroamericans in the area advocated excluding the Chinese completely, the immigrants nonetheless found a place in the young mining district. Still, local miners succeeded in prohibiting them from ever taking employment in the mines, relegating the Chinese to less lucrative pursuits. Prejudice often kept them apart from the rest of society. In spite of having only a few families and being separated from the core of the economy and society, the Chinese thrived and built one of their most important communities in the West: Virginia City's Chinatown numbered over one thousand at its peak in the mid-1870s (Chung "Chinese Experience," "Their Changing World"; Chan).

An 1877 lithograph illustrating Virginia City's Chinatown provides vivid details of life in that ethnic neighborhood. Druggists prepare medicine; a priest performs a ceremony; a barber cuts a patron's hair; cooks make sausage while other workers clean laundry and repair shoes. It is a thriving diverse place, an image that the census reinforces. Enumerators for the federal census, for example, recorded merchants, doctors, a phrenologist, as well as laborers, carpenters, masons, peddlers, and wood cutters. Chinatown had its own Chinese laundries, teachers, prostitutes, restaurants, gambling houses, and opium dens. Others occasionally enjoyed these services, but the ethnic enclave that the Chinese established served itself primarily.

It happens that women were relatively rare in most nineteenth-century North American Chinatowns. Federal law inhibiting Chinese women from immigrating accentuated a problem that had already existed among Asian immigrants. Culturally and often legally discouraged from marriage outside their ethnic groups, most Chinese men faced a lifetime of bachelorhood. It is nevertheless clear that they lived in a community that provided emotional and economic support.

The Cornish are another group that fits less obviously into the idea of community. As pointed out above, they immigrated with fewer women than the Irish, for example. They also tended to leave a mining district as soon as they exhausted the resource. Similarly, the Cornish reluctantly came to a western boom town, aware as they were that such phenomena only rarely met expectations. Boom towns usually failed shortly after grabbing the region's attention. The Cornish were, consequently, the last to arrive and the first to leave the Comstock. They established a Methodist church and brought a few families, but they usually did not sink deep roots. When they finished exploiting the Comstock's riches, most left. Their church, one of four in Virginia City by 1876, fell into disrepair. While the other three continue to stand, it long since vanished from the historic district's building stock (Shade).

Given this profile, it would be easy to conclude that the Cornish failed to establish a community on the Comstock and did little to contribute to one while there. Upon further examination, however, it seems that the Cornish were part of a community, the importance of which is not diminished by the fact that it is less obvious from a conventional view point. The Cornish were citizens of the mining frontier, a vast network of interconnected islands strung out across the globe. Their community had outposts in Wisconsin, Colorado, California, British Columbia, Australia, South Africa, South America, Mexico, and Ireland. One Cornish family underscores the possibilities: its children were born in Cornwall, Bolivia, California, and then the Comstock. An occupation in mining demanded movement, but it did not prohibit the growth of community. Wherever the Cornish traveled, they found former neighbors, relatives, friends, or at least the friends of friends. This formed a solid bedrock for a transient existence, and certainly these connections eased the stress of a life constantly changing and on the move.

While the lifestyle of the Cornish might make it appear that they had no community, their social fabric played a crucial role in making their life palatable. Arguably, their community was more significant to them than to those with a more sedentary lifestyle, for it was certainly profoundly important, withstanding challenges unknown to others. People frequently called Cornish miners "Cousin Jacks," a term of disputed etymology. Whatever its origin, the name underscores the significance of relationships for these immigrants (Todd, Rowe).

The Cornish were one of the more famous of the temporary inhabitants of the typical mining West town. Others moved nearly as frequently. In the midst of this transience, there were many ways to maintain continuity. Groups besides the Cornish encouraged the growth of ethnic organizations that provided ready-made companions in any city, regardless of how unfamiliar the setting and its people. Thus the Irish had the Fenian Brotherhood, the Ancient Order of Hibernians, and the Irish Land League. The Scots could join the local Caledonian Club; the Germans had their athletic organizations; and in a place as large as Virginia City, societies existed for Italians, Mexicans, Poles, Scandinavians, and the Welsh, to name a few.

Churches and temples similarly provided a ready-made network to ease moving. Fraternal organizations also functioned in this capacity. A Freemason, an Odd Fellow, or a Pythian each knew that a new home on the mining frontier would include initiated brothers and an accommodating lodge. The Comstock's many cemeteries offer striking evidence of the power of these relationships on the mining frontier. Although there are examples of family members interned side-by-side, for the most part, one's kin moved away before more than a few if any relations could be buried there. Instead, graves are grouped by fraternity, church, and ethnicity.

Here, then, are several examples of community that existed while perhaps failing to meet what one might expect from the conventional definition. There is an undercurrent, however, running throughout this discussion that needs to be addressed directly. Intuition might tell us that a community depends on a mix of men, women, and children, but for thousands of years cloistered monks and women religious have demonstrated that this is not the case. The military and prisons also point in this direction. Simply because the earliest roots of Comstock history were nearly all male does not mean that the place was not a community. Similarly, if only men had inhabited Chinatown, it still would have fulfilled the definition. To assert that a mix of men and women is necessary to form a community is sexist, and in the case of the nineteenth-century Chinese immigrants, it borders on racism.

Sex ratios, transience, and an absence of churches and government, then, do not mean that society lacked an internal fabric. During the 1850s, the almost all male placer miners who searched the canyons of what would be known as the Virginia Range were transient, lacking churches and formal government. Still, anecdotes from the period clearly indicate that there was a feeling of camaraderie and the building of community.

With the strike in 1859, it is clear how the earliest miners could respond to the promise of growing population. They quickly drafted rules to regulate themselves, electing officers and establishing the first forms of government (Lord). When preachers came by, the miners showered them with gold. Transience dominated this earliest, largely male society and yet it was a community. What followed built on this foundation.

A vivid expression on the Comstock comes from perhaps one of the most unlikely sources. During the early 1990s, archaeologist Donald Hardesty excavated the site of O'Callahan and Shanahan's Hibernia Brewery and Saloon. The popular image of the wild west saloon would lead to an image of a place of unshaven, hard drinking men, accustomed to violence and often seeking it: a row of these toughs drinking while standing along a bar while others play poker at a table, until the inevitable accusation of cheating leads to a shooting. Drinking, together with the piano playing from the corner, pause for the brief, deadly altercation, then quickly resume. This is the image Hollywood has imprinted on our national psyche.

Hardesty's excavation reveals a place removed from cliché. Among the remains, there are the expected large quantity of broken glasses and whiskey, wine, ale, and champagne bottles. The poker chips and die reinforce the stereotype. There were also, however, soda bottles, broken doll parts, marbles, and the remains of other toys. The saloon clearly had a kitchen and served meals. Women's buttons and the remnants of a perfume bottle also count among the artifacts recovered (Hardesty).

Clearly, this was a place more complex than the saloon of movies and television. The Hibernia Brewery and Saloon was the nineteenth-century equivalent of a pizza parlor where families came for a meal, a drink, and an evening with friends. A single spent bullet may hint at the limits of civility, and yet the meaning of an isolated artifact will remain elusive. Ultimately, even the remnants of a saloon reinforce the idea that community was part of the western mining frontier.

While the cliché of the nineteenth-century mining West claims it lacked the fabric of proper society, careful examination of the evidence demonstrates that a sense of community was integral to the newly founded, and sometimes transient towns of the region. Places like Virginia City and Gold Hill took pride in excellent schools, well-built churches, and law enforcement that kept crime at a minimum. People went to great lengths to establish connections through ethnicity, religion, and other organizations to provide their fluid world with the connections taken for granted in a well-established place. The energy spent creating community in the mining West is evidence that this was hardly an expendable trait of human existence. In fact, community was one of the first cornerstones laid in the newly founded societies of the region.

REFERENCES

Angel, Myron, ed. *History Of Nevada: 1881*. Oakland, California: Thompson and West, 1881.

Chan, Loren B. "The Chinese in Nevada: An Historical Survey, 1856-1970." *Nevada Historical Society Quarterly* 25 (Winter 1982): 266-314.

Chung, Sue Fawn. "The Chinese Experience in Nevada: Success Despite Discrimination." *Nevada Public Affairs Review* 2 (1987): 43-51.

———. "Their Changing World: Chinese Women on the Comstock, 1860-1910" Ed. Ronald M. James and C. Elizabeth Raymond. *Comstock Women: The Making of a Mining Community*. Reno: University of Nevada Press, 1998.

Del Papa, Frankie Sue. *Political History of Nevada*. 9th ed. Carson City: Nevada State Printing Office, 1990.

Elliott, Russell R. *History of Nevada*. Lincoln: University of Nebraska, 1987.

Hardesty, Donald L. "Public Archaeology in the Virginia City Landmark District: The 1993 and 1994 Field Seasons." Carson City: Report for the Nevada State Historic Preservation Office,

1994.

James, Ronald M. "Women of the Mining West: Virginia City Revisited." *Nevada Historical Society Quarterly* 36:3 (Fall 1993): 153-177.

――――. *Temples of Justice: County Courthouses of Nevada.* Reno: University of Nevada Press, 1994.

――――. "Defining the Group: Nineteenth-Century Cornish on the Mining Frontier." *Cornish Studies:* Vol. 2. Ed. Philip Payton. Exeter, UK: University of Exeter, 1994.

James, Ronald M., Richard D. Adkins, and Rachel J. Hartigan. "Competition and Co-existence in the Laundry: A View of the Comstock." *Western Historical Quarterly* 25:2 (Summer 1994):164-184.

Lapomarda, Vincent A., S. J. "Saint Mary's in the Mountains: The Cradle of Catholicism in Western Nevada." *Nevada Historical Society Quarterly* 35: 1 (Spring 1992): 58-62.

Lord, Eliot. *Comstock Mining and Miners.* 1883. San Diego, California: Howell-North Books, 1959.

Rowe, John. *The Hard-Rock Men: Cornish Immigrants and the North American Mining Frontier.* New York: Barnes and Noble, 1974.

Shade, Rose Marian. "Virginia City's Ill-Fated Methodist Church." *Journal of the West* 8:4 (October 1969): 447-453.

Todd, Arthur Cecil. *The Cornish Miner in America.* Spokane, Washington: Arthur H. Clark, 1995.

United States Census. 8th U. S. Manuscript Census, 1860, Utah Territory, Roll 1314, Microfilm 653, RG 29, Nevada State Library and Archives, Carson City, Nevada.

Wright, William [Dan De Quille pseud.]. *The Big Bonanza.* 1876. New York: Alfred A. Knopf, 1953.

American Canyon
A Chinese Village

DAVID VALENTINE

Figure 1. Chinese placer miner with his rocker. Courtesy of Nevada Historical Society.

In the early days of Nevada history, the relationship between Euro-Americans and Chinese often was a bigoted, hostile affair. EuroAmericans feared that the Chinese willingness and ability to work for low wages threatened their livelihood, and they reacted to these fears. After the passage of the Chinese exclusion act in 1882, the Chinese population dropped to the point where they were no longer seen as an economic threat. At this time, Euro-American attitudes toward the Chinese slowly began to shift. Chinese were now seen as a potential source of additional income to Euro-American businessmen,

David Valentine has worked as an archaeologist in Nevada since 1989 and became interested in American Canyon after working on several cultural resource projects in the area for the Bureau of Land Management.

and many Euro-Americans and Chinese began to enter into business relationships that worked to the mutual benefit of both parties. From 1884 to 1900, American Canyon, located in northern Nevada on the eastern flanks of the Humboldt Range in Pershing County was the site of a bustling Chinese community based on placer mining. The history of American Canyon reflects the change in attitude toward the Chinese by their earlier persecutors.

Chinese Placer Mining in the United States

The processes of erosion are blind to the materials that humans consider valuable. A gold vein is as susceptible to erosion as any other rock. As particles of gold are eroded from a source, they are redeposited in streams, hillside colluvial deposits, and glacial till with gravel. Gravel deposits containing gold or other minerals (such as cinnabar, diamonds, garnets, jade, platinum, tin, tungsten and turquoise) are known as placer deposits. The 1849 gold discovery at Sutter's Mill in California was a placer deposit.

The discovery of gold in California attracted Chinese as much as any other group. Chinese argonauts, lured by the promise of easy wealth and pushed by deplorable conditions at home, joined the California gold rush. In the early 1850s, 85 percent of California Chinese were involved in placer mining (Rohe, "After").

The search for gold often led to the discovery of "mother lodes"—the original gold veins from which the placer deposits derived. To mine gold veins in unweathered rock requires machinery and extra labor to tunnel through hard rock and to separate gold from rock and other minerals. A substantial outlay of capital is required to procure necessary machinery and extra labor prior to commencement of mining. Lacking large sums of money for the initial outlay, most Chinese were prevented from starting hard rock gold mines. Antagonism from Euro-American miners and mine laborers, who feared that the Chinese would lower their standard of living by working more cheaply, prevented many Chinese from acquiring jobs at hard rock mines. Due to these pressures, many Chinese switched from mining-related jobs to service industries such as cooking or running laundries. The Chinese who stayed in the mining industry tended to specialize in placer mining.

A further specialization developed by Chinese to avoid antagonism with Euro-American miners was the reworking of placer claims thought to be "worked out" by Euro-Americans. Late nineteenth century Euro-American miners generally expected a claim to pay a minimum of four dollars per day. Once the easily obtainable gold was removed by Euro-American miners, they were willing to sell or lease their claims to patient and enduring Chinese placer miners who recovered smaller nuggets and gold dust left behind (Liestman).

The tool kit most often used by the Chinese placer miner consisted of the "pan" and "rocker." A gold pan is a large pan in which gold-bearing gravel and water are swished around in an effort to separate lighter sand and gravel from the heavier gold particles. It is most often used in initial prospecting efforts when the miner is looking for pockets of gold-bearing materials. The rocker, first developed by Mexican miners in California, generally consists of an open wooden box mounted on rocker legs, vaguely resembling an infant's cradle. Inside the box is a screen for removing large material, a deflecting apron to direct the flow of water and gravel, and a riffled bottom to catch the gold. The device is rocked to keep the gravel moving through the box and to concentrate the gold in the riffles (Vanderburg 37-41). Materials to construct a rocker were inexpensive, and the rocker was easily portable, contributing to its desirability by thrifty and mobile Chinese placer miners. (See Figure 1, page 107.)

A less portable device for placer gold recovery is the sluice box, which resembles a flume through which gold bearing gravel is moved with a continuous stream of water. Riffles on the bottom of the sluice box concentrate the gold. Diversion dams and ditches were often constructed to provide the constant source of water needed for a sluice box. Hydraulic mining arose as a technique for sluicing large volumes of auriferous gravel. Chinese miners used sluice boxes and hydraulic mining techniques when sufficient water and capital were available for construction and operation of the sluices, ditches, etc. (LaLande; Rohe "The Chinese").

As prospecting and mineral discoveries spread north and east from California, so did Chinese placer miners. The first Chinese placer miners appeared in the 1850s in that portion of the Utah Territory which later became Nevada, in the Gold Canyon District near Dayton. Dayton, before it received its current name, was known as Chinatown (Angel; Mack). By the mid 1870s, Chinese placer miners were operating across Nevada, located in the Island Mountain and Tuscarora Districts in Elko County; the Klondyke, Tule Canyon and Tokop Districts in Esmeralda County; the Bald Mountain District in White Pine County; and the Rebel Creek, King's River, Rosebud, Sierra, Kennedy, and Indian Districts in Humboldt County (Pershing County was created out of Humboldt County in 1919) (Vanderburg 62-173).

Arriving in American Canyon

Chinese people reached the Humboldt Range in the 1860s. The earliest mention of Chinese in the area is a newspaper article from Unionville in 1863 (Marden). It is possible that some Chinese were working placer gold deposits found in Buena Vista Creek, the stream running through Unionville (Vanderburg 162), even though the 1870 census did not list any placer miners amongst the Chinese.

Some Chinese obtained work in the hard rock mining industry in Unionville. In an effort to reduce costs, John C. Fall of the Arizona mine hired Chinese labors to work in the mine mills. The cheaper labor allowed him to process ore previously determined to be unprofitable (Raymond 187-88). However, this move was not well received by the Euro-American mining community.

Two Euro-American miners, W. S. Bonnifield and L. F. Dunn, helped form the Workingman's Protective Union to "protect the interests of the white workingman against the encroachment of capital and Coolie labor, and to use all legal means of ridding the country of Chinamen." This Union was responsible for the armed expulsion of forty-six Chinese from Unionville on January 1, 1869. When a federal jury charged Dunn and W. S. Bonnifield with the "crime of violation of the Treaty between the Empire of China and the United States of America" (the Burlingame Treaty), M. S. Bonnifield, a lawyer serving in the state senate at the time, rushed to his younger brother's defense. The charges against the two men were eventually dropped, largely due to the refusal of local officials to follow through with any legal action (Lingenfelter), because the treaty was not yet ratified (Rusco, E.)

The Workingman's Protective Union was initially unsuccessful in its efforts to rid Unionville of Chinese. The Chinese trickled back into town, and resumed work in the mill—sorting ore, feeding stamp batteries and attending amalgamation pans (Raymond 187-88).

In 1875 placer gold deposits were found in Spring Valley, roughly four miles north of American Canyon and twelve miles south of Unionville. Spring Valley was initially included within the boundaries of the Indian District. After discovery of placer gold, and later hard rock gold and mercury deposits, the district was reorganized as the Spring Valley District (Johnson). The Spring Valley placer deposits were soon being worked by about thirty Euro-Americans and as many as 125 Chinese. They used a long tom (a modified sluice box) in the winter when water supplies were adequate. During the rest of the year, rockers were used. Newspaper accounts from 1877 reported there were two hundred Chinese in Spring Valley living in a camp that supported four stores ("Chinese Placer Miners"). The 1880 Census counted 127 Chinese in Spring Valley, one hundred listed as placer miners. In addition to miners, there were: one merchant, two doctors, one wood chopper, three cooks, three mill workers and one laundryman. The occupations of thirteen Chinese were not listed.

Placer deposits were found in American Canyon in 1881. They were first worked by Euro-American miners who reportedly recovered one million dollars before beginning to lease claims to Chinese miners in 1884 (Vanderburg 159-62). Hoback Kong was the first to lease a placer claim (from M. S. Bonnifield) in American Canyon (Claim Records). Toi Lee, Wong Kee and Hong Hing soon followed suit in leasing claims. In addition to Bonnifield, claims were leased from Dunn, a miner and saloon operator from Spring Valley; Sam Jones, a blacksmith from Spring Valley; R. C. Ruddell, a prominent Lovelock rancher; and Thomas Harper, another miner (American Mining District 10-11; Humboldt County Contracts and Records Book A; "Placers Leased"). (On the following page is a map showing American Canyon and environs [Base map U.S.G.S., Nevada, 1:500,000 topographic]).

Chinese Mining in American Canyon

Wong Kee appears to have been the principal leader of the Chinese placer mining in American Canyon. In addition to

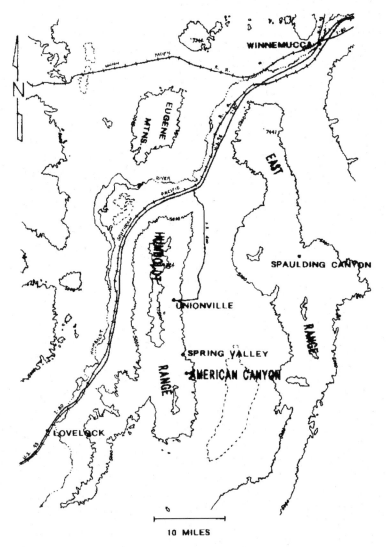

Figure 2.

leasing placer claims, he was responsible in 1885 for construction of ditches from the head of the Canyon to the placer
grounds (Nevada State Water Engineer). An addition to Wong
Kee's ditch system, consisting of a water tunnel in South
American Canyon (a tributary of American Canyon) and ditch
leading to American Canyon, was constructed in 1892 by Toi

Lee in partnership with miner Thomas Harper ("Still in the Ring").

Wong Kee's ditches provided up to six miner's inches of water—fifty-four gallons per minute (Wells). This was not sufficient to run a sluice box, but provided ample water for domestic use and for washing pay gravel with rockers (Nevada State Water Engineer). Water distribution appears to have been implemented by selling buckets of water to individuals as they needed it. The archaeological record shows the remains of a dugout alongside the ditch contains dozens of cans modified into buckets.

With the construction of ditches, large scale placer mining began, and the Chinese population of the area began to shift from Spring Valley to American Canyon. By 1887, one hundred Chinese were mining in American Canyon ("Chinese Placer Miners"). The population increased to 120 for the years 1891 and 1892, with an additional five Chinese in neighboring Dry Gulch and a dozen remaining in Spring Valley ("The Heathen Chinese"; "Still in the Ring"). The reason so many Chinese decided to move south to American Canyon is not clear. It is possible that they exhausted all of the placer gold in Spring Valley; however, Spring Valley continued to produce placer gold for many years and was the site of the first gold dredge operation in Nevada in 1910 (Walker). Another possible impetus for the exodus of Chinese from Spring Valley was increasing Euro-American interest and presence there, caused by a switch from placer mining to hard rock gold and mercury mining.

In American Canyon, Wong Kee, Toi Lee, Hong Hing and Hoback Kong subleased twenty foot by twenty foot sections to individuals or small groups (Vanderburg 159-60). Household groupings listed in the 1900 Census manuscript indicate that individual subleases were most likely the norm, but that groups of two to four individuals were common. Partners in these small groups often shared the same surname, indicating they were based on family, clan or district associations.

Shafts were excavated on each of the small leases. These shafts, many of which still exist, varied in depth from ten to one hundred feet. The shallower shafts were located in the upper reaches of the canyon where the depth to bedrock also is shallow. Depth to bedrock, and corresponding shaft depth, increased toward the mouth of the canyon. Drifts were dug along pay streaks on bedrock and false bedrock clay layers.

All mining by Chinese in American Canyon was by hand. Shovels, picks, pans and rockers were effectively used for gold recovery. Over two miles of the canyon bottom are honeycombed with shafts and tunnels gouged through the tightly packed alluvial gravel. This work was dangerous, and at least two Chinese miners in Spring Valley and one in American Canyon were killed by cave ins. The man killed in American Canyon was reported to be "green"; he did not understand the importance of shoring. This would indicate that not all Chinese who came to American Canyon were experienced placer miners ("Chinamen Killed," 1880; "Chinaman Killed," 1892).

The Chinese Community

Various authors have placed the Chinese population in American Canyon during the period 1884 to 1895 from between three hundred to three thousand individuals (Basso; Bragg; Mordy and McCaughey; Paher 130; Vanderburg 159). It would appear that most, if not all, of these figures are exaggerated. The census count for the critical year of 1890 indicated that the entire Chinese population for Humboldt County was 377 (United States Department of the Interior, Census Bureau [DOI, CB] 1894). The census manuscripts for that year have been destroyed, and the exact population in American Canyon is unknown. Newspaper articles report the population of American Canyon in 1887 to be one hundred, and in both 1891 and 1892, around 120. These figures include only six Chinese women ("The Heathen Chinese"; "Still in the Ring"). Articles in the Winnemucca, Nevada newspaper *Silver State* also count additional Chinese in Spring Valley and Dry Gulch north of American Canyon and Chinese in Spaulding Canyon in the East Range, roughly forty miles to the northeast. It was reported that the Chinese were constantly coming and going. It is possible that populations of Chinese were moving between American Canyon and other mining districts and that the figure of three hundred for Chinese placer miners was regional.

This indicates that American Canyon was a very significant Nevada Chinese community during its peak. During the period between 1880 and 1900 the total Chinese population of Nevada declined. Even though the overall Chinese population of Nevada was diminishing, the ranking of the Chinese population in Humboldt County compared to the rest of the counties in the state was increasing. Humboldt County went from having the sixth highest number of Nevada Chinese in 1870 to the second highest in 1890 and 1900 (DOI, CB 1892; DOI, CB 1901). Before discoveries in American Canyon, the only other large Chinese population centers in Humboldt County were in two mining towns, Spring Valley and Unionville, and two railroad towns, Lovelock and Winnemucca. Even though the 1890 census manuscripts have been destroyed, an idea of the Chinese population of these communities can be determined by examining the census data for 1880 and 1900 and by looking at other sources. Lovelock's Chinese population increased from thirty-one in 1880 to thirty-nine in 1900 (Rusco, M). Most of the 127 Chinese in Spring Valley left, leaving less than a dozen in 1892 ("The Heathen Chinese"; "Still in the Ring"). Unionville's Chinese population plummeted from an estimated seventy-six in 1880 to none in 1900 (USCM 1900b). Winnemucca's Chinese population also declined, from eighty-one in 1880 to fifty-eight in 1900 (Au). American Canyon, with a population of 120 in 1891-92, was the largest Chinese community in Humboldt County during most of its existence.

Perhaps the best way to see the influence American Canyon had on Nevada communities is to follow the activities of some of its merchants and other businessmen. Commerce among the Chinese thrived in American Canyon, and from 1886 to 1903 at least two stores, and often as many as four, were operated by Chinese in American Canyon. These stores sold traditional Chinese goods (imported through San Francisco), lumber, and foodstuffs such as swine, chicken, wheat, tea, coffee, tobacco, ham, sardines, sugar, onions, and potatoes, often purchased from Euro-American Lovelock merchant S.R. Young. Two wagon loads of these goods were shipped to American Canyon once a week by Euro-American teamster Simon Billups ("The Heathen Chinese"; "Still in the Ring").

Hong (Hung) Hing owned one of the stores, operating it from 1890 through 1898. The Humboldt County Assessor's Rolls indicate that Hong Hing's store carried the most merchandise in American Canyon for most of the period of its operation. This would indicate Hong was one of the wealthier Chinese in American Canyon. In addition to running a store, Hong Hing leased mining claims from Euro-American placer miners. On December 11, 1895, he leased the Spring Garden Placer claim from Sam L. Jones for forty dollars. The lease was to run for twenty years unless "sooner forfit [sic]." On the same day, he leased an unnamed claim from S. Billup. This lease was to run for twenty years but was considerably more expensive at ten dollars per foot for a 1500 foot long claim (American Mining District 10-11).

A Hong Hing also operated a store in Eureka, Nevada. While in Eureka, that Hong Hing was reported to be worth forty thousand dollars. He also challenged the Nevada opium laws in court after being arrested for possession of a pipe (Caressi). While there is no proof that the Eureka Hong Hing is the American Canyon Hong Hing, the Eureka Hong Hing left Eureka shortly before the American Canyon store was opened. To be able to operate one of the richest stores in American Canyon, and to lease claims costing fifteen thousand dollars, is something possible by someone worth forty thousand dollars.

It appears as though another merchant, Sin Yuen, bought out Hong Hing and ran the store until 1903. "Sin Yuen" might have been the store name, or else the name of an absentee owner, since in 1900 a Lee Long was enumerated as a store keeper. This name does not appear in the County Assessor's Rolls or in any newspaper articles. Lee was a relative newcomer to the United States, arriving in 1885. In 1900 he was forty-four years old and single.

Another of the major operators in American Canyon was Wong Kee. Wong Kee immigrated to the United States in 1873, at the age of twenty-five. Contrary to Chinese custom, Wong Kee brought his wife, Ahe Ho, with him. He first arrived in American Canyon in 1885. He told census enumerators that his profession was placer miner (USCM 1910), but other historical records reveal that he was a shrewd businessman with interests in many different activities.

Wong Kee built most of the water ditches in American Canyon, and eventually ended up owning them all (nearly seven miles). The main line of the ditch system was constructed between July and November of 1885 (Nevada State Water Engineer). This water allowed full-scale placer mining to take place in American Canyon. By owning the ditches and controlling the water, Wong Kee had considerable power among the Chinese placer miners.

Wong Kee sold the ditches to white miner J. W. Wenzel in 1905 (Nevada State Water Engineer). Wenzel apparently did not have the full purchase price, and the debt was carried by Wong Kee for several years under a mortgage agreement (Humboldt County Assessor's Rolls). Wenzel continued using the ditches for mining and domestic water purposes, eventually replacing the open ditches with buried iron pipe.

Even though newspaper accounts do not mention that Wong Kee ran a store, the Humboldt County Assessor taxed him for merchandise from 1896 through 1906. Wong Kee operated this store until he left American Canyon late in 1906. From 1904 until 1906, this was the only store in American Canyon.

Wong Kee disappears from northern Nevada records for a short while, again surfacing in Lovelock in the spring of 1908. He purchased a lot from Fong Sing and his wife Ling Kao, and opened a laundry (Humboldt County Deeds 415; Humboldt County Assessor's Rolls). This business must have been prosperous, because in 1914 Wong Kee constructed a two story concrete building to house his enterprise (Hart 17).

Wong Kee sold his business interests and left Lovelock in 1917. Where he went has not been determined. A letter addressed to Wong Kee in Lovelock, postmarked May 15, 1916, is on display in the "Beyond Gum San" exhibit in the Nevada State Museum. This letter is from the Canton State Bank in San Francisco. Considering that it is postmarked the year before Wong Kee left northern Nevada for good, it is possible that he was wrapping up his affairs for a move to San Francisco or back to China, possibly Canton, via San Francisco.

What Wong Kee was doing during his hiatus from northern Nevada in 1907 and the early part of 1908 is unknown. However, in January of 1908, the residents of Rhyolite, Nevada, were excited by the visit of a Chinese businessman, a Wong Kee from Barstow, California, to their city. Euro-American labor interests were concerned that he was there to scout locations for Chinese laundries or to provide cheap labor for the mines. Wong Kee was not there for any of those reasons— he had business with Walter Scott, the famous "Death Valley Scotty." He told reporters that he was there to warn Scotty

Figure 3: Walter Scott (Death Valley Scotty) and Wong Kee in Rhyolite, Nevada, January 1908.

that a special train Scott was promoting would be hijacked in Barstow by creditors attempting to recover their loans. It was also reported that Scotty owed Wong Kee $300, and speculated that if Scotty could arrange a special train, he would have enough money to pay his debt to Wong Kee ("Wong Kee"). While Wong Kee is a fairly common name among Chinese, it is probable that the "Barstow" Wong Kee is the "American Canyon" Wong Kee. (Figure 3)

While operating in Spring Valley, Chinese imported hogs from as far away as Paradise Valley ("Paradise Hogs"), and they may have continued to do so while working in American Canyon. One Chinese who may have been buying these hogs is Toi (Toy) Lee. In an 1891 newspaper article, Toi Lee was referred to as a "pioneer merchant" who is now engaged in the butcher business ("The Heathen Chinese"). The Humboldt County Assessor's Rolls showed a Toi Lee taxed for merchandise in 1887, but did not show him being taxed for merchandise at any other time. He was, however taxed for possession of hogs in 1891 and 1892, part of his butcher business.

On October 11, 1897 Toi Lee purchased lot 13, Block 22 in Lovelock from Kin Kee for $25 (Humboldt County Deeds 581-82). Toi Lee operated Young's Hotel Cafe in Lovelock until he passed away during a trip to China in 1900 (Hart 24).

Ah Jake (China Jake, Woo Jake) was another man who got his start placer mining in and near American Canyon. He first appears in the historic record in Spring Valley in 1880 (USCM 1880), twenty-four years old, married and listing his profession as placer miner.

Like other successful Chinese, Ah Jake had many dealings with Euro-Americans in the region, however his early dealings were a bit unusual. In 1881, Ah Jake and Ah William acquired 1,000 feet of placer mining ground in Dry Gulch, a drainage between Spring Valley and American Canyon. The property was turned over to them by Henry Pfluger and W. C. Ruddell. No money changed hands, and the only conditions for acquiring the property were that they excavate and prospect ten shafts to bedrock and keep "their noses clean" (Humboldt County Contracts and Records). One suspects that Pfluger and Ruddell owed Jake and William money and turned over the claim in lieu of cash.

In 1887 China Jake was assessed $2.70 for a house. The exact location of the house was unrecorded, but it most likely was in the Spring Valley/American Canyon region (Humboldt County Assessor's Rolls).

By the mid 1920s, Ah Jake was one of the principle owners of the Hop Jake Company in Lovelock. This firm was the largest Chinese-American business in Lovelock and owned much property, including several restaurants. In 1936, Ah Jake sold out his shares and moved back to China (Hart 17).

Simon Billups was not the only provider of freighting services into American Canyon. Ah Lem owned a wagon (two in 1893 and 1894), and provided additional freighting services between American Canyon and Lovelock. In addition to hauling stores to American Canyon, he also hauled American Canyon gold to Lovelock to purchase supplies or for safe keeping (Murbarger). The County Assessor collected taxes from Ah Lem in both American Canyon and Spaulding Canyon (where he owned mining claims), another placer mining area in the East Range roughly twenty-four miles northeast. This indicates that he also provided freighting services between

American Canyon and other smaller, satellite Chinese communities.

Wood for fuel and building purposes was provided by Yen Chin. Yen was born in 1848, and immigrated to the United States in 1868. According to the 1900 Census, he was married for twenty-five years, but lived alone in American Canyon (USCM 1900). In addition to buying lumber from S. R. Young, he may have also harvested timber from the juniper woodlands growing above 5,600 feet in the Humboldt Range. Numerous old and weathered axe and saw cut stumps in the region testify to timber harvesting.

Clues to the everyday business of American Canyon are also found in the historic and archaeological records. For example, not all foodstuffs were purchased through S. R. Young's Lovelock store. Other sources of pork, chicken and vegetables included Euro-American truck farmers operating in the Humboldt Range, and Chinese who tended their own gardens and raised their own pigs and chickens (Murbarger). There is archaeological evidence for Chinese gardens in American Canyon, including a hoe blade and levelled areas with no structural remains.

Chinese often formed various societies. In addition to providing housing, food, and medical care during lean times as well as avenues for religious and social activities, some of these societies were also established as political organizations working toward the overthrow of the Manchu rulers of China. Meeting and religious halls for these societies, known as *joss houses*, were constructed in every major Chinatown in the West. A joss house was established in American Canyon and may have been a local headquarters for the Chee Kong Tong (Chung 170). It was reported to have been decorated with peacock feathers, gilded paint and pictures of dragons and devils (Basso 4). A Chinese man who stayed in the area until his death in 1928 was employed to guard and care take the joss house.

There was some time available to pursue distractions from the hard and dangerous work of mining. One such distraction was gambling. A newspaper article reports Chinese playing a lottery in American Canyon ("Still in the Ring"), and fan tan counters have been found in the archaeological deposits. Others appear to have sought diversion with drugs and alco-

Figure 4. Dugout structure in American Canyon occupied by Chinese. Only the stone foundation remains. Photo courtesy of the Nevada State Museum and Historical Society.

hol. Fragments of "Tiger Whiskey" (Chinese ceramic alcoholic beverage bottles) and champagne bottles, opium cans and ceramic opium pipe bowl fragments scattered among the ruins give testimony to their consumption.

The American Canyon War

Groups of Chinese immigrating from the same region in China tended to band together and form *tongs* (Tong means society or association). Within these associations members could speak their own language and dialects and practice customs as they would at home. The associations also provided assistance to members, such as food and housing during lean times, and made provisions for removing the bones of deceased members back to China for final burial. They also regulated the actions of their members, including establishing locations and prices for stores and laundries and setting rules of conduct. Chinese who broke these rules were often punished by the association, independently of United States' laws and customs. Conflict often arose between different associations competing for resources in the same areas.

Chinese belonging to the *Samyi* (from the vicinity of Guangzhou [Canton]) and the *Longdo* (from the Xiangshan or Zhongshan region near Hong Kong) associations operated peacefully for many years in American Canyon, to the surprise of local newspaper reporters (Chan; Lai et al.; "Still in the Ring"). However, in late spring of 1893, trouble began. Two groups, one led by Lee Ing (or Hing) and the other by Hong Gee, began to squabble over a claim.

In May, Hong Gee filed charges against Lee Ing and two of his men (Lee Do Toy and Lee Hong Ott) for stealing several ounces of gold and smashing up his house. The three men were arrested on a charge of "riot" and hauled off to Lovelock for "examination" ("Trouble Among Chinese"; "The Chinese Case"). It is interesting to note that their defense lawyer was M.S. Bonnifield. The defendants were all found guilty as charged, and paid fines and court costs totalling $96 (Union Township Justice Docket 125-127). The brush with the local legal system failed to resolve the issue among the Chinese, and less than a month later, several Chinese were again in jail, and a man was dead.

On May 31, the two groups fought a gun battle. One man in Lee Ing's party was wounded during an attack by the Hong Gee faction. When the Ing group returned fire, a Gee man was killed and that party was routed ("War in American Canyon").

Lee Yek, a reputed highbinder (hired thug) in the service of Ing, turned himself into the authorities in Lovelock. He freely admitted that he was responsible for the killing. Initial newspaper reports suggested that the dead man had been shot twice in the back. This conflicted with Yek's story that the shooting was done in self defense ("The Chinese Trouble"). A manhunt was initiated for Ing. He was found hiding under a house in the Winnemucca Chinatown and arrested ("Another Chinaman Arrested").

The *Silver State* reported on the inquest held on June 9 in Lovelock. Testimony by Thomas Harper (a Euro-American claim owner in American Canyon) shed new evidence on the incident. According to Harper, Ing was in lawful possession of the claim. Harper's testimony also established that the dead man was a highbinder employed by Gee. The highbinder brought up "four new and the largest sized revolvers" from San Francisco prior to the shootout. These weapons were to be used in the attack against the Ing party. The authorities decided that Yek had acted in self defense. All charges were dropped, and both Ing and Yek were released ("The Chinese Cases").

The court records for the incident are considerably less dramatic than the newspaper account. They state:

> M. S. Bonnifield appeared for the defendant, and moved that the defendant be discharged from custody. The District Attorney appearing in the part of the state, and not being ready to proceed with the examination and knowing of no legal cause why the defendant should not be discharged, said motion is granted and the defendant herein is hereby ordered and is discharged from custody. (Union Township Justice Docket 133)

Nevada has had a tradition of ignoring crimes committed between members of ethnic minorities (Zanjani). It appears as though the law would clamp down on the members of a minority as long as there was potential for levelling fines, but would ignore transgressions between members of the minority if the perceived result was going to be an expensive trial. The American Canyon War is a striking example of the unequal apportionment of Euro-American law on the western frontier.

Decline of the American Canyon Chinese Village

With passage of the 1882 Chinese exclusion act, fewer young Chinese men came to American Canyon to work in the mines, and the aging population began to leave American Canyon to return to China or larger Chinatowns for protection or to retire. All the shallower deposits had been exhausted, and ever deeper shafts were required to recover gold. Euro-American miners were once again becoming interested in American Canyon, not only for placer gold, but also hardrock mercury and silver deposits. With renewed interest in American Canyon, the American District was organized out of the Spring Valley District in June of 1893 (American Mining District).

These factors were responsible for the rapid decline in the Chinese population after 1895. The 1900 Census only counted fifty-eight Chinese in the entire district. In 1905, after a visit to the area, the Humboldt County Assessor reported fewer than ten Chinese living in American Canyon. These men were said, "to be too old to be of any account anywhere else and are left to die" (Bragg 21). One of the men was Wong Kee, running the sole remaining store. He indicated that he would soon leave American Canyon for Spring Valley. A geologist reporting on mercury deposits in Nevada did not mention any Chinese in American Canyon during a visit in 1908 (Ransome 37). Only four aged Chinese placer miners were counted in American Canyon in the 1910 census. These men were eighty-year-old Lee Hog Ming, seventy-four year old Lee Ming, seventy year old Quong Che, and sixty-two-year-old Ching Yin. Lee Hen, Lee Lim and Lee Ley, brothers ranging in age from forty to fifty-five, lived in nearby Dry Gulch. Two Chinese men were reported to be "on the ground" in 1913 working with a rocker (Schrader). No Chinese were counted in the district during the 1920 census; however Vanderburg reported that a lone Chinese man died in South American Canyon about 1928 (159). Since the majority of Chinese counted in the district during the 1910 census were Lees, it is possible that this man was a Lee. He stayed in American Canyon as caretaker of the Joss House, and may have indulged in some placer mining as his other duties allowed.

Conclusions and Discussion

The Spring Valley District, which once again includes American Canyon, is considered the best placer gold mining ground in the State of Nevada (Koschmann and Bergendahl; Vanderburg 159). Estimates for total placer gold production for the Spring Valley District between 1881 and 1895 vary from five million dollars to twenty million dollars. The Wells Fargo and Company estimates it hauled nine million dollars worth of gold on its stage lines during this period. A Chinese man living in the area in 1913 reported that his people removed twenty million dollars (Schrader 325-72). An exact amount will probably never be known since the Chinese were reluctant to discuss such matters with Euro-Americans, and much of the gold they mined was sent to China. A reasonable and much quoted estimate puts the figure at ten million dollars (Koschmann and Bergendahl; Vanderburg 159).

Euro-Americans in the United States often feared the Chinese. They felt that Chinese willingness to work for lower wages (always at most half of that offered to an Euro-American) threatened to destroy their standard of living, or that the hard working Chinese placer miners would recover all the gold before they could. Differences in appearance, language and custom made it easy for Euro-Americans to hate the Chinese. Bigoted Euro-Americans often went to extremes to discourage Chinese miners. They initiated exorbitant foreign miners' taxes, wrote mining district laws outlawing claim possession by Chinese miners, passed other legislation unfavorable to Chinese, and often resorted to mob violence. This persuaded many Chinese placer miners to seek employment in areas less likely to antagonize Euro-Americans (Rohe). This antagonism led not only to the Chinese Exclusion Act in 1882, but also was felt in mining regulation throughout the United States. Prior to the California gold rush, the Federal Government had attempted to control exploitation of minerals on federally controlled land through leases administered by the War Department. This system was corrupt and difficult and expensive to administer. When the regulations expired in 1840, they were not renewed, leaving the Federal Government with no mining law. Miners in California and Nevada used a system based on Spanish mining law, in which miners claimed minerals as their own. Groups of miners would organize mining districts and establish rules for staking claims and for general conduct (United States Department of the Interior, Bureau of Land Management). It was common for Chinese miners to be excluded from claim ownership. This was the case when the first mining district was organized in Nevada (Utah Territory) at Gold Canyon in 1859 (BeDunnah). When the Federal Government finally created mineral and mining laws in 1866 and 1872, much of the flavor of these early district rules was incorporated into these laws, including the provision that a miner must be, or affirming the intention of becoming, a citizen of the United States (30 U.S. Code § 22). Since alien Chinese were excluded from United States citizenship (Salyer), they technically had no legal right to claim ownership. While this aspect of the Federal mining law was often ignored or unenforced, it was initially upheld in an 1890

Idaho court case. District court judge Willis Sweet ruled that "Chinese have no rights whatever on mining lands in the United States" (James 22).

After passage of the 1882 Chinese Exclusion Act and its renewal in 1892, the Chinese population in the United States began to decline. With fewer Chinese working in the United States, the perceived threat felt by Euro-Americans that Chinese would take over all the available jobs or force wage scales to a lower level was lessened. Perceived economic threats also lessened as Euro-American settlers began to secure their own economic positions. Toward the turn of the century, Euro-Americans began to show a measure of tolerance for the remaining Chinese in the United States. This is demonstrated in American Canyon by the ability of Wong Kee and Hong Hing to readily enter into a wide variety of business deals with Euro-Americans, including leases, loans and mortgages. Eventually, respect for their accomplishments was shown (BeDunnah). Vanderburg's 1936 report of placer mining in Nevada reflects this when he states, "Mention should be made of the important role taken by the Chinese in developing the placer deposits in the State in the early days"(16).

During the various western gold rushes of the late nineteenth century, once a claim was considered played out by an Euro-American miner it would be offered to the Chinese. In most cases, this was done to procure additional income from the claim instead of merely abandoning it, but often was done so that Chinese placer miners working the claims would be around to provide additional customers to Euro-American businesses. Miners in a district would reverse, or ignore, district edicts and Federal law against Chinese owning mining claims in an effort to attract Chinese to a declining district (James 19). Many Euro-Americans, exploiting loopholes in the federal mining law, leased claims to Chinese.

Many Chinese miners in Spring Valley were still purchasing unpatented mining claims from Euro-American miners, technically an illegal act which did not afford them any protection from claim jumpers. A *Silver State* article dated January 17, 1877, concerning the placer ground in Spring Valley reads, "The ground, or at least a part of it, was purchased by them of the whites, but we believe there is no law to prevent white men from working in the diggings if they felt disposed to do so." By the time the Chinese began to work in American

Canyon, they were leasing claims. This provided an advantage to the Chinese, in that so long as the leased claims were providing income to the Euro-American claimants, the claim holders would go to extra lengths to protect their, and hence Chinese, interests. This is nicely demonstrated by Thomas Harper's willingness to testify for Ing during Ing's court appearances, and by M. S. Bonnifield's legal representation of Chinese on numerous occasions.

Another example of tolerance through removal of economic threat, is the willingness of M. S. Bonnifield and L.F. Dunn to lease claims to the Chinese. These two men were actively engaged in the expulsion of Chinese from Nevada, especially in 1869 when the Workingman's Protective Union chased the Chinese from Unionville under threat of arms. Fifteen years later, when they were comfortable pillars of the community, they willingly leased claims to Chinese miners.

American Canyon, with its miles of open shafts and placer tailings and the scattered ruins of a once thriving community, gives testimony to the persistence and hard work of Chinese placer miners and the positive impacts they had on several Nevada communities. A look at the historic record for the area gives testimony to the lessening of tensions after many years of bitter hatred by Euro-Americans against the Chinese. Reduction of tension finally allowed Euro-American and Chinese miners and other businessmen to begin to work together for their mutual benefit. Unfortunately it came too late for the Nevada Chinese to realize the full benefits of United States citizenship, a goal they would not be able to attain for nearly another half century.

ACKNOWLEDGEMENTS

I would like to thank Dr. Sue Fawn Chung, University of Nevada, Las Vegas, for her encouragement and excellent instruction. Mr. Jay Marden of Winnemucca aided me greatly by finding early newspaper articles concerning the American Canyon Chinese and sharing this information. Mrs. Ruth Danner assisted me with finding materials in the Humboldt County Courthouse and Recorder's Office.

REFERENCES

American Mining District. Recorders' Book A. Humboldt County Recorder's Office, Winnemucca, Nevada, 1893-1905.

"Another Chinaman Arrested." *Silver State* [Winnemucca, Nevada] 5 June 1893: 3.

Angel, Myron, ed. *History of Nevada.* Oakland, California: Thompson and West, 1881. Berkeley, California: Howell-North, 1958.

Au, Beth A. "Home Means Nevada: The Chinese in Winnemucca, Nevada, 1870-1950, A Narrative History." Master's thesis. University of California, Los Angeles, 1993.

Basso, Dave. *Ghosts of the Humboldt Region: A Glimpse Into Pershing County's Past.* Sparks, NV: Western Printing and Publishing, 1970.

BeDunnah, Gary. *A History of the Chinese in Nevada, 1855-1904.* Thesis University of Nevada Reno, 1966. San Francisco, California: R & E Research Associates, 1973.

Bragg, Allen C., ed. *Humboldt County 1905.* Winnemucca, NV North Central Nevada Historical Society, 1976.

Caressi, LuAnn. Telephone interview. Las Vegas, Nevada, 1996.

Chan, Sucheng. *Asian Americans: An Interpretive History.* Boston, MA: Twyane Publishers, 1991: 5.

"Chinaman Killed." *Silver State* 21 Dec. 1892: 3.

"Chinamen Killed." *Silver State* 1 Oct. 1880: 3.

"Chinese Miners." *Silver State* 17 Jan. 1877: 3.

"Chinese Placer Miners." *Silver State* 23 July 1881: 3.

"Chinese Placer Miners." *Silver State* 20 June 1887: 3.

Chung, Sue Fawn. "Destination: Nevada the Silver Mountain." *Origins and Destinations.* Los Angeles, CA: Chinese Historical Society, 1994.

Claim records. Humboldt County Recorder's Office, Winnemucca, Nevada, 1881-1905.

Hart, Philip D., "Chinese Community in Lovelock, Nevada: 1870 to 1940." *Archaeological and Historical Studies at Ninth and Amhurst, Lovelock, Nevada,* Vol. 1. Ed. Eugene M. Hattori, Mary K. Rusco, and Donald R. Tuohy. Carson City, NV Nevada State Museum, 1979. 11-43.

Humboldt County Assessor's Rolls [HCAR]. Humboldt County Recorder's Office. Winnemucca Nevada, 1876-1916.

Humboldt County Contracts and Records. Book A: 400. Humboldt County Recorder's Office. Winnemucca, Nevada.

Humboldt County Deeds. Book 43: 415. Humboldt County Recorder's Office. Winnemucca, Nevada.

———. Book 33: 581-82. Humboldt County Recorder's Office, Winnemucca, Nevada.

James, Ronald L. "Why no Chinamen are Found in Twin Falls." *Idaho Yesterdays* 36.4 (1993): 14-23.

Johnson, Maureen G. " Geology and Mineral Deposits of Pershing County, Nevada." *Nevada Bureau of Mines and Geology, Bulletin* 89 (1977): 78-81.

Koschmann, A. H., and M. H. Bergendahl. "Principal Gold Producing Districts of the United States." *United States Geological Survey Professional Paper* 60 (1968).

Lai, Him Mark, Joe Huang and Don Wong. *The Chinese of America.* San Francisco, CA: Chinese Culture Foundation, 1980.

LaLande, Jeffery M., "Sojourners in Search of Gold: Hydraulic Mining Techniques of the Chinese on the Oregon Frontier." *Industrial Archaeology* 11 (1985): 29-52.

Liestman, Daniel. "The Chinese in the Black Hills, 1876-1932." *Journal of the West* 27 (1988): 74-83.

Lingenfelter, Richard. *The Hardrock Miners: A History of the Mining Labor Movement in the American West, 1863-1893.* Berkeley, CA: University of California Press, 1974.

Mack, E. M. *Nevada: A History of the State From the Earliest Times Through the Civil War.* Glendale, California: Aurthur H. Clark, 1936.

Marden, J. P. Personal interview. Winnemucca, Nevada, 1993.

Mordy and McCaughey. *Nevada Historical Sites.* Reno, NV: Western Studies Center, Desert Research Center, 1968.

Murbarger, Nell. "Chinese Ghost Town in the Humboldt Range." *Desert* (November 1958): 4-7.

Nevada State Water Engineer. Proof of the Appropriation of Water No. 0730. Carson City, April 22, 1909.

Paher, Stanley. *Nevada Ghost Towns and Mining Camps.* Las Vegas, NV Nevada Publications, 1970.

"Paradise Hogs." *Silver State* 13 December 1877: 3.

"Placers Leased." *Silver State* 17 May 1893: 3.

Ransome, Francis L. "Notes on Some Mining Districts in Humboldt County, Nevada." *United States Geological Survey Bulletin* 414 (1909).

Raymond, Rossiter W. *Statistics of Mines and Mining in the States and Territories West of the Rocky Mountains.* Washington, D.C.: Government Printing Office, 1870: 187-188.

Rohe, Randall. "After the Gold Rush: Chinese Mining in the Far West, 1850-1890." *Montana: Magazine of Western History* 32.4 (1982): 2-19.

———. "The Chinese and Hydraulic Mining in the Far West." *Mining History Association Annual* 1 (1994): 73-91.

Rusco, Elmer R. *Chinese and the Law in Nevada: Race and Class in a Western State* (in press).

Rusco, Mary K. "Counting the Lovelock Chinese." *Archaeological and Historical Studies at Ninth and Amhurst, Lovelock, Nevada,* Vol. 1. Ed. Eugene M. Hattori, Mary K. Rusco, and Donald R. Tuohy. Carson City, NV: Nevada State Museum, 1979: 44-56.

Salyer, Lucy E. *Laws Harsh as Tigers: Chinese Immigrants and the Shaping of Modern Immigration Law.* Chapel Hill, North Carolina: U of North Carolina P, 1995.

Schrader, F. C. "The Rochester Mining District, Nevada." *United States*

Geological Survey Bulletin 580 (1915): 325-72.

"Still in the Ring." *Silver State* [Winnemucca, NV] 18 January 1892: 3.

"The Chinese Case." *Silver State* [Winnemucca, NV] 25 May 1891: 3.

"The Chinese Cases." *Silver State* [Winnemucca, NV] 10 June 1893: 3.

"The Chinese Trouble." *Silver State* [Winnemucca, NV] 3 June 1893: 3.

"The Heathen Chinese." *Silver State* [Winnemucca, NV] 21 August 1891: 3.

"Trouble Among Chinese." *Silver State* [Winnemucca, NV] 23 May 1893: 3.

30 US Code. Sec. 22, 17 Statute 19. 1872 (1976)

Union Township Justice Docket. Humboldt County Courthouse, Winnemucca, Nevada, 1892-1893.

United States Department of the Interior, Bureau of Land Management. Notes on the history of mining law provided for training course 3000-48, Inspection and Enforcement for Locatable Surface Management. Phoenix, Arizona, Apr. 1992.

United States Department of the Interior, Census Bureau. *Compendium of the Eleventh Census, Part 1 - Population.* Washington, DC: Government Printing Office, 1892.

———. *Abstract of the 11th Census: 1890.* Washington, DC: Government Printing Office, 1894.

———. *Census Reports Vol. 1, Twelfth Census of the United States Taken in the Year 1900, Population.* Washington, DC: United States Census Office, 1901.

United States Census Manuscript, Nevada, Humboldt County, Buena Vista Township, 1870.

———. *Nevada, Humboldt County, Spring Valley/Indian Township,* 1880.

———. *Nevada, Humboldt County, Foltz Precinct,* 1900.

———. *Nevada, Humboldt County, Unionville Township,* 1900.

———. *Nevada, Humboldt County, Foltz Precinct,* 1910.

———. *Nevada, Humboldt County, Lovelock Township,* 1910.

Vanderburg, William O. "Placer Mining in Nevada." *Nevada Bureau of Mines and Geology Bulletin* 27 (1983).

Walker, H. G. "First Gold Dredge in Nevada. *The Engineering and Mining Journal* 91 (1911): 1210-1211.

"War in American Canyon." *Silver State* 1 June 1893: 3.

Wells, J. H. "Placer Examinations: Principles and Practice." *United States Department of the Interior, Bureau of Land Management, Technical Bulletin* 4 (1973).

"Wong Kee of Barstow Comes to Warn 'Scotty.'" *Bullfrog Miner* [Rhyolite, Nevada] 1 February 1908: 8.

Zanjani, Sally. "Hang Me if You Will: Violence in the Last Western Mining Boomtown." *Montana: The Magazine of Western History* 42.2 (1992): 48.

African American Communities on the Western Frontier

ROGER D. HARDAWAY

During the late nineteenth century, several thousand African Americans left the South to live in the American West. Many of these migrants— especially soldiers and cowboys— experienced a nomadic existence on the frontier; they moved often and were not bound to the land. Others, however, were less likely to roam over the Great Plains, the Rocky Mountains, and the Pacific Slope. These latter pioneers wanted to settle and feel a sense of attachment to this new section of the country in which they had chosen to make their homes. Moreover, they usually settled together—in parts of existing cities, in all-black towns, and in agricultural colonies. These transplanted black southerners helped each other survive in their new, often inhospitable environments. This cooperation and mutual support helped create and foster within each group the sense of community that is necessary for immigrants anywhere at any time to feel that they belong in the place to which they have moved.

The biggest impetus for African Americans to make the move to the western frontier was the racism and discrimination that permeated southern society during the post-Reconstruction era. Many ex-slaves and other black southerners voted with their feet when Reconstruction ended in 1877 and the northern Republicans who had "guaranteed" them equality under the Constitution abandoned their cause. In exchange for four more years of White House control (under Rutherford B. Hayes), the Republican Party was willing to leave southern

Roger Hardaway holds the juris doctor from the University of Memphis and the doctor of arts in history from the University of North Dakota. He is associate professor of history at Northwestern Oklahoma State University, and has done much research and writing on the African American presence in the American West.

African Americans to the mercy of those who hated them. As white Democrats "redeemed" their states from the control of the GOP, they proceeded posthaste to enact laws that undid many Reconstruction reforms. Blacks found themselves disenfranchised and segregated in the white-dominated society. Their collective condition—political, social, and economic—deteriorated quickly. While many African Americans remained in the Jim Crow South, others left. Most of the migrants headed north, but several thousand opted for the opportunity to make a fresh start in the American West (Savage; Katz; Hardaway).

The first state on the western frontier to which many southern blacks were drawn was Kansas. They knew that slavery had never existed in the Sunflower State, and many were aware of the antislavery exploits of John Brown and other militant abolitionists in Kansas in the decade preceding the Civil War. Kansas, therefore, became a symbolic "promised land" of freedom to African Americans who had become disheartened when the expectations of Reconstruction proved to be illusions (Athearn; Painter). But neither Kansas nor any other western state or territory, for that matter, was the promised land. The frontier was, however, a place where African Americans could settle, live, work, and raise families in an atmosphere that was more racially tolerant and less discriminatory than the South. Several thousand black sojourners chose to stay in Kansas while others moved south to Oklahoma or on west to New Mexico, Arizona, Colorado, Nevada, Montana, Washington, California, and other jurisdictions. The result of these migrations was that while the number of western African Americans was, relatively speaking, never great— less than one percent of the populations of most western states and territories (a notable exception, of course, being the former slave state of Texas)—they had an impact upon the character and development of the western American frontier. This influence can best be seen by examining the places in which they settled and the factors that caused them to develop the types of communities they did (Crockett; Hamilton).

Several self-appointed leaders of African American migrations to the West envisioned blacks living in utopian societies—racially segregated and isolated towns or agricultural colonies where residents could prosper and run their own affairs without fear of being controlled by Caucasians. One of the best-known of these enthusiastic promoters was an ex-slave from Tennessee named Benjamin "Pap" Singleton. After the Civil War, Singleton decided to help his fellow African Americans adjust to freedom by assisting them in locating land on which to establish farms. Finding Tennessee acreage too expensive for impoverished blacks, Singleton decided to lead his followers west where land was more readily available at cheaper prices. He and several business associates set up a real estate company and began in the mid-1870s to recruit black Tennesseans willing to migrate to the promised land. Singleton charged colonists to relocate them and for helping them negotiate land purchases. Apparently, Singleton was motivated as much by the desire to see ex-slaves succeed as he was by the urge to make a profit. This enthusiasm, however, caused him to overstate to his recruits the prospects that existed in Kansas for them to enjoy economic prosperity and freedom from racial prejudice.

Singleton's first attempt at establishing an agricultural colony in Kansas was not successful. Several hundred blacks settled in Cherokee County in the southeastern corner of the state in the 1870s. While some of these colonists were followers of Singleton, not all were. Moreover, while Kansas land was much less expensive than that in Tennessee, ten dollars an acre was a common price at that time in Cherokee County. Most of the migrants, therefore, lacked the capital to buy sufficient land and necessary equipment to establish successful farms. Many had to become day laborers for area white farmers and many—including Singleton—grew disillusioned (Entz).

In 1878 Singleton withdrew his support for the idea of founding an agricultural colony in Cherokee County. Instead, his focus shifted to east central Kansas where the government was opening up some former Indian lands in Morris County to homesteaders. This, of course, meant that the land could be acquired for only a small administrative fee. However, the land that was available to Singleton's colonists was hilly, rocky, and not rich enough for sustained agricultural use; it was better suited for grazing cattle than for planting crops. Consequently, many people also became disenchanted with this settlement—called Dunlap—and moved away after a short time. Still, this second Singleton colony was much more successful than the first. Settlers at Dunlap, with help from the local Presbyterian organization, set up a church and a school. They also established several social organizations. New residents—often encouraged by state officials in Topeka—continued to arrive at the colony even as others moved out. Another problem for the Dunlap settlers was that they experienced some discrimination from their white neighbors even as they had to work for them to make enough money to survive. As time passed, the population of the colony continued to decline. The school closed in the 1890s; and—like several similar experimental settlements—Dunlap ceased to exist as a viable community after the Great Depression of the 1930s (Hickey).

Perhaps the best-known of the all-black frontier communities was Nicodemus in western Kansas. W. R. Hill, a white professional town promoter, and several former slaves founded the settlement in the summer of 1877, only months after the compromise that ended southern Reconstruction and made Hayes president. The town fathers set up an organization called the Nicodemus Town Company with W. H. Smith, an African American, as president. Hill chose a site for the town and filed a claim for 160 acres of public domain land in the name of the promoters' group. Smith and Hill then sent out literature and made recruiting trips to attract settlers to their new town. Several hundred immigrants came to Nicodemus from eastern Kansas and several former slave states—especially Tennessee and Kentucky. In addition to the social and political equality that living in Nicodemus would afford, these colonists (like Singleton's followers) were drawn to the settlement by its boosters' exaggerated claims that great agricultural possibilities existed on the arid Kansas prairie.

The founders of Nicodemus, like Singleton and other promoters of western settlement, charged the settlers fees for helping them to relocate and file homestead claims. They sold some of them housing lots carved from the land they had obtained for free from the U. S. government. But while financial considerations may have been uppermost in their minds when they established Nicodemus, they nevertheless hoped that the town's new residents would enjoy living there. Thus, they encouraged them to establish organizations to enhance the quality of life in the frontier community. Not surprisingly, given the historical importance of religion in the development of African American society, three churches (two Baptist and one Methodist) were among the first institutions organized by the Nicodemus colonists.

By 1880 the population of Nicodemus was almost three hundred; many residents, however, had come and gone since 1877, driven elsewhere by the harsh Kansas environment. Most of those who stayed were forced to live in dugouts or sod houses—dirt being a more plentiful commodity than wood or other building material on the Kansas frontier. These rudimentary homes were often heated by burning cow dung, which was also more readily available than any other type of fuel. African Americans, like other western pioneers of the late nineteenth century, had to adapt to the frontier environment in which they were trying to plant their roots.

Another problem for the settlers of Nicodemus was obtaining enough food to feed their families. They farmed, of course, but many of them (like the colonists in other western all-black settlements) had to work for nearby white families in order to earn money to buy provisions. In addition, a lack of funds to purchase plow horses and farm implements left most of the residents using hoes and shovels to prepare the earth for planting or having to pay others to help with the farm work. Over time, however, the settlers' thrift and industry allowed them to buy more equipment and livestock. By far the largest crop grown at Nicodemus was corn, but farmers also raised wheat, millet, and other grains. Livestock included horses, mules, cattle, and hogs (Schwendemann; Crockett; Hamilton).

The African Americans who settled in Kansas were able to survive because they worked hard. In addition, they were able to become politically important because their numbers were great enough for the major political parties—especially the GOP—to court their votes. In the all-black communities, of course, blacks routinely held governmental positions. In towns dominated by whites—like Lawrence and Topeka—blacks constituted enough of the populations that they also had some political clout. On the state level, the Republican Party often appointed blacks to patronage positions in the governor's office and the state legislature (Cox; Woods). In 1882 and 1884, Edward P. McCabe, a former resident of Nicodemus, was elected Kansas state auditor— the highest office outside the Reconstruction South to which any African American had been elected up to that time.

McCabe's political ambitions also caused him to lead many blacks from Kansas south to Oklahoma Territory. Nicodemus failed in the mid-1880s as a major blizzard convinced the town's struggling pioneers to move to cities and seek steady, paid employment. Meanwhile, in 1886, McCabe lost a bid to be the Republican nominee for a third term as state auditor. These events coincided with the U. S. government's efforts to open up the western half of Indian Territory to non-Indian settlers in 1889; the government officially designated this area "Oklahoma Territory" in 1890. Many blacks—former slaves of Indian planters— already lived in Indian Territory. McCabe reasoned that if he could lead a significant number of blacks to Oklahoma Territory, he might wangle a presidential appointment as governor of the combined jurisdictions. This would encourage other African Americans to move to Oklahoma and whites not to locate there, allowing the area to become virtually an all-black (and Indian) state (Robinson; Dann). McCabe's ultimate vision failed, of course, but thousands of blacks did migrate to the two territories (which merged in 1907 to become the state of Oklahoma) where they proceeded to found a number of all-black communities (Hill; Tolson; Carney).

Several of Oklahoma's all-black towns still exist. Perhaps the best-known of these municipalities is Langston, the site

OKLAHOMA'S ALL - BLACK TOWNS

Map courtesy of Oklahoma State University Cartography Service and Dr. George O. Carney, Professor of Geography.

Public officials. Residents of all-black communities exercised much political power free of white domination. Pictured are the members of the town council of the all-black town of Boley, Oklahoma, circa 1907-1910. Courtesy of Oklahoma Historical Society.

of Langston University, a state-supported institution that is Oklahoma's only historically black college. Also significant is Boley, a town praised by Booker T. Washington who visited the community in 1908 and extolled the productivity and industriousness of its African American residents. In Langston, Boley, Taft, Clearview, and others of Oklahoma's original thirty all-black settlements, African Americans owned all of the businesses, held all of the political offices, and were able to grow and develop free—at least on the local level—from discriminatory treatment by whites (Crockett; Hamilton; Gray; Patterson).

A few other all-black communities were established in the American West during the first few years of the twentieth century. In 1901 Francis Boyer and Dan Keyes, black men from Georgia, homesteaded on the plains of eastern New Mexico. About twenty-five black families eventually settled in the vicinity, creating the rural African American community of Blackdom. Residents of the settlement established a post office, a general store, and a community building where they conducted educational, religious, and social activities.

All of Blackdom's citizens engaged in agriculture to some extent. They raised crops (wheat, hay, vegetables, and fruit—especially apples) and livestock (chickens, turkeys, geese, ducks, hogs, and sheep) while supplementing their diets by hunting antelope, quail, doves, and rabbits. Eventually, however, lack of water doomed the community; alkali built up in the soil, causing it to lose its productivity. Many of Blackdom's residents began working for white farmers while others relocated. In 1920 Boyer and his wife, Ella, tried to establish a town— also called "Blackdom"— on forty acres near the abandoned homesteads. But the Boyers moved away the following year and their town soon disappeared from the map. Many of the African American pioneers who settled Blackdom moved into Roswell and other New Mexico towns where their descendants live today (Gibson).

In 1908 Allen Allensworth, a retired U. S. Army chaplain, established an all-black colony in California that developed into a town that bore his name. Allensworth was born a slave in Kentucky in 1842 and became an ordained Baptist minister after serving in the U. S. Navy during the Civil War. In 1886 President Grover Cleveland appointed him chaplain in the all-black Twenty-fourth Infantry. In addition to religious duties, Allensworth's responsibilities included teaching reading, writing, and other basic subjects to the soldiers in his unit. After twenty years of service, he retired in 1906 as a lieutenant colonel—the highest military rank achieved by an African American up to that time.

Allensworth wanted to create an all-black community to show U. S. white leaders that African Americans were capable of managing their own affairs and making positive contributions to American society. By building and maintaining a successful all-black colony, African Americans could prove to whites that they were deserving of the right to vote and the other privileges of citizenship. Allensworth also hoped that several retired soldiers would settle in his town to serve as living examples of what blacks could accomplish when given the opportunity.

The colony, which was located in central California north of Bakersfield, was successful for several years. By the mid-1910s, it had two hundred residents living on nine hundred acres. They grew grains and sugar beets while raising cattle and chickens. The community's citizens had built several stores, two churches, a school, a public library, a post office, a hotel, a restaurant, and other businesses. Moreover, they had established several organizations including sewing, debating, and theater clubs for adults and a glee club and other groups for the town's youth. An Allensworth resident, Oscar Overr, had been elected California's first African American justice of the peace.

Things soon began to deteriorate for Allensworth, however. The colonel was killed in September 1914 when he was hit by a motorcycle while crossing a street in Monrovia, California. Since he was the driving force behind the colony from the beginning, his death left its future in doubt. Other events conspired at the same time to doom the all-black settlement. The railroad company that had serviced the town built a bypass around it in 1914. The following year, the California legislature defeated a proposal that would have built a publicly funded Tuskegee-type industrial institute in Allensworth. A final blow was the difficulty the community's residents had pumping water from the arid region's low water table. Those who did not abandon the settlement during the economic hard times of the 1920s and 1930s left to find work in the new industries built in the Golden State during World War II. Today, Allensworth survives only as an historic site operated by the state of California (Hamilton; Bunch).

In 1910 Oliver T. Jackson founded the African American community of Dearfield, Colorado. Jackson and the other Dearfield residents experienced many difficulties in establishing an all-black colony on the barren plains northeast of Denver. Chief among the colonists' problems was the lack of money. Many of them had to borrow from Jackson the filing fees necessary to claim their homesteads. Others could not afford to build homes for awhile. Thus, they lived in tents and dugouts, and they hired their labor out to neighboring white farmers until they had enough money to construct permanent residences. Dearfield was primarily an agricultural colony. The people who lived there raised hogs, chickens, ducks, geese, and turkeys while growing such crops as corn, squash, beans, oats, barley, alfalfa, potatoes, beets, pumpkins, and melons. Some had horses and cattle, and they raised hay to feed their livestock. The settlers could not afford to irrigate, although they were near the South Platte River, so they used the dry-land farming methods typical of most home-

An agricultural community. Oliver T. Jackson (on left, holding child) founded the all-black agricultural colony of Dearfield, Colorado, in 1910. He is pictured with one of the settlement's families standing in a cornfield. Courtesy of Denver Public Library.

steaders in the arid West. They burned cow chips, sagebrush, and driftwood from the river for fuel.

The Dearfield residents did several things to create a sense of community in their settlement. They helped each other plant, cultivate, and harvest their crops; this, of course, made them reliant upon each other and, consequently, brought them closer together. The Denver office of the Presbyterian denomination built a church in Dearfield and supplied the town with a student pastor. Jackson and his neighbors built a few businesses for those settlers who wanted to live in Dearfield without farming. These included a store, a boardinghouse, a lumber and coal yard, and a cement block manufacturing company. Jackson himself operated a service station with a grocery store attached, a restaurant, and a dance hall.

Dearfield grew and prospered until farm prices fell after World War I. The community's seven hundred residents of 1921 had dwindled to twelve by 1940. Many, fleeing depression and drought, sold their Dearfield homes in the 1930s for as little as five dollars. The town's businesses closed and the surrounding farm houses stood empty and deteriorating (Johnson; Waddell).

As was the case with Dunlap, Blackdom, Allensworth, and Dearfield, the Great Depression and the Dust Bowl drove African Americans from many of the West's other all-black towns and agricultural colonies in the 1930s. Many of these experimental communities were—like Nicodemus and the Cherokee County colony in Kansas a half-century earlier— abandoned by their discouraged residents and almost obliterated by the prairie dust that blew over their vacant buildings and deserted fields. Others, like those in Oklahoma mentioned earlier, have survived. But even those communities that have disappeared served important functions as has been indicated. They gave African Americans opportunities to run their own social, economic, and political affairs generally free from racial discrimination. Most failed not because their founders lacked vision or determination, but because of environmental factors and because the settlers lacked the capital to invest in land, equipment, and businesses.

Perhaps the most significant thing about the West's all-black settlements was that they allowed African American pioneers to develop and cultivate community institutions that helped to make their lives more enjoyable and fulfilling. Additional studies have shown, moreover, that western black residents of white-dominated towns were also able to create those entities that fostered a strong sense of community. In 1910 Helena, Montana, was a city of 12,500 residents including a black community numbering over four hundred. Just as in all-black towns, church activities were at the center of African American life in Montana's capital city. As early as the 1880s, members of an African Methodist Episcopal congregation spawned such organizations as a literary society and a woman's club. Black Helenans also organized a library, fraternal lodges, various social clubs, a newspaper, and several businesses.

Montana's white citizens—like those in most other states during the frontier era— demanded racial segregation in most social matters (although Helena had integrated schools because of the prohibitive cost of maintaining a separate educational system for only a few African American students). Helena blacks responded positively to forced segregation by developing their own community within a larger, white-controlled one. And while their political clout was minimal, African Americans in Helena were nevertheless instrumental in

African American policeman, Helena, Montana. Pictured is William C. Irvin, in a photograph made by James Presley Ball, an African American who operated a studio in Helena from 1887 to 1900. Courtesy of Montana Historical Society.

getting a black man, William C. Irvin, appointed to the city police force for several years (beginning in 1888) and in forcing white politicians to consider blacks' opinions on laws and governmental actions that particularly affected them (Lang).

Black community-building activities also occurred in such frontier towns as Los Angeles, San Francisco, Seattle, Denver, Phoenix, Dodge City (in Kansas), and Virginia City (in Nevada). Much like their counterparts in Helena, African Americans in these cities built schools and churches, founded literary and civic societies, created fraternal and social organizations, fielded baseball teams, published newspapers, organized clubs and charitable associations, voted, lived, loved, married, worked, had children, grew old, and died among people who shared something with them besides skin color (de Graaf; Daniels; Taylor; Dickson; Luckingham; Haywood; Rusco). That something was the desire for a better life than they would likely have had if they had stayed in the South. For many African Americans of the late nineteenth and early twentieth centuries, then, the western frontier offered the best opportunity the United States had available for them to live contented lives. And while the West was generally good for them, they were generally good for the West; that section of the country grew and developed into a more culturally diverse and, therefore, a richer place because of the African American pioneers who chose to settle on its soil.

REFERENCES

Athearn, Robert G. *In Search of Canaan: Black Migration to Kansas, 1879-1880*. Lawrence: The Regents Press of Kansas, 1978.

Bunch, Lonnie G., III. "Allensworth: The Life, Death and Rebirth of an All-Black Community." *Californians* 5 (November/December 1987): 26-33.

Carney, George O. "Historic Resources of Oklahoma's All-Black Towns: A Preservation Profile." *Chronicles of Oklahoma* 69 (1991): 116-133.

Cox, Thomas C. *Blacks in Topeka, Kansas, 1865-1915: A Social History*. Baton Rouge: Louisiana State UP, 1982.

Crockett, Norman. *The Black Towns*. Lawrence: The Regents Press of Kansas, 1979.

Daniels, Douglas Henry. *Pioneer Urbanites: A Social and Cultural History of Black San Francisco*. Berkeley: U of California P, 1990.

Dann, Martin. "From Sodom to the Promised Land: E. P. McCabe and the Movement for Oklahoma Colonization." *Kansas Historical Quarterly* 40 (1974): 370-378.

de Graaf, Lawrence B. "The City of Black Angels: Emergence of the Los Angeles Ghetto, 1890-1930." *Pacific Historical Review* 39 (1970): 323-352.

Dickson, Lynda F. "African-American Women's Clubs in Denver, 1890s-1920s." *People of Color in the American West.* Ed. Sucheng Chan, Douglas Henry Daniels, Mario T. Garcia, and Terry P. Wilson. Lexington, MA: D. C. Heath and Co., 1994.

Entz, Gary R. "Image and Reality on the Kansas Prairie: 'Pap' Singleton's Cherokee County Colony." *Kansas History* 19 (1996): 125-139.

Gibson, Daniel. "Blackdom." *New Mexico Magazine* 64.2 (1986): 46-47, 50-51.

Gray, Linda C. "Taft: Town on the Black Frontier." *Chronicles of Oklahoma* 66 (1988-89): 430-447.

Hamilton, Kenneth Marvin. *Black Towns and Profit: Promotion and Development in the Trans-Appalachian West, 1877-1915.* Urbana: U of Illinois P, 1991.

Hardaway, Roger D. *A Narrative Bibliography of the African-American Frontier: Blacks in the Rocky Mountain West, 1535-1912.* Lewiston, NY: The Edwin Mellen Press, 1995.

Haywood, C. Robert. " 'No Less a Man': Blacks in Cow Town Dodge City, 1876-1886." *Western Historical Quarterly* 19 (1988): 161-182.

Hickey, Joseph V. "'Pap' Singleton's Dunlap Colony: Relief Agencies and the Failure of a Black Settlement in Eastern Kansas." *Great Plains Quarterly* 11 (Winter 1991): 23-36.

Hill, Mozell C. "The All-Negro Communities of Oklahoma: The Natural History of a Social Movement." *Journal of Negro History* 31 (1946): 254-268.

Johnson, Frederick P. "Agricultural Negro Colony in Eastern Colorado." *Western Farm Life* 17 (May 1, 1915): 5, 12.

Katz, William Loren. *The Black West.* 4th ed. New York: Touchstone Books, 1996.

Lang, William L. "The Nearly Forgotten Blacks on Last Chance Gulch, 1900-1912." *Pacific Northwest Quarterly* 70 (1979): 50-57.

Luckingham, Bradford. *Minorities in Phoenix: A Profile of Mexican American, Chinese American, and African American Communities, 1860-1992.* Tucson: U of Arizona P, 1994.

Painter, Nell Irvin. *Exodusters: Black Migration to Kansas After Reconstruction.* New York: Alfred A. Knopf, 1977.

Patterson, Zella J. Black. *Langston University: A History.* Norman: U of Oklahoma P, 1979.

Robinson, Jere W. "Edward P. McCabe and the Langston Experiment." *Chronicles of Oklahoma* 51 (1973): 343-355.

Rusco, Elmer R. *"Good Time Coming?": Black Nevadans in the Nineteenth Century.* Westport, CT: Greenwood Press, 1975.

Savage, W. Sherman. *Blacks in the West.* Westport, CT: Greenwood Press, 1976.

Schwendemann, Glen. "Nicodemus: Negro Haven on the Solomon." *Kansas Historical Quarterly* 34 (1968): 10-31.

Taylor, Quintard. *The Forging of a Black Community: Seattle's Central District From 1870 Through the Civil Rights Era.* Seattle: U of Washington P, 1994.

Tolson, Arthur L. "The Black Oklahoma Towns." *The Black Oklahomans, A History: 1541-1972.* New Orleans: Edwards Printing Co., 1972.

Waddell, Karen. "Dearfield. . . . A Dream Deferred." *Colorado Heritage* (1988, no. 2): 2-12.

Woods, Randall Bennett. *A Black Odyssey: John Lewis Waller and the Promise of American Life, 1878-1900.* Lawrence: The Regents Press of Kansas, 1981.

Nevada's Pioneer Portuguese Communities
A Pictorial History

DONALD WARRIN

Figure 1. Pico Island as seen from the island of Faial, Azores, 1988. Photo by Donald Warrin.

Immigration from Portugal to the United States in the nineteenth century was relatively modest. In fact, most Portuguese from continental Europe chose to emigrate to their former colony, Brazil. Only because Portuguese immigrants chose to concentrate in two regions, New England and the

Donald Warrin is an emeritus professor in the Department of Modern Languages and Literatures, California State University, Hayward. He specializes in the history and literature of Portuguese immigrants in the western United States.

West Coast, can we speak of any significant Portuguese presence in this nation.

The experience of any American ethnic group, viewed closely, is unique, and that of the Portuguese in the western United States is no exception. Virtually all of them originated, not from the European mainland, but from the Portuguese Atlantic archipelagoes of the Azores, Cape Verde, and Madeira. In the late 1700s American whaling ships began to stop at these islands to replenish crews and supplies. The most frequently visited islands were those in the central and western portions of the mid-Atlantic Azores: Pico, Faial (Figure 1), São Jorge, Flores, and tiny Corvo. Serving on a whaler offered the islander economic opportunity and the possibility of emigration. An extended whaling voyage provided many hardships but also the opportunity to learn English and to experience the world as few others had. In the early nineteenth century whaling ships began to cruise the Pacific. On some ships Azoreans formed a significant portion of the crew. Thus, in mid-century, these men were strategically placed to participate in the California Gold Rush. And so began a tradition of Azorean immigration to the West Coast. Following a general tendency of immigrants to cluster according to their place of origin, the majority of Portuguese in Nevada—particularly the earliest settlers—originated from one island, Flores.

The discovery of vast deposits of silver and gold in 1859 in what became known as the Comstock Lode precipitated a rush of humanity into the area. The principal towns on the Comstock were Virginia City and Gold Hill (Figure 2). Little remains today of the latter, but in the mid 1870s it could boast of a population of some ten thousand. At the time the Portuguese community on the Comstock consisted of almost 150 people, including several women married to Portuguese men (Census). (It is quite likely that the Portuguese community was larger than indicated at the time. The 1875 state census was particularly unreliable in its counting of foreign ethnic groups. And the fact that the year previous fifty-seven Portuguese were naturalized in Storey County, on the Comstock, suggests a larger number [Index]).

Most of the Portuguese on the Comstock lived in Gold Hill and worked at the mines. But many tended to express

Figure 2. Gold Hill, Nevada, 1875. Courtesy of Nevada Historical Society.

their industrious and independent nature by choosing occupations such as storekeeper and barber. The latter was a favorite occupation, for the center of social life for the Portuguese male was more commonly the barbershop than the saloon.

Many Portuguese immigrants to the West adopted the name Joe King, from the Portuguese first name Joaquim, because of its similarity in pronunciation ("Zhwahking"). One of these was a Gold Hill miner and friend of Nevada politician C.C. Stevenson. When Stevenson became governor and moved his residence to Carson City in 1887, he deeded his spacious Gold Hill home (Figure 3) to Joe King (Deeds).

Prospectors, including many Portuguese, soon moved farther inland in search of new deposits of silver and gold. One of the principal new mining areas was located around Grantsville in present-day Nye County. Grantsville (Figure 4) and nearby Ione were the center of the small Portuguese community in the area, which dates from the late 1860s.

One of the early Portuguese in the Grantsville area was John Weeks, who established a ranch at what is still known as Spanish Springs, in the hills above Ione. Weeks also engaged in mining, as can be seen by the arrastra he was using

Figure 3. Joe King, his wife, Mae, and son, George, in front of their Gold Hill home, ca. 1900. Courtesy of Mrs. Wilber D. Gordon.

Figure 4. Grantsville Ruins, 1991. Photo by Donald Warrin.

Figure 5.
Arrastra of John
Weeks, Spanish
Springs,1991.
Photo, Donald
Warrin.

Figure 6. Frank Frates
(from State Resources)
Courtesy of Bancroft Library.

in the 1870s (Figure 5) to grind ore (Assessment, Nye, 1875; "Census," Nye, 1880).

In the early 1860s, as the Central Pacific Railroad inched across the Sacramento Valley and into the Sierra foothills, it became apparent to many Portuguese gold miners that construction work was a surer way of making a living. Before the hiring of thousands of Chinese laborers, the Portuguese formed a significant part of the work crews (Payroll). Many worked their way into Nevada and settled there. Frank Frates, from São Jorge Island, shipped out of Nantucket on a whaler in 1852; on his second and last voyage, from1856 to 1859, he was second mate on the *Sea Ranger*. Frates reached the diggings near Auburn, California, in 1861. Two years later, as tracks for the Central Pacific were being laid nearby, he signed on as a laborer. His years of experience directing men at sea were quickly rewarded. Not long after starting he was a foreman and later became an assistant to James H.Strobridge, the superintendent of construction. After completion of the transcontinental line at Ogden, Utah in 1869, Frates moved to Winnemucca and took charge of the railroad line through central Nevada. Later he served the Central Pacific and its successor, the Southern Pacific, in various capacities in Nevada and California (Frates; *State*).

Railroad work brought other Portuguese into Humboldt County, Nevada, at about the same time that Frank Frates (Figure 6) arrived. Antone Joseph was a Central Pacific employee, but, like other Portuguese in the region, he soon tried cattle ranching. Antone and his brother Manuel were owners

THE TIGER,

JOS. MENDES, PROPRIETOR.

This saloon has been fitted up with a view to comfort, unsurpassed by any similar establishment in the State. To a stranger it is a perfect mystery. Up stairs and down, turn as you will, you always find yourself before a bar, supplied with the choicest brands of **Wines, Liquors and Cigars.** Experienced and attentive bar-keepers are always on hand to serve the patrons of the House. San Jose Fredricksburg Beer constantly on draught. Also XXX English Porter, German Wine, St. Louis Beer, Milwaukee Beer, and the celebrated Culmbach Beer on tap.

Figure 7. Advertisement for "The Tiger," 1878. Eureka and its Resources.

in the mid 70s of a bridge at Golconda across the Humboldt River (Assessment, Humboldt, 1875; Census, Humboldt, 1870; Truett).

Joseph Mendes came from the island of Flores and settled on the Comstock in 1864, where he became one of the early members of the progressive Gold Hill Miners' Union ("Constitution"). Five years later he began mining near the eastern Nevada town of Eureka. As was typical of the Portuguese, Mendes managed by thrift to accumulate a sizable amount of capital and became an entrepreneur with interests in a brewery, racetrack, theatre, and saloons. One of his establishments was the notorious Tiger Saloon (Figure 7) in Eureka where legend says many a gunfight took place (*Eureka's*). Mendes was the most influential member of the local Portuguese community (Assessment, Eureka, 1873, 1880, 1883; *Eureka Daily*; McKenney; *White*, 11 September 1886).

Guilherme (William) F. Mendes (Figure 8) arrived in 1872 as the last of the four Mendes brothers to settle in Nevada. For a time William attended school in Eureka. But three years later, Joseph, George, and Jesse decided that the quieter life

Figure 8. Sketch of William Franklin Mendes, 1909. Reno Evening Gazette.

*Figure 9. William Mendes (right) and family, with friend
(left), Duckwater, early 1900s. Courtesy of Lynn M.
Maxfield.*

of remote Duckwater, to the south, would better suit the im-
pressionable young man; so Joseph purchased a 600-acre
ranch there for him. William prospered as one of the most
influential men in the region, the "father of Duckwater." The
large, irrigated Mendes ranch—eventually almost one thousand acres—fed horses and cattle and supplied fruits and
vegetables to the mining towns of the region (Figure 9). William and his wife, Mary Jacques Mendes, sent their three children to Salt Lake City for schooling; and son William attended
the University of Santa Clara (Assessment, Nye, 1900; Dugan;
Mendes; Notable).

The prodigious water supply flowing out of Big Warm
Spring and into Duckwater Creek was constantly fought over,
both literally and figuratively, by the inhabitants of Duckwater.
The sketch of William Mendes appeared at a time when he
was visiting Reno to defend a challenge to his water rights
(Boudway; Irwin; Reno; Strait; White, 14 May 1903).

A second mining boom hit Nevada soon after the turn of
the century. Berlin (Figure 10) was the site of one of the new
bonanzas. It was a company town, only a few miles from the

older mining camp of Grantsville. However, because of the low wages the company paid, it had difficulty hiring and retaining English-speaking miners (Daggett). The great majority of its workers were southern Europeans: Basques, Italians, and especially Portuguese. On March 7, 1906, the *Tonopah Daily Sun* announced, "Race War in Berlin Averted." Warned of trouble in the camp, the Nye County sheriff and four deputies borrowed an automobile and drove the seventy-five miles from Tonopah. Arriving with revolvers drawn, they arrested several dozen armed Basques and Portuguese, who were threatening each other over the company's hiring policies. After paying hefty fines the disputing parties, including the Portuguese mine foreman, Mr. Gomez [Gomes], were ordered to leave camp (Bruner; Tonopah).

John Avila Gomes (Figures 11, 12) was born on the island of Terceira, Azores, in 1870. Facing compulsory military service as a teenager if he remained, at the age of eleven he emigrated with his mother and four sisters, dressed as the fifth daughter. Settled with his family in Nevada, he attended school, buckarooed for several years, and worked as constable

Figure 10. Berlin, early view. Foreman's house is the white building, partially hidden in the upper right, 1901-1902. Courtesy of Central Nevada Historical Society.

Figure 11. John A. Gomes, wife Lottie, and son George with their Cadillac, ca. 1912. Courtesy of John M. Gomes.

Figure 12. General store of John A. Gomes, Golconda, ca. 1912. Courtesy of John M. Gomes.

in Battle Mountain. Borrowing $1,000 from future senator George Nixon he established a general outfitting store in Golconda. Later businesses included a saloon, several mines, and the Cadillac seen here that he used as a motorized stage between Golconda and the mining town of Midas. The general store was the gathering place for the Portuguese community of Humboldt County, where a new arrival from the islands could sleep in the bunkhouse, take English lessons from Gomes, and be directed to a job in the cattle or sheep industry, or in the mines (J. Gomes; *Humboldt;* Manhã).

John's wife, Lottie, from St. Louis, had less tolerance for the desert and its influence. She expressed her feelings in these verses taken from "To Some Men I Know" (L. Gomes):

> On the desert wide
> Where the sagebrush blooms
> And the coyote wails at night
>
> . . . .
> Behold the barbarian man,
> Loving the plains as a strong man can,
> No women's shops to distress his mind
> All things to him are dear and kind,
> No pretty church, with its open door,
> Cushioned pews and velvet floor,
> But the doors of Saloons are open wide
> And over the sage for miles men ride
> To eat, to drink, to live for the day,
> Seems to make (some) men happy,
> Seems to be (some) men's way.
> Music, and flowers, shops, and art,
> In their life takes no vital part
> But the days are grey
> and we miss the things so far away,
> And women can never tell
> How the desert makes of our life a hell.

Sheep were common in the Azores in the nineteenth century and probably were an important factor in the Azorean presence in the western sheep industry. Sheepherding was an arduous and lonely task, but Portuguese immigrants often preferred it as a means of accumulating the funds necessary to obtain their own flocks or to enter some other line of

Figure 13. Portuguese sheepherder, Central or Eastern Nevada. Courtesy of John M. Gomes. Photo by Manuel Azverado, a Portuguese photographer who arrived in White Pine County in 1897, where he maintained a studio for several years. Azevedo was also active in the Monitor Valley in central Nevada. Some time later he published a collection of photos from the California Gold Country, entitled Pictural Tuolumne. *(Tuolumne, CA: Author, n.d.).*

business. Portuguese activity in the Nevada sheep industry was centered in Elko, Humboldt, and Lander counties (Figure 13).

Joe C. Mello was a sheep foreman for the Golconda Cattle Co. In 1915 he and three of his Portuguese herders visited the Pan-Pacific Exposition in San Francisco and had their picture taken for a postcard seated in this automobile (Figure 14). All look somewhat uneasy in the big city in their Sunday best. The card was addressed to John A. Gomes, Golconda, and said, in Portuguese: "Friend Gomes, I hope you are in good health. I tell you to tell 'Maneta' ["One-arm"] that if he needs a man to drive the automobile I know how to drive. Your friend, J.C. Mello" (J. Gomes).

Portuguese were particularly active on the ranches of the legendary Scotsman, John G. Taylor, who at one time owned some 75,000 sheep and could boast that he had so many ranches he couldn't count them (Figure 15). Both Frank

Figure 14.

Joe Mello (at the wheel) and companions, Pan-Pacific Exposition, San Francisco, 1915. Courtesy of John M. Gomes.

Figure 15.

John G. Taylor and Frank Mancebo, ca. 1915. Nevada Nomads: A Story of the Sheep Industry. *Courtesy of Nevada Historical Society.*

Mancebo, from the island of Flores, and Manuel Moreira, from the island of Santa Maria in the Azores, were sheep foremen for Taylor in the first decades of this century. Women from the Azores often worked on the Taylor ranches, especially as cooks (Sawyer). The Taylor headquarters in Lovelock were an important factor in attracting Azorean settlement there.

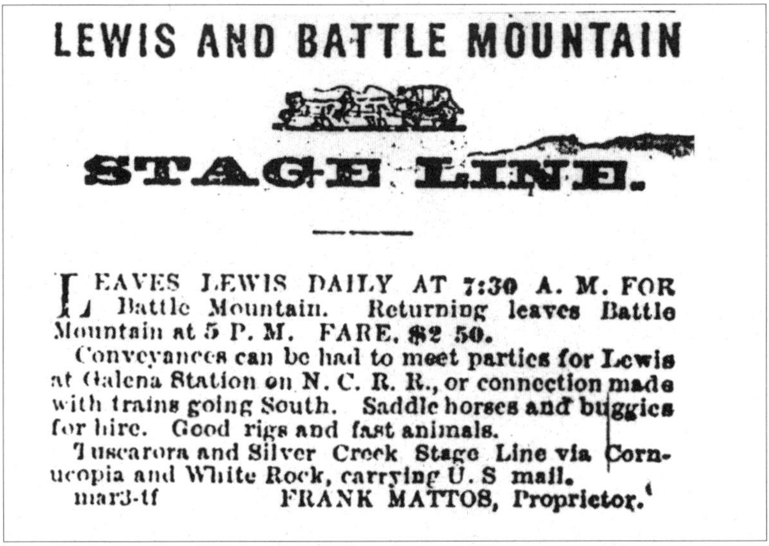

LEWIS AND BATTLE MOUNTAIN

STAGE LINE.

LEAVES LEWIS DAILY AT 7:30 A. M. FOR Battle Mountain. Returning leaves Battle Mountain at 5 P. M. FARE, $2 50.
Conveyances can be had to meet parties for Lewis at Galena Station on N. C. R. R., or connection made with trains going South. Saddle horses and buggies for hire. Good rigs and fast animals.
Tuscarora and Silver Creek Stage Line via Cornucopia and White Rock, carrying U. S mail.
mar3-tf   FRANK MATTOS, Proprietor.

Figure 16. Advertisement for the Portuguese-owned Lewis and Battle Mountain Stage Line.

Portuguese in Nevada were especially attracted to the transportation industry. Some were stage drivers; many drove—and owned—teams of horses carrying goods to and from the mines; and others were railroad workers. The Mattos brothers were successful entrepreneurs in transportation in the State. Joseph operated a stage major line out of the town of Taylor, in White Pine County, while Frank's stage (Figure 16) ran between the two Lander County towns of Lewis and Battle Mountain (*Battle; White*, 27 Apr. 1889).

Frank Mattos was also the operator of a freight hauling business in Austin. In 1889 he owned eighty-one horses and one hundred cattle, a three-hundred acre ranch in Lewis, and the American Exchange Hotel in Battle Mountain, along with a stable, blacksmith shop, and corral (Assessment, Lander, 1889).

As the twentieth century approached, the older Portuguese settlements in the central and eastern portions of the state, and on the Comstock, began to disappear as the Portuguese population moved into the growing towns of Fallon, Lovelock, Reno, and Yerington. Dairying, in which the Portuguese had participated in Nevada since the 1870s, became a popular occupation, particularly in and around Reno. By the 1920s it was estimated that the Portuguese controlled 25% of the dairy industry in Nevada. Reno alone had a couple of dozen dairies run by Portuguese. Given that historically in California they have controlled over one-third of the dairy industry, the Nevada figure should not be surprising (Castello; Graves; Harrington; Personal).

Occasionally we find a Portuguese woman operating a dairy or ranch. Such, in 1910, were the widows Mary Azevedo, a "dairyman" in Golconda, and Isabella Gomes, farmer in Stillwater (Census, Churchill; Census, Humboldt). Even if not officially in charge, Portuguese women frequently had a major role in ranch operations.

Representative of those who moved from the old to the new settlements is Joseph De Braga. Born in 1870 on Santa Maria Island in the Azores, he came to Austin, Nevada, twenty years later. De Braga later mined near Grantsville and, in 1918, settled with his wife and six children in Stillwater, Churchill County (their seventh surviving child would be born the following year). There they ranched and operated a dairy (*Fallon*; Osgood; Census, Churchill, 1890). Portuguese commonly married within their ethnic group. If not, they most often married other Catholics, usually Irish Americans, such as Margaret Kennedy (Figures 19a,b).

Albert B. Silva left the island of São Jorge, Azores, in 1910 and, in 1917, settled in Yerington where he ran a dairy with his wife Wilma, the daughter of Portuguese immigrants (Nevada). Dairying was a preferred occupation among the Portuguese and Italians of the town (Figure 17).

In a pattern often followed by immigrants, Frank Martin left the island of Flores in 1876 with a ticket paid by a Nevada sheepman from his home town. After working off his passage, Martin soon had his own sheep and ranch in Lander County. Martin, his wife Ellen O'Leary Martin, and children eventually moved to Sparks where, among other ranching enterprises, they operated a dairy (Figure 18). After visiting the 1915 Pan-Pacific Exposition, Martin brought in the first milking machine and constructed the first silo in the Reno area. All five of their surviving children, including three daughters, graduated from college (four from the University of Nevada, Reno) and became teachers (Assessment: Humboldt 1884-1895, Lander 1890, Washoe 1913; Machado; Machado and McClaskey).

Many Portuguese invested their savings from mining, sheep, or cattle in a commercial establishment. Antonio J. Manhã in Reno started in the grocery business with ex-sheepman Frank Penque. Later Penque and sheepman Frank Mancebo established the Azores Mercantile Company in Lovelock and the Azores Store in Fallon (Manhã; Mateas and Moura).

At the turn of the century the bicycle was an important mode of transportation and the bicycle race a major sporting event. The Reno Wheelmen, founded in 1896 by a group of cyclists, grew to be the city's most prominent social and fraternal club. In 1905 the Wheelmen defeated the New Century Wheelmen of San Francisco and the Garden City Wheelmen of San Jose, California, regaining the Pacific Coast Bicycling Championship they had lost in 1902 (Earl).

Two of the team cyclists were Martin and Manuel Simas Jr. (Figures 20a,b), the sons of Manuel Simas, a foreman at the Reno Water Company, who had immigrated from Portugal in 1865. Although the Portuguese in Nevada were almost always politically conservative and Republican, Manuel Simas (father, age 57 or son, age 27) ran unsuccessfully in 1904 for the State Assembly on the Socialist ticket (Political Directory; Census, Washoe, 1910). The year 1905 marked the last year of competition for the Reno Wheelmen cycling team. The enthusiasm of the public for racing was shifting to the automobile and the motorcycle.

The Portuguese community of Reno has disappeared along with the dairies and sagebrush, displaced by today's casinos, industries, and shopping centers. Modest communities of Portuguese Americans continue to exist, however, in the rural

Following pages: A Portugese family album: Albert and Wilma Silva family, Frank and Helen Martin family, Joseph and Margaret DeBraga, Martin and Manual Simas, A. J. Manhan and sons.

Figure 17. Albert and Wilma Silva with son Ed, Yerington, ca. 1925. Courtesy of Ed Silva.

Figure 18. Frank Martin, wife Helen O'Leary Martin, and children, Sparks, Nevada, ca. 1910. Courtesy of Edith Martin Machado.

Figure 19a. Margaret Kennedy De Braga, wedding photo, 1901. Courtesy of Churchill County Museum & Archives Photo Collection.

Figure 19b. Joseph De Braga, wedding photo, 1901. Courtesy of Churchill County Museum & Archives Photo Collection.

Figure 20a. Manuel Simas with the Reno Wheelmen, 1904-1905. Courtesy of Nevada Historical Society.

Figure 20b.. Martin Simas with the Reno Wheelmen, 1904-1905. Courtesy of Nevada Historical Society.

Figure 21. Manhan Grocery Store, 4th and Virginia Streets. Owner A. J. Manh and sons Albert (standing) and Tony, kneeling. (1922). Courtesy of Fred Manhã.

Figure 22. Festival parade, Fallon, 1930. Courtesy of Churchill County Museum & Archives.

towns of Fallon, Lovelock, and Yerington. And, in spite of small numbers, they continue to honor their Portuguese heritage through the celebration of the unique Holy Ghost Festival (Figures 22, 23).

The Festa do Espírito Santo, or Holy Ghost Festival, is a medieval celebration of the Holy Spirit, suppressed by the

Figure 23. Ellie Kent, Festival queen, Fallon, 1942. Courtesy of Churchill County Museum & Archives, Eleanore Kent Collection.

Catholic Church centuries ago on the European continent, but still flourishing in the Azores and also among Portuguese communities in California, Nevada, and Idaho. The Holy Ghost Festival was brought originally to California in the last century by Portuguese immigrants. The first celebration of the Holy Ghost Festival in Nevada took place in Yerington in 1919 under the auspices of the União Portuguesa do Estado da Califórnia (U.P.E.C.). It continues to be celebrated in May or June, during Pentecost, in Fallon, Lovelock, and Yerington. The parade from the Catholic church to the community hall is one part of this two-day celebration. Other major events are the crowning and blessing of the "queen," a free dinner of "sopas" for the community (beef, broth, and bread), an Azorean round dance (the "chamarrita"), and an auction to raise money for the next year's Festival. In recent years young, non-Portuguese women occasionally have been chosen as the festival queen.

With active immigration to the state from Portugal greatly diminished for almost three quarters of a century, it is only through the efforts of the descendants of these Nevada pioneers that this significant aspect of Azorean culture has been maintained.

REFERENCES

Assessment Rolls (Counties of Eureka, Humboldt, Lander, Nye, and Washoe).

Battle Mountain Messenger, 17 Mar. 1883.

Boudway, Becky. *Treasure in the Dust: Enduring Gold and Silver's Century of Divorce*. Fresno, Calif.: Panorama West Books, 1985. 93-116. [Expresses the viewpoint of Mendes's brother-in-law and rival, Joseph Tognoni.]

Bruner, Firmin. Interview by author, Fallon, Nevada, 14 June 1990.

———. *Some Remembered—Some Forgot: Life in Central Nevada Mining Camps*. Carson City: Nevada State Park Natural History Association, 1974. 8 [Expresses the Basque viewpoint.]

Castello, Antonio. Interview by author, 28 July 1988.

Census Manuscripts, U. S. (Counties of Churchill, Humboldt, Nye, and Washoe).

"Census of the Inhabitants of the State of Nevada, 1875." 2 vols. Appendix to Journals of Senate and Assembly, of the Eighth Session of the Legislature of the State of Nevada. Carson City, 1877.

"Constitution, Bylaws, Order of Business, and Rule of Order of the Miners' Union of Gold Hill, Nevada. Organized December 8th, 1866." Special Collections, University of Nevada, Reno.

Costa, John. Interview by author, 26 July 1988.

Daggett, Ellsworth. "Appendix A to the Report upon the Condition of the Nevada Co.'s Property in Berlin, Nevada, February 1st, 1908." Special Collections, University of Nevada, Reno.

Deeds, Storey County. Book 50, 524-525. Special Collections, University of Nevada, Reno.

Dugan, Inez. Telephone interview by author, Murray, Utah, 8 Apr. 1990.

Earl, Philip I. "The Reno Wheelmen, 1896-1909." *Washoe Rambler* 5.2 (Summer 1981): 28-45.

Eureka and Its Resources. 1879. Reno: Univ. of Nevada Press, 1982.

Eureka Daily Sentinel , 7 Jan. 1873.

Eureka's Yesterdays; A Guide to a Historic Central Nevada Town. Reno: Nevada Historical Society, 1988. 33.

Fallon Eagle, 9 Jan. 1943.

Frates, Frank. "Dictation" 19 July 1888, for "California As It Is," a project of H.H. Bancroft, ms. Bancroft Library.

Gomes, John M. Interview by author, Reno, Nevada, 19 Dec. 1989.

Gomes, Lottie. "Sagebrush Soliloquies." Reno: *Nevada State Journal*, 1919. 8

Graves, Alvin R. "Immigrants in Agriculture: The Portuguese Californians, 1850-1970s." Diss. UCLA, 1977. 172.

Harrington, Scott B. "Economic Survey of the Dairy Industry in Nevada." Thesis. Univ. of Nevada, 1925. 20.

Humboldt Miner, 1 Mar. 1902.

"Index to Names of Persons Naturalized in the First Judicial Court, 1861-1906." Special Collections, University of Nevada, Reno.

Irwin, Louisa v. J.C. Tognoni et al.

McKenney, L. M. *Pacific Coast Directory for 1886-87.* San Francisco: L. M. McKenney Co., 1886. 880.

Machado, Edith Martin. Interview by author, Hayward, Calif., 9 Mar. 1989.

———, and Mary McClaskey. Interview by author, Hayward, Calif., 20 Oct. 1990.

Manhã, Fred. Interview by author, 29 July 1988.

Manhã, Maria and Vivian. Interview by Geoffrey Gomes, Turlock, Calif., 11 Mar. 1989.

Mateas, Rosaline, and Virginia Moura. Interview by author, 30 Jan. 1987;

Mendes, William E. Interview by author, Minden, Nevada, 15 Nov. 1987.

Nevada, The Silver State. 2 vols. Carson City: Western States Historical Publishers, 1970. II:967.

Notable Nevadans: Snapshots of Sagebrushers Who Are Doing Things.

Reno: [n.p.], 1910, [n. pag.].

Osgood, Marguerite. Interview by author, 3 Nov. 1990.

Payroll Records, Central Pacific Railroad. California State Railroad Museum Library, Sacramento.

Personal Property Rolls, Washoe County, csp. 1928.

Political Directory, Nevada Historical Society.

Reno Evening Gazette, 4 Aug. 1909.

Sawyer, Byrd Wall. *Nevada Nomads: A Story of the Sheep Industry.* San Jose, Calif.: Harlan-Young Press, 1971. 60-65.

State Resources, 2.7 (1891). Oakland, Calif.: Resources Publishing Co. 392-393.

Strait, B. B. et al. v. C.A. Bron et al.

Tonopah Daily Sun, 8 Mar. 1906.

Truett, Velma S. *On the Hoof in Nevada.* Los Angeles: Gehrett-Truett-Hall, 1950. 139, 197.

White Pine News [Taylor and Ely].

Between Feast and Famine
Coal Communities
in the American West

ERIC MARGOLIS

See, when this town started it started with the Simpson
Mine, Lafayette Miller— they had 'em open that mine
up—and all Johnny Bulls, Englishmen. Then the Welsh
come in, naturally, because—next county over. Then
the Wops come and the Bohunks come. Then the Bul-
garians come, the Greeks come—all just a wishwash—
because there was work here, hell there was 22 mines
here at one time.

Interview with Henry (Welshy) Mathias, 1975.

Coal mines were first opened around 1860 in Utah and Colorado but it wasn't until the 1870s that production reached
the boom level. The native population was too small to satisfy
the mines' voracious appetite for labor. As demand soared,
experienced miners were sought in England and Wales. During the 1870s, the Welsh coal mining valleys were in an economic depression; many thousands came to American seeking work (Ginzberg 8). Mormon missionaries were active in
south Wales and brought experienced miners to eastern Utah.
These experienced miners developed the mines and many
became bosses and foremen.

Demand continued to increase, and armies of coal diggers arrived from all over the world. Mining introduced ethnic
diversity to much of the rural West. By 1901 thirty-two nationalities were living in the Colorado Fuel and Iron (CF&I)
company towns and twenty-seven different languages were

*Eric Margolis teaches in the Division of Educational Leader-
ship and Policy Studies at Arizona State University.*

being spoken (Scamehorn 152). Finns, Greeks, Italians, and Slavs predominated in eastern Utah mines; Polish and Slavish miners settled around Sheridan, Wyoming; Finns, Slovenes, Italians, Scots and Asians worked along the Union Pacific line near Rock Springs. Blacks from the Deep South found their way West, and Mexican immigrants crossed the border to work the mines. By 1900, more than sixteen thousand men were mining coal in Colorado, New Mexico, Wyoming and Utah. Many had been brought in as strike breakers. During the Colorado strike of 1913, Welshy watched them bring immigrant strikebreakers to the mines:

> They'd come in trains and the windows would be whitewashed or chalked up till they got up right to the mines, drive the goddamn train coach right to the mines and unload 'em right at the mines.

The accompanying graphic[1] shows coal mine employment for Colorado, New Mexico, Utah and Wyoming between 1885

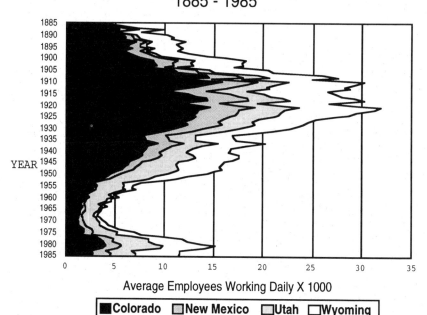

Coal Mine Employment by State
1885 - 1985

YEAR

Average Employees Working Daily X 1000

■Colorado □New Mexico □Utah □Wyoming

and 1985. The data indicate a steady increase in the number of miners, which lasted from the turn of the century through the early 1920s. The periods of decline appear to be indication of strikes in 1903-04, 1913 and 1919. Despite ups and downs, employment hovered around 25,000 from 1907-1926. This defines the period of full employment that the miners remember as "the good old days."

The Coal Town in the American West:
Structures and Functions

There were two types of coal town: hub cities and coal camps. Each of the coal fields had an incorporated city serving as the metropolitan hub of the region. These towns experienced population growth that makes the boom towns of the 1970s seem weak by comparison. The population of Walsenburg, Colorado increased an average of 66 percent every ten years between 1890 and 1940. The population of Price, Utah, doubled every decade from 1890 to 1930. Rock Springs, Wyoming, soared from 763 people in 1880 to 3406 in 1890 (Census data).

Figure 1. Little Italy at Sopris. A coal camp in the Purgatory River valley west of Trinidad, Colorado, prior to 1915. Courtesy of Glen Aultman.

Numbers cannot tell the whole story. The boom towns of the first coal age were isolated, unregulated and composed of people from many different lands and cultures. Life was cheap and violence on both the individual and organized level was common. The miners explained the level of violence by pointing out that a mule was worth more than a man. In those days before workman's compensation a mule had to be purchased while workers were freely available. Donald Mitchell, interviewed in 1978, put it this way in describing his experiences during the 1930's:

> DM: Here come the super in a hurry down there: "Any mules killed?" "No." "Any men killed?" That's what — And then they put that compensation law, see. And he said this himself, he come down on a day when the trip got away, he said: "Any men killed?" "No." "Any mules?" He said, "It used to be the other way." He said, "We used to have to buy another mule; it cost us $250.00, it didn't cost nothing, we just hired another man." That's what he told us. (Chuckle) Super told us that.

The Amicarella brothers, Claude and Lawrence, used their account to underscore the racism inherent in corporate hiring practices:

> CA: If a mule was accidentally killed —
> LA: Oh, you got hell.
> CA: You got hell, and they closed that end of the mine down.
> LA: Let a man get hurt, they'd say, "Oh well, they'll hire another Mexican."
> CA: Yeah. That's right.
> LA: That's just the way it happens, fellows.
> CA: There was no respect given at all.
> (Interview with Claude and Lawrence Amicarella, 1978)

Many boom town effects were felt. Drinking was one of the few forms of recreation; red light districts served the large population of single miners; gamblers flocked in to separate miners from their paychecks. Child abuse was complicated by the fact that boys as young as twelve worked in the mines (see Figure 4, following) while girls of that age served in boarding houses or took care of the babies. There were few jobs for women. Alex Bisulco (interviewed in 1978) described the life that wives lived, this way:

> AB: When I look back and see how those women could raise those kids, and do the housework, I can't see how they did it. I don't see how they could not go bugs. Washing clothes by hand on the board, you know, go haul the water, go haul the buckets, you see. No hydrants, no water in the house, an old two seater can out back, and all that kind of stuff. I don't see how they did it.

Hub cities were dominated economically and politically by the industry to which they owed their existence. During the 'teens and twenties Walsenburg, Colorado, was controlled by the Republican Party under a corrupt sheriff named Jefferson Farr. The political situation was eloquently expressed by miners who remembered:

> Dan: When Jeff Farr run this town, anybody that said they were a Democrat, hell they shot 'em. There was no Democrat. And when they didn't have enough votes, they took all the names of the mules—Walsen had about 33 mules, Ideal the same and they all got a different name—if they didn't have enough votes for the Republican to win, they put all the names of the mules down.
> Johnny: They voted the mules.
> Nick: At that time Colorado Fuel and Iron Company, they say everything here.
> (Interview, Biondi's Sporting Goods)

Walsenburg was not atypical. Helen Papanikolas characterized Price, Utah, as the "coal operators town" (266). James B. Allen said of Rock Springs that "Although it was never company-owned the Union Pacific controlled it in almost every way" (179).

Hub cities were surrounded by towns built on private property, owned and controlled by a single company. During the 1880s and 1890s, miners had been encouraged to build their own houses, "squatting" on company property. Early photo-graphs show a variety of "natural" constructions, including adobe ranchitos, tar-paper shacks and dugouts. Independent entrepreneurs were offered concessions to open stores and bars and provide goods and services. Privatization saved the company capital at a time when they were developing the prop-erty. But private homes and stores had drawbacks.The com-pany could only collect minimal ground rent, and if the min-ers went on strike, the company couldn't easily evict them to make room for strike breakers. As soon as possible, company houses were built to replace this "vernacular" housing. Dur-ing the 1903 strike in Utah and Colorado, for instance, strik-ing miners and their families were forced out of their homes and the houses were burned or blown up by company guards, clearing the way for uniform rows of company housing (Wright 338).

The coal companies depicted company towns as "model" communities, using them as advertisements and inducements to attract labor (Scheick, Hubbell et al. 40). By 1910, accord-ing to Allen (188), the operators were becoming aware that town planning and social welfare could increase work effi-ciency and lead to better public relations.

Figure 2. Tobasco, Colorado, circa 1913. Photo courtesy of Harvey Phelps, M.D.

The interrelation of structures and functions in the model coal camp produced a total institution. The dominant structures were industrial—the tipple where coal was loaded on train cars, and in some areas long strings of beehive coke ovens. Scattered throughout the industrial plant were houses for the workers. Most common were square, four-room, single-family camp houses with a distinctive peaked roof, laid out in rows with neighborhoods separated from one another. There was frequently an area of larger houses called "Silk-Stocking Row," where the foremen and bosses lived. Silk-Stocking Row was usually equipped with indoor plumbing and was located above the rest of the town where dust, noise and smoke were less obnoxious. As well as reflecting class distinctions, coal towns reproduced ethnic divisions as well. Neighborhoods had names like: Greek Row, Little Italy (see Figure 1), Hunkey Town, Snake Town, Chihuahuaita.

There was a general store selling tools of the trade, food and most other necessities of life. Company stores were either owned by the coal company or were run as concessions. Almost every camp had bars, saloons, pool halls, and dance

Figure 3. Charles Niccoli Saloon in the setting of Hastings, Colorado. Photo by L. C. McClure. Courtesy of Denver Public Library.

halls. As Kate Livoda (interviewed in 1980) put it: "And then
they had a company store, and a company saloon. And if they
didn't get them one way they got them the other." Gambling
and prostitution were not unheard of. Some camps had
churches staffed with a minister paid by the company, and a
school with a company-paid teacher. Most included a post
office, a movie theater, a railroad station, shoe repair and
barber shops. Really large camps like Dawson, New Mexico,
also had a hospital, a mortuary and a cemetery. There was
little crime, but each camp had a marshal in the pay of the
coal company. Their major role was to keep out union orga-
nizers, radicals and other "undesirables." During strikes it
was common practice to fortify the towns and hire scores of
armed guards.

Company towns served several interrelated functions. They
were practically a necessity for resource development in an
underdeveloped area. As waves of immigrants were brought
in they accomplished socialization and acculturation, transforming agricultural peasants into wage workers by teaching
industrial discipline and how to march to the rhythms of the
coal economy. When strikes stirred the coal fields the coal
camp made it easy to control access to the work place. The
company town similarly functioned to limit information about
bad working conditions and the frequent accidents which
killed and maimed miners. There were no independent newspapers in the coal camps. Only the largest explosions in which
scores were snuffed out in a single blast were loud enough to
pierce the silence and reach the world outside.

The CF&I instituted the West's most comprehensive system
of company towns, manifesting a peculiarly modern concern
with "human resources" and boom town conditions which
might interfere with production. A revealing 1905 article is
entitled "Uplifting 17,000 Employees: The Human Story of
Workers Who Were Led by the Colorado Fuel and Iron
Company from Conditions of Drunkenness and Dirt to Well-
Ordered Living . . ." (Lewis). The article, written for the business
publication *World's Work* by the editor of CF&I's company
magazine *Camp and Plant*, presented the company rationale
for the model coal town. The author used three vignettes on
boom town social problems to "illustrate the environment the
workmen made for their children, the dwellings they provided
for themselves, the manner in which they handled the liquor

problem, and the way they amused themselves when left to their own devices. . . . "

In the first story an Italian cuts his wife's throat with a razor and two Mexicans kill each other in a knife fight while the children of the coal camp look on. The second story depicts an "adobe bunkhouse" not built on company ground but maintained by a *padrone*: "In this noisome place, in addition to vermin of all sorts, lived thirty-eight Italian workmen, each drawing from $60 to $80 a month. . . . They slept in two 'shifts'—those who worked by day crawling into the places just vacated by those who worked at night." The bunkhouse had been "discovered" by the company doctor who was investigating the cause of sickness among coke workers at El Moro.

The third incident concerned a Fourth of July drinking spree:

> The result of the celebration by the "coal diggers" was the suspension of work in the mine for five days—the temporary shut-down of a bank of coke ovens at Redstone where some of the product of the Coalbasin mine is burned to coke, with a loss to the company of thousands of dollars due to delay in shipments of fuel and to the non-productiveness of capital invested in mines, railway, and coke ovens, and a loss of thousands of dollars to the men in wages. (Lewis 5939)

It was clear to CF&I managers that boom town conditions were interfering with production. A rational approach dictated that something be done and the concept of using applied sociology to solve human resource problems in an industrial setting was new and promising. Anticipating the social impact assessments of the 1970s, but in response to the coal strike of 1901, the CF&I created a "Sociological Department" under direction of the company's chief surgeon (Scamehorn 146). The Sociological Department instituted programs in "education, social training and industrial training, housing and communication. . . . Its objective was to benefit employees and their families by educating children, improving relations in the home, molding better citizens, and fostering an appreciation for labor" (Scamehorn 150-51).

One of the photographs in Lewis' 1905 article, showing a group of children, was captioned "Some 'Raw Material' for

Kindergarten" (See photo, following pages.) According to
Scamehorn (152), Dr. Corwin, the head of the Sociological
Department, believed "Most of the children were destined to
become miners or the wives of coal diggers." Therefore "girls
were taught to maintain neat homes and to prepare savory
meals, while boys acquired proficiency in technical pursuits
that would enable them to command good wages. . . ." By
1903-04 kindergartens were operating in thirteen camps and
the company was beginning to transfer the operating expenses
to local school districts. Courses were also offered for "mothers and housewives, working adults, and the elderly." Included were night classes in English and hygiene. In addition
to education, the Sociological Department built and maintained model houses, opened reading rooms, began local cot-
tage industries for women (lace production at El Moro, bas-
ket-weaving at Primero), and wrestled with the alcohol problem (Scamehorn 151).

No less important than social control and Americanization
was the function of the company town to make a profit. Capital
invested in housing, stores and services was expected to
produce a return in the same way as the capital invested in
mining machinery. James B. Allen (188-89) analyzed figures
from a 1920 report by the Bureau of Labor which included a
study of sixteen coal camps in Colorado and Wyoming which
Allen suspected were owned by the CF&I. Allen estimated that
the average house cost $700 to build and rented for eight
dollars per month. He assumed that half of the rent went to
community maintenance. Thus the capital investment would
be repaid in about fourteen years, after which the building
would return 6.8 percent per year. Allen's assumptions should
be viewed as conservative; it is unlikely that the coal companies
invested that much in maintenance over the life of the town.
Furthermore, depreciation must take into account the fact
that when the towns closed, the houses were frequently sold,
recouping about half of the original construction costs. Rental
properties, company stores, and public utilities substantially
reduced the mine company's cash flow and need to borrow,
therefore enabling the more rapid accumulation of capital.
Although John Valdez didn't start mining until the depression,
he described a situation which was characteristic of the coal
fields:

John Valdez: When I started in it was pretty damn rough, I'll tell you. And then we used to trade at the company store. Well, you had to eat. Statement day, sometimes you get a dollar or a dollar and a half. Sometimes you get the snake, and that happened many-a-time.

Interviewer: A what?

John Valdez: A snake. Nothing coming. Company kept it all.

Interviewer: Why did you call it a snake?

John Valdez: Cause they just put a little line like that. Just like that, you know, where it says balance due? Cause they take your powder, they take your groceries what you bought. Everything came out on your statement—lights and all and everything. House rent. Everything if you rented a house, they took everything before you saw your statement.

(Interview with John Valdez, 1978)

Allen (197), termed the company town "benevolent exploitation" because:

. . . avarice seems to have been more the exception than the rule, and in many company towns good living conditions and adequate public services were provided from the beginning. . . . Nevertheless, all of the services were in part exploitation, for they were designed to produce more satisfied employees and hence more productive employees.

This gives a subtle modernist interpretation of the term exploitation— one which neglects the analysis of those actually living in those towns. For Allen, exploitation was a psychological manipulation, for the miners it was simply appropriation. As Lawrence Amicarella, a miner, put it: "they paid for the operation of their mine out of the sweat of the coal miner" (Interview). In fact, the company town with its store, scrip system, political domination and use of company guards became a specific grievance which along with demands for the eight-hour day and higher wages were cited as reasons for strikes. In part, the demand for union recognition may be seen as an attempt to establish a countervailing power to total corporate control. In the 1903 Colorado strike:

Figure 4.

School boys at Sopris.
Children in company
schools were frequently
posed like this.
Courtesy of Glen
Aultman

> The miners claimed that higher prices were charged in the company stores than in other places. . . . They objected to being forced to live in the houses of the coal company. . . . Employees of the Victor Fuel Company objected to deductions made from every man's wages—$1 a month for medical attention. . . . They alleged that while the company deducted from their total wages $1,800 to $2,000 monthly for medical attention, the cost to the company for such service did not exceed $700 a month. . . . (Wright 331-332)

Similar demands were put forth in the 1903 strike in Utah (Powell 127), and again in the 1913 Colorado strike:

> We demand the right to trade at any store we please and the right to choose our own boarding place and our own doctor. . . . We demand the abolition of the notorious and criminal guard system which has prevailed in the mining camps of Colorado for many years. (Beshoar 60)

The Period of Full Production

From 1909 to 1926, employment fluctuated around 26 thousand. The graphic on the facing page displays coal production for the West during the period 1890-1986. In 1910, production reached an all-time high and remained high until 1914 when production dropped as copper smelters switched from coke to fuel oil. Despite the drop, the price remained stable and after 1915 demand began to pick up again (MRUS, 1919, 589).

Production increased to record levels during World War I, then dropped temporarily in response to the end of the war and the nationwide strike of 1919. In the unionized Wyoming mines, the strike was 95 percent effective despite the use of troops to force miners back to work in Sheridan (Kuzara 142). Wyoming production declined by almost 25 percent that year. Even in Colorado's non-union mines the strike was more than 50 percent effective (MRUS—Part II, 1921 506). As a result of the strike, the daily rate in union mines nationwide was raised from $6.00 to $7.50, the highest wage yet. The miners received another raise when the Bituminous Coal Commission provided a $.24 a ton increase. This was the high point for western miners (MRUS—Part II, 1921, 457). Donald Mitchell remembered:

    Mitchell: The time we made 7.75 was some of the best time in the mine. . . . I'll tell you why, why I mean by that. I was making 7.75 and if the boss told you to go back—there'd be places they'd want the water pumped out, see—go down and pump that water out. Well you'd go down and pump out water, you got a shift no matter how long. Maybe you was only down there 2 or 3 hours at the most. I'd put as high as 23 shifts in 15 days.

    Interviewer: Wow.

    Mitchell: I bought a brand new Plymouth car, paid for it in three months, kept it for my wife and two kids, er, three kids. You try that now. so I said that was the best time we had.

    Interviewer: When was that?

    Mitchell: That was around in the '20's, let's see that'd be around '22, '23 along in there

             (Interview with Donald Mitchell, 1978).

Coal Production by State
1885 - 1985

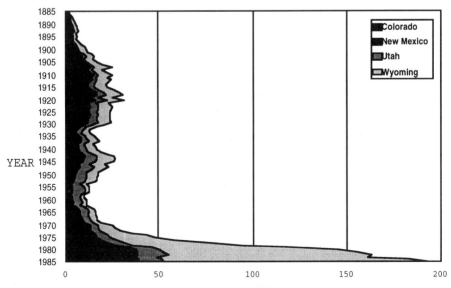

The people of the coal camps remember good times, especially during the period of full production. Every mine camp had a baseball team and competition helped give each camp an identity. As in any small town, people made their own social events:

> We used to go on Saturday nights, we get together, you know, we bundle up our kids and somebody know how to play accordion, you know, and make and go and take everything out of one room and we dance all night and then we have coffee and somebody had a ham, and somebody had, make a good lunch, you know. And throw the babies on the bed and they sleep you know, and we had a lot of fun.
>
> (Interview with Gertrude Ferraro, 1978).

During periods of strife, when the miners lived in strikers' tent colonies or explosions devastated entire towns, the various ethnic groups learned to pull together. Integrative bonds of interdependence and mutual aid were forged. Community was formed. As the older immigrants learned English and became naturalized citizens, their children grew up, attended school and brought home American customs. Ongoing processes of socialization, acculturation and integration united the community and gradually ethnic conflicts were set aside:

> Martha Todd: Well, everybody from the camps they did the shopping in the camps during the week. But Saturday night they came to town. They did their shopping, and go to the movies and the young folks went to a dance. There was a dance every Saturday night in different places and the most favored dances that everybody liked to go to—I'm going to use the word they used in those days—the Hunkey dances.
>
> Interviewer: What were they?
>
> Martha Todd: They were the dances given by Slavish people. Then they used to refer to the Wop dances. Now you know what that was. And the Mexicans had their dances, but we all didn't go to the Mexican dances. We were a little bit afraid of them. We weren't wanted.
>
> (Interview with Martha Todd, 1978)

The use of terms which are considered derogatory today was explained by one man who grew up in a coal camp as follows:

> There wasn't all this racial undertone at the time. I know I grew up as the dumb Swede and I suppose Ernest was the Wop, but we never worried about it. I was in his home at any time. I was welcome and he was in mine. I had friends from south of the border and Slavic people, we had lots of them in Morley, and nobody paid any attention to it .
>
> (Unidentified speaker, Public meeting, 1978)

As immigration slowed and older miners became citizens, the acculturation function of the coal camp had been fulfilled. In Sheridan over one hundred persons applied for citizenship in 1924 (Kuzara 199-200). By 1921 more than 32,000 miners were at work in the four western states, and towns like Trinidad, Helper, Rock Springs and Gallup were prosperous communities:

> Chenoweth: Trinidad was essentially a coal mining town. At one time the Chamber of Commerce of the United States designated Trinidad as the outstanding city of its size for business in the entire United States. We showed a trading area of 30,000.
>
> Interviewer: What was Trinidad like then?
>
> Chenoweth: A booming town. A booming town in every respect. There were streetcars running between a number of the coal camps, trains—see, the railroad bringing it in—C&W railroad bringing in miners. Stores opened till 10:00 at night. Saturday night, midnight. A boom town. Lots of business. Lots of money. . . . It was a wide open town. Everything was here. I suppose largely due to catering maybe to the coal mining interest. They worked hard all week, they wanted to come in, they wanted a little relaxation in Trinidad. They could find anything they wanted here.
>
> (Edgar Chenoweth, Public Meeting, 1978)

Private automobiles began to be seen in the coal camps and increased mobility meant the inevitable end of the company store's monopoly. Movie theaters and later radio brought news of the outside world ending the isolation. For a decade it appeared that prosperity would solve the coal miner's problems, but social and technological changes were occurring which would make the situation worse.

The Bust

World War I had encouraged productive capacity to outstrip demand, but the seriousness of the problem was masked in the early 1920s by high prices and nationwide strikes in 1919 and 1922. There had been temporary recessions and depressions, but the demand for coal had been increasing for a century. Nevertheless in 1921 the growth in demand had stopped (MRUS, 1925, 393-95). At first neither operators nor miners expected this to be different from other temporary slumps. Industry responded, not by laying off miners but by cutting the average days worked. Before the war, miners worked an average of 215 days; by 1923 this was down to 179. But the expected upturn in demand never occurred. Major changes in coal mining and the national energy economy produced a fifty-year bust period with only a brief respite during World War II (MRUS—Part II, 1925 398).

Along with problems due to overproduction, the industry was plagued by underconsumption. The rising cost of coal induced consumers to conserve. Thus, while in 1910 it took 3.2 pounds of coal to produce one kilowatt hour of electricity, by 1929 a kilowatt hour could be produced with half that (MRUS 395). Competition from other fuels cut heavily into the coal market. While coal consumption increased 3.3 percent from 1913 to 1925, natural gas increased 105 percent, petroleum 211 percent, and hydroelectric power increased 119 percent (MRUS, 1925 395). In 1926-27 natural gas lines reached Denver, and even coal towns like Sheridan, Wyoming were switching to gas (Kuzara 205). The Arizona copper smelters replaced coke with fuel oil. Of the 818 employees in Dawson in 1928, only 500 remained in 1932 (Melzer 311).

Throughout the West employment levels fell dramatically, from 32,000 in 1921 to 23,500 in 1929. During the depression pressures to buy at the company store increased. Miners were docked for rocks that were loaded with the coal, and company weighmen were encouraged to record short weights. Timbering was kept to a minimum; equipment was allowed to deteriorate. There were frequent layoffs and wage cuts. More than one miner's family remembered the hardships with bitterness:

> Bazanele: During the depression we have three kids and I remember in mines that work, oh maybe two, three months in the wintertime and then nothing. Maybe one day a week, and with one day a week you got to pay the rent . . . so we got our men go down the canyon where the mine used to be and dig up lead and copper you know and go sell it . . . to buy flour and potatoes. . . . We used to go for jack rabbits and squirrels and prairie dogs and everything else.
> (Interview with Josephene Bazanele, 1978)

> Diamante: We've had some very, very lean years. Very lean years! You go through summer months when maybe a coal miner wouldn't work 10 days in 4 months.
> Interviewer: How did you live?
> Diamante: You just couldn't. They raised . . . they had a garden, they had a few children, some of them went fishing or go deer hunting or do some manual jobs here and there. They just didn't . . . I remember when we were kids we ate potatoes and macaroni and the only eggs we ate we got out of a chicken coop and we had a cow we milked. . . . This is in the, oh, in the late 20's and the early 30's. See, that's when the depression hit.
> (Interview with James Diamanti, 1978)

During the late 1920s, many of the old timers who had immigrated in the eighties and nineties were forced out of the industry. Mines struggled to modernize and machinery brought unemployment to thousands of coal diggers. Immigrant miners had trouble adapting to the new technology.

Walt Cielinsky explained how the machines took his father's job:

> Cielinsky: And then the way they knocked dad out, ... they brought the first coal loading machines into the fields. . . . Well, these old timers like that they were skilled craftsmen with their hands. Buddy, they could do anything with their hands. You take a man in his, well late 50's or early 60's, been working all his life with his hands and then tell him, "Well, Bill, here's a machine. That's all the job you got left." Now they didn't say, "Now Bill, starting tomorrow, you go with Charlie there and he's going to break you in." Now if you was buddy-buddy that's the way it would work, but if they wanted to get rid of you they'd say, "There's your machine, you're supposed to be a miner, get in there and cut it." You couldn't do it, you didn't know how to run the machine or nothing. You'd hurt your-self, kill yourself probably. So he wasn't qualified for it and that's all we have so goodbye.
>
> (Interview with Walt Cielinski, 1976)

Kesel (238) showed that the percentage of foreign born in Colfax County, New Mexico, declined from 29.4 percent in 1910 to 8.2 percent in 1930. Too old for the Civilian Conservation Corps camps, some went back to the old country, others retired and moved away. In the 1930's when the first wave of mine and camp closings hit, people deserted the coal camps for the hub cities, frequently buying their houses from the company and hauling them to town. Between 1920 and 1930, the population of coal mining counties increased only slightly while hub cities registered large increases. For example: Huerfano County, Colorado increased by 1.08 percent while Walsenburg increased 54 percent; Carbon County, Utah increased 14.91 percent but Helper's population increased 68.56 percent (Census Data). Young people raised in the coal camps left seeking employment opportunities elsewhere, doubtless telling themselves that they would return when things got better. But this generation that might have been coal miners would find no place in the declining industry. Melzer (331) described the situation in Dawson:

The young seemed particularly hard hit in the 1930's. Unable to go directly in the mines from high school, as most had done in the past, young males searched for temporary odd jobs, went off to the Civilian Conservation Camps or waited for a chance to work in town. . . . Others left never to return as Dawson gradually lost its youth and showed further signs of aging.

When the depression finally eased, coal production increased from 1934 to 1937. Depleted stockpiles were rebuilt and industrial production began to recover. However, it was not until the war that the coal mines began to see a real change:

> John Valdez: Well, I mean, people just suffered it out. They used to give onions and potatoes here to the people that wasn't working. Then till they come out

Figure 5. Union Pacific Coal Company, July 1946, Stansbury Mine, Rock Springs, Wyoming. Original caption, "Women pick foreign matter out of coal as it is carried on conveyor thru tipple." Photo by Russell Lee. Courtesy of National Archives.

with the WPA, they changed some, things changed a little bit. They used to give some of the people, used to give them, I guess it was the county or the state, I don't know, they used to give them welfare orders. I mean, no money or nothing, just orders to the stores. You know, every store that. . . . But it got pretty rough till, well, I hate to say this, but while I don't like to see a war, but that's the only thing when things started picking up.

(Interview with John Valdez, 1978)

World War II increased the demand for coal but hastened the exodus of young people from the coal fields. Melzer (313) estimated that by 1944, 6 percent of Dawson's population was serving in the armed forces. There was a labor shortage and less experienced miners were recruited. Photographs taken in 1946 record women working in "outside" positions at the Union Pacific Mines in Wyoming. Mechanization was proceeding apace. During 1944 machine production reached 78 percent in Colorado; 99 percent in Utah and in 96 percent in Wyoming. In the peak year of wartime production, employment actually remained below depression levels. The number of miners continued to decline until 1968. The company town was finished. Immigration had ceased, the older miners had become acculturated, solidarity had been achieved through unionization, the private automobile ended the company town as a total institution and miners like everyone else were free to live one place and work another (often driving fifty or seventy-five miles to work). The towns of the first coal age began with a boom but ended with a whimper. Melzer's description of Dawson was typical of the end:

The miners' credit at the Company store was cut off, and their outstanding debts to the store were deducted from their last paychecks, leaving them with less money for moving expenses. Transfers to other branches of the company were rare, and no one received much aid from the local unions. . . . The state welfare director meanwhile told the miners that they were eligible for relief only if they qualified for old-age

assistance or met the stringent requirements for direct aid. Unemployment checks were available for a
few weeks, and some veterans could still draw on
theHir bonus checks from World War II. . . . The miners complained that although the United States could
invest millions of dollars in the Marshall Plan to save
war-torn Europe, no federal funds could be spared to
save their hometown. (319)

NOTES

[1]Data on production and employment were drawn from three
government sources. *Mineral Resources of the United States* was
published from 1866 to 1931. It was followed by *The Minerals Yearbook* which was published by the Bureau of Mines until 1993. Since
then, these data are available from the National Energy Information
Center <infoctr@aia.doe.gov>.

[2]For example, after the 1910 Starkville explosion that killed 56,
E. H. Weitzel, the manager of CF&I's fuels division, forbid reporters
access to the site. See McGovern and Guttridge (64-65). Dawson,
New Mexico, suffered catastrophic explosions in 1913 and 1923, which
left 383 dead, yet was recorded only in the most cursory newspaper
reports.

[3]Helen Papanikolas (119) cited a similar sociological concern from
the chief engineer of the Utah Fuel Company. "These companies are
headed by wide-awake businessmen, all of a kindly nature. They are
doing everything possible for their employees that is 'businessly' possible . . . . They pay splendid wages, study the sociological side of
their men and try to anticipate their wants. . . . Mine workers are
well cared for."

ACKNOWLEDGEMENTS

The research was supported by grants from the National Endowment for the Humanities, Grant No. 76-070210-481, and
the Colorado Humanities Program, Grant No. P68-0276-32.
The author would like to thank the coal miners of Colorado,
New Mexico, Wyoming and Utah for their willingness to share
their wisdom.

REFERENCES

Compendium of the Census, 1890, 1900, 1910, 1920. *Data from
the Department of the Interior.* Washington, D.C.

Allen, J. B.. "The Company-Owned Mining Town in the West: Ex-
    ploitation or Benevlolent Paternalism." *Refelctions of West-
    ern Historians.* Ed. J. A. Carroll. Tucson: U of Arizona P, 1967.
    177-97.
Beshoar, B. B. *Out of the Depths: The Story of John R. Lawson, a
    Labor Leader.* Denver: Golden Bell Press, 1943.
Ginzberg, E. *Grass on the Slag Heaps: The Story of the Welsh Min-
    ers.* New York and London: Harper and Brothers, 1942.
Kesel, R. H. "The Raton Coal-Field: An Evolving Landscape." *New
    Mexico Historical Review* 60.3 (1966): 231-250.
Kuzara, S. A. *Black Diamonds of Sheridan.* Cheyenne, WY: Pioneer
    Printing and Stationary Co., 1977.
Lewis, L. "Uplifting 17,000 Employees: The Human Story of Work-
    ers Who Were Led by the Colorado Fuel and Iron Company
    from Conditions of Drunkenness and Dirt to Well-Ordered
    Living." *World's Work* 9 (1905).: 5939-50.
McGovern, G. S. and L. F. Gutteridge. *The Great Coalfield War.* Bos-
    ton: Houghton Mifflin, 1972.
Melzer, R. "A Death in Dawson: The Demise of a Southwestern Com-
    pany Town." *New Mexico Historical Review* 55.4 (1980): 309-
    330.
MRUS. *Mineral Resources of the United States.* Washington, D.C.:
    U.S. Government Printing Office, 1892-1931.
Papanikolas, H. Z. "Unionism, Communism and the Great Depres-
    sion: The Carbon County Coal Strike of 1933." *Utah Historical
    Quarterly* 41 (1973): 254-300.
Powell, A. K. "The 'Foreign Element' and the 1903-4 Carbon County
    Coal Miners' Strike." *Utah Historical Quarterly* 43 (1975): 125-
    54.
Scamehorn, H. L. *Pioneer Steelmaker in the West: The Colorado Fuel
    and Iron Company 1872-1903.* Boulder, CO: Pruett Press,
    1976.
Scheick, C., L. Hubbel, et al. *Historical/Archaeological Inquiry Into
    Coal Mining Remains in New Mexico.* State Historic Preserva-
    tion Bureau: 1981
Wright, C. D. *A Report on the Labor Disturbances in the State of
    Colorado, from 1880 to 1904, Inclusive.* Washington, D.C.:
    U.S. Government Printing Office, 1905.

INTERVIEW SUBJECTS

Amicarella, Claude and Lawrence. February 21, 1978. Lafayette,
    Colorado.
Bazanele, Josephene. August 20, 1978. Berwind Canyon, Colo-
    rado.
Biondi's Sporting Goods. February 3, 1978. Walsenburg, Colorado.
Bisulco, Alex. June 27, 1978. Aguilar, Colorado.

Chenoweth, Edgar. Public Meeting. April 28, 1978. Trinidad, Colorado.

Cielinski, Walt. May 1976. Boulder, Colorado.

Diamanti, James. April 24, 1978. Price, Utah.

Ferraro, Gertrude. May 23, 1978. Cokedale, Colorado.

Livoda, Kate. September 20, 1980. New Orleans, Louisiana.

Mathias, Henry. July 2, 1975. Lafayette, Colorado.

Mitchell, Donald. February 5, 1978. Walsenburg, Colorado.

Todd, Martha. February 6, 1978. Walsenburg, Colorado.

Unidentified Speaker. Public Meeting. April 28, 1978. Trinidad, Colorado.

Valdez, John B. February 7, 1978. Walsenburg, Colorado.

Catholics in Nevada

KEVIN RAFFERTY

Religion has always played a prominent role in the historical development of any American territory, and Nevada was no different in this regard. As soon as portions of Nevada were opened by mining and other economic developments, and immediately after the miners, gamblers, and prostitutes established camps and towns, religious figures carrying the fire of religious fervor followed. At times religion's presence was in the form of itinerant evangelists and revival missions, but often as not the established religions attempted to develop social and spiritual structures and institutions in such places to meet the needs of their adherents who had relocated to those towns.

In the cyclical development, rise, and ultimate abandonment of towns based on mining was mirrored the fate of the larger denominations. Churches relocated personnel and sometimes physical plants to meet the need for spiritual services that new population aggregations required. These institutions often served as the focus of social life for towns and the nearby mining camps and ranches, provided social and charitable services and institutions, and often served as a familiar haven for immigrants from Europe looking for a safe harbor amidst the storm of social and geographical change in a foreign land (Wren; Trout ; Shepperson, *Restless Strangers*; Dwyer; Kosso; Eterovich).

The impact of the Roman Catholic Church and its followers on the development of the United States has been far reaching. Histories of the Catholic Church and its development

Dr. Kevin Rafferty is Professor of Anthropology at the Community College of Southern Nevada, located in Las Vegas. He has been conducting archaeological and historical research in the eastern Mojave Desert since 1980.

nation-wide have been undertaken (McAvoy), yet the role of the institutional church has yet to be explored in any depth as it pertains to Nevada. Much of the story of Catholics in Nevada comes from documents written by and for the Nevada Catholic Church (Gorman; Walsh; WPA; Salpointe; Caviglia), or from articles or biographies of important historical per- sonalities in the history of the Roman Catholic Church in California and Nevada (Dwyer; McGloin). In the last twenty years various articles on the ethnic groups that composed the Roman Catholic population in Nevada have been written and can flesh out the pictures developed in the cold, dry his- tories. However none of them touch on the larger develop- mental picture state-wide.[1]

Pre-Territory Era to 1859

Institutionally the territory that became Nevada was attached ecclesiastically to Spain, and later (after 1821) to Mexico. It was originally part of the Diocese of Sonora and later under the Diocese of the Two Californias under Bishop Garcia Di- ego y Moreno from 1840-1846. This portion of the territory contained no settlements and had no missions to administer, so this fact is merely an historical oddity in the history on the Nevada Catholic Church. The real history of the Catholic Church in Nevada begins only after the American occupation of the region in 1848 after the Mexican War (Gorman).

Paradoxically this does not mean that there was no Catho- lic presence in the region prior to 1848, although it was ephem- eral. Historical rumors persist of evidence that Spanish min- ers, and specifically Franciscan padres, may have been in southern Nevada in the Eldorado Canyon area along the Colo- rado River and in the Las Vegas Valley. Davis and Lincoln note that Mrs. Helen Stewart of the then Las Vegas Ranch stated that a silver rosary and silver coins dated to 1770 were recovered in the Las Vegas Valley and at one of the mines in the area (Davis; Lincoln; Weir). Unfortunately the artifacts have not survived and there appears to be no documentary evidence from Spanish or Mexican archives regarding activ- ity in the region. Townley suggests that this does not pre- clude the possibility that such expeditions occurred, but merely means that no historical records have yet to be lo- cated.

Townley also cites another source that supports the idea of the Spanish establishing mines in the Eldorado Canyon area. He cites an informant in Riggs who stated that Mexican miners came into the Eldorado Canyon area in 1882 carrying an old Spanish map of the area that pinpointed a large mine then existing in the Eldorado Mining District. Townley tentatively accepts this report based on the reputations of the informants who had talked to Riggs.

Father Francisco Garces, a Franciscan padre, is another candidate for the title of being the first European to traverse Nevada. He was a member of an expedition looking for routes of travel through what was then northern New Spain. Evidence suggests that he entered the extreme southern portion of Nevada on March 4, 1776, and quickly departed (Bancroft; Hafen and Hafen). Claims have also been put forward for the Dominguez-Escalante expedition of 1776 having entered southern Nevada, but these claims have generally been dismissed based on the historic evidence (Bancroft; Hafen and Hafen). Both the Garces and the Dominguez-Escalante expeditions explored portions of the route that would later be completed through Nevada and would be called the Old Spanish Trail, a major corridor of travel and communication between new Mexico and California between 1829 and 1848.

Early on in northern Nevada, the Catholic impact was even slighter. Many of the members of the Peter Skene Ogden and James Bridger fur trading expeditions that rendezvoused in northern Nevada in 1825 were French and Irish, and thus presumably Catholic (Bancroft). This religious identification had no lasting impact on the subsequent development on the state's history.

The greatest early impact on Nevada history by those of Catholic extraction was the blazing of the Old Spanish Trail through southern Nevada by two Mexican nationals, Antonio Armijo and Rafael Rivera. Rivera served as a scout for Armijo's 1829-1830 expedition from New Mexico to southern California, and was the first *known* non-Native American to cross through the Las Vegas Valley into the Amargosa Desert. The efforts of Rivera and Armijo, both Catholic, finalized the route of the Old Spanish Trail/Mormon Road through southern Nevada by identifying adequate water sources in the Las Vegas Valley that would sustain future travel and communication through the area as well as the first settlement by Mormon missionaries in 1855. These springs also spurred the founding of Las Vegas in 1905 as a whistle stop on the San Pedro, Salt Lake, and Los Angeles Railroad (Hafen and Hafen; Roske; Warren; Fletcher; Paher). This initial trail blazing activity had repercussions far beyond what anyone could have foreseen in terms of the future history of the state of Nevada.

The institutional history of the Catholic Church in Nevada begins in 1850, when Sadoc Alemany, a Spaniard, was named Bishop of the Diocese of Monterey on June 30. This diocese included Nevada, which at this time had a very small European population. On July 29, 1853, the diocese was split, with Bishop Alemany becoming Bishop of the Diocese of San Francisco, which included Nevada within its borders. The administration of Nevada was a simple affair until the late 1850s when the Comstock silver strike created a rush of people into the area. In 1859 Bishop Alemany sent two priests to the Genoa-Silver City region of northern Nevada to minister to the spiritual need of Catholic miners in the area; thus the official history of the Catholic community of Nevada begins in earnest (Gorman).

The history of Catholics in Nevada, in particular during the Comstock Era, is inextricably linked to the institutional church and the Irish. The earliest bishops, the majority of the priests, and much of the early Catholic population of Nevada was Irish, and it was the Irish that had the greatest impact in terms of Catholic development within Nevada. Thus the Irish and the institutions of the church are emphasized in the early historical periods. It is at the end of the pre-Territorial Era that the Irish connection in Nevada begins. In 1851, Eugene O'Connell, an Irish priest from All Hallow's Seminary in Dublin, Ireland, arrived to serve as a pastor. He returned to Ireland in 1854, but he had made a favorable impression on the Bishop, who recommended he be appointed Vicarate Apostolic of Marysville, north of San Francisco, in 1860. It was O'Connell's connections to All Hallow's Seminary that served as a pipeline for Catholic priests from Ireland to enter Nevada, placing an indelible Celtic stamp on the institutional church during its first seventy-one years of existence in the state (Gorman; Caviglia; Dwyer).

The Comstock/Early Mining Era, 1859-1880

The Rush to Washoe occurred in earnest in 1859. In that year two Irishmen, Peter O'Riley and Patrick McLaughlin, helped create the initial rush and they were followed by thousands of other miners, the majority of whom were Irish (Lord; Olson). Other ethnic groups that were heavily Catholic were also attracted to the Comstock: French, Germans, and Mexicans. Gabriel Maldonado, a Mexican national, was in the Virginia City area in 1859 and staked out what became known as the Mexican Claim. Gold Hill, near Virginia City, contained a large contingent of Mexican miners, many of whom worked at the Mexican claim (Bancroft).

Where Catholics entered, their church was not far behind. In 1858 Bishop Alemany sent Fr. Joseph Gallagher to Dayton, Nevada, but nothing permanent came of this visit. Fr. Hugh Gallagher, Joseph's brother, was sent to the Virginia City-Genoa area in 1860 and established the first Catholic churches in the state. He built St. Theresa's in Carson City, St. Mary's in the Mountains in Virginia City, and a little chapel in Genoa. The latter was abandoned in late 1860 (Angel; Davis; Olson). This Genoa pattern of mining boom, population explosion, chapel building, stabilization, and often decline and abandonment set the pattern for the church (and mining) in Nevada in the late nineteenth and early twentieth centuries (Olson).

In this Comstock Era the Catholic Church established its formal administrative hierarchy and territorial organization. The basic structure was a three-tiered arrangement. Where there were enough communicants in a defined geographical area a *parish* was established, usually with a church building and a resident pastor. Once parishes were established, many set up *missions* in areas where stable bodies of Catholics had settled. A mission may or may not have had a building but the mission could expect to receive regular visits from the pastor or assistant pastor of the closest parish. Finally there were *stations*, areas where there was a sparse Catholic population that tended to be transient. There was no formal chapel, and visits by priests (and therefore performance of the mass) were irregularly scheduled. In many areas of northern and western Nevada, and later southern Nevada, the transition from station to mission to parish occurred with some regularity. However eastern Nevada experienced extremely rapid boom and bust cycles, making this transition quite difficult and in some areas impossible (WPA; Olson).

The Celtic nature of the Catholic Church was also established on the Comstock. Eugene O'Connell was appointed Apostolic Vicarate of Marysville on September 18, 1860, partially over his own objections. He asked to be released from this burden by the current Pope, Pius IX, but was refused. He was then quoted as having replied to the refusal "Damnus sum ad metalla"—condemned to the mines. He was more of an academic than an administrator but stayed true to his vow of obedience. His Vicarate, upgraded to diocese status in 1868 and based in Grass Valley, California, covered the territory west of the Utah border to the Pacific Ocean and north of the thirty-ninth parallel; essentially California north of San Francisco and northern Nevada. He had just five priests to cover this vast territory. Southern Nevada remained under the jurisdiction of the Diocese of San Francisco (Gorman; WPA; Caviglia; Dwyer).

At this point Bishop O'Connell began importing Irish priests from the seminary at All Hallow's in Dublin. He received Patrick Manogue, later Bishop of Grass Valley, in 1862 and sent him to Virginia City, which by 1866 had seven thousand Catholics and three parishes (Dwyer). By 1878 the list of priests that had served, or were serving, in Nevada included the following men: Patrick Manogue, Frs. Joseph and Hugh Gallagher, John Nulty, William Clark, Thomas Grace, Patrick O'Kane, Lawrence Scanlan, Luke Tormey, Joseph Phelan, Daniel Meagher, Danny O'Sullivan, Carnelius Delahunty, William Gleeson, Patrick O'Reilly, Edward Kelley, William Moloney, James J. Hynes, and James Callan. Non-Irish religious figures included Frs. Dominic Monteverde, John Mevel, Leon Haupts, and Vincent Riera. In addition, from 1863-1865 the Passionist fathers from Italy had a "monastery" at Gold Hill (Gorman; WPA; Dwyer).

The essentially Celtic nature of the communicants in Nevada was also established early. The 1841 census of Ireland showed a population of 8,175,124, a figure which may have been undercounted by twenty percent. During the potato blight and famine of 1845-1850, that number was greatly reduced by deaths or emigration to essentially the United States

(Dwyer). This wave of immigration changed the essential nature of the Catholic Church in both Nevada and throughout the United States. For hundreds of years in Ireland the Catholic Church served not only its basic religious function but as a rallying point for Irish cultural and religious nationalism against British attempts at cultural genocide. Their Catholicism became the national and religious identity of the Irish, and when they came to America this pattern continued. Irish immigrants met prejudice from the native Protestants on the East Coast, and the immigrants tended to live in Irish neighborhoods that were centered around their parish (Dwyer; McAvoy).

Out West the Irish met less prejudice, since Nevada frontier society had not had the time to develop rigid social or religious constraints. The Irish flourished in this atmosphere and came to dominate the early politics and economics of the Silver State. However Irish social life still tended to be centered around their parish, which had fraternal and secret societies as social adjuncts. On the Comstock the Irish formed societies such as the Fenians, the Irish Benevolent Society, and the Knights of the Red Branch, plus military companies. The various guard companies, including the Emmet, Sarsfield, Sweeney, and Montgomery Guards on the Comstock, and the Wolf Tone Guards at Hamilton, Nevada, had their beginnings in this period. These military societies formed a major component of the official Nevada Guard that was organized in 1883 (James).

Catholics played a pivotal role in the development of the Comstock silver boom. In 1869 the mining firm of John W. Mackay, James G. Fair, James C. Flood, and William S. O'Brien bought the Consolidated Virginia Mine property. Between 1870 and 1875 this firm was responsible for the "Great Bonanza" that took millions of dollars in silver out of the mines. Mackay, Fair, and O'Brien were born in Ireland and emigrated to the United States in the 1840s. Their efforts, both ethical and unethical, created the last major boom in mining on the Comstock before the last bust set in. After 1900 the Mackay family would become very important in the development of higher education in Nevada (see next section) (Angel; Bancroft; Scrugham).

Other Irish Catholics involved in the Virginia City-Reno-Carson City area included E. D. Sweeney, who helped to stake out and develop Carson City; Peter Cavanaugh, an Irish contractor who was responsible for the construction of the Nevada State capitol; John McCone, who built several gold foundries in the Virginia City area; and William Mooney, who was a prominent liveryman in Virginia City (Angel; Bancroft).

Lest it be thought that only Irish Catholics were in the Comstock region, Shepperson's book *Restless Strangers* underscores the fact that Catholics of all nationalities were instrumental in developing the infrastructure of the Virginia City-Reno-Carson City area. French-Canadians became lumberjacks in the Lake Tahoe area; French nationals became important elements of the Virginia City medical establishment between 1860 and 1870; and numerous other Catholic nationalities became businessmen in the region. Shepperson's examination of the 1880 census of Virginia City revealed that the following nationalities had established businesses on the block north of the International Hotel, centered on C and Union Streets: six Germans, four Irishmen, four Austrians (probably Yugoslavians), four Italians, three Frenchmen, two Canadians, two Swiss (probably of Italian background), one Scotsman, and one Portuguese. One southern European, Andrew Milatovich from Dalmatia (a heavily Catholic region), ran one of the most cosmopolitan stores in Virginia City and opened one of the first stores in Reno in 1868. His family and their descendants ran stores in the Reno area for years.

The majority of the southern Europeans (Italians, Swiss, Slavs) and the Irish and Portuguese were almost certainly Catholic in background, as were the French and French-Canadians. The Germans very likely contained some Catholics in their numbers as well.

The institutional Catholic Church was also prominent in the establishment and development of educational, social, and health facilities that benefitted the whole Washoe region. Fr. Patrick Manogue, Pastor of St. Mary's of the Mountain in Virginia City, was the catalyst for the building of St. Mary's school and an orphanage by 1865, and getting it staffed by the Sisters of Charity out of San Francisco. St. Mary's Hospital in Virginia City was opened in 1877, and served the residents of the Comstock until 1897, when it was taken over by Washoe County (Walsh).

As mines were opened and developed elsewhere in northern and eastern Nevada, Catholics and their institutions followed. Austin in central Nevada developed a parish in 1864 (St. Augustine's) and served several missions and stations in the area. Belmont was the site of St. Patrick's Mission in 1873, which lasted into the 1890s. In White Pine County the silver rush of the 1860s produced a flurry of Catholic activity. Hamilton became the location of SS. Peter and Paul Parish under Fr. Dominic Monteverde, who also established a mission at Cherry Creek and stations at Treasure Hill and Piedmont. By 1880, due to a cyclical mining bust, the Hamilton area was downgraded to a mission (WPA; Olson).

Other parishes founded in eastern Nevada included St. Lawrence's, established in 1869 in Pioche by Fr. Lawrence Scanlon, later Bishop of the Diocese of Salt Lake City. He developed a small church, a miner's hospital, and organized the miners into a benevolent society before his departure in 1873, which coincided with the end of the mining boom in Pioche and the downgrading of the parish to a mission (Angel; WPA; Olson).

At Eureka, another parish was founded in response to the silver boom. Father Dominic Monteverde visited the town in 1871, and Fr. James Hynes established St. Brendan's Parish in 1872. This parish served as the "mother church" for missions and stations in Ruby Hill, Palisade, Pinto, and Pine Valley in Eureka County. This parish also served several areas in White Pine County: Egan Canyon, Piedmont, Schellbourne, Ward, Newark Valley, Mineral City, and White River Valley. Additional stations and missions served by the parish included Cortez in Lander County, Tybo in Nye County, and several spots in Elko County: Elko, Ruby Valley, Spruce Valley, Secret Canyon, and Mound Valley (WPA; Olson). Priests in this era had to be individuals with sound physical constitutions and a desire to travel over the vast territories that their parishes covered.

This boom attracted not only Irish miners but Italian immigrants in significant numbers as well. Italians in the Eureka area specialized in being *carbonari*, producers of charcoal for the smelters in the Eureka area. Archival evidence places Italian nationals in the Eureka area as early as 1869. Many of the households of *carbonari* included several adult males, all related, often from the same village in southern Switzerland or northern Italy. Archaeological research has recorded a number of *carbonari* ranches and households in the Mt. Hope area, approximately twenty-five miles north of Eureka, confirming the archival evidence (Zeier).

The Italians in Eureka engaged in what was called Nevada's "Italian War." In reaction to the low prices paid for their charcoal by local mines, low wages, and attempts by mine and smelter owners to drive charcoal prices down even further, the *carbonari* created a protective association whose aim was to increase charcoal prices and improve general working conditions. The *carbonari* sometimes employed force to prevent charcoal from other burners from reaching the smelters, and the owners reacted in kind. Serious violence ensued, causing the deaths of five *carbonari* and injuries to several others. This violence broke the back of the association and allowed businesses to proceed with their normal course of affairs (Earl; Cofone "Themes in the Italian Settlement of Nevada").

As Catholics entered the state, their influence grew. Individuals who had an influence on the course of events in the state included Manuel San Pedro, a pioneer miner who helped develop the silver strikes in Humboldt and Nye Counties; J.B. Gallagher, a Nevada State Senator and Assemblyman from Mason Valley in Esmeralda County (Angel); and numerous other Catholics who toiled in the mines and worked developing and laboring in the infrastructure of the economy and political system of the state. For example, in Hamilton in 1870, the Census noted the following groups and professions: an Irish lawyer and an Irish policeman, seven Polish merchants, 234 Germans, and prostitutes from Costa Rica, Peru, Chile, Mexico, Ireland, France, and Germany. The *Daily Inland Empire*, the Hamilton paper, was published by James Ayres (a Scotsman) with an all Irish printing and technical staff (Shepperson, *Restless Strangers*).

The first Basques also moved into Nevada at this time. Pedro Altube, a Spanish Basque from the Pyrenees Mountains, established the Spanish Ranch in the Elko region in 1859. He then began bringing over many other Basques to join him. This was the predecessor to the Basque wave of migration in the 1870s and 1880s that helped to establish the sheep raising industry in the state (Douglass "The Basques of the American West"; "The Basques of Nevada"; Hulse *Nevada Adventure*).

The end of the era saw Catholics distributed throughout Nevada in significant numbers, except for in southern Nevada where there were only a few Euroamericans. The next era would see a maturation and consolidation of the Catholic Church in its original area of operation in western Nevada, and its struggle for survival in eastern Nevada following a general depopulation of the area. Southern Nevada does not become important until the modern era, but the seeds of its importance are sown in the early twentieth century with the founding of Las Vegas. The late mining and consolidation era was important to Nevada Catholics and was presaged by a change in the hierarchy and structure of authority in the region.

Late Mining/Consolidation Era, 1880-1931

For the institutional church this era begins with a change in hierarchy and later a change in jurisdictions. Father Patrick Manogue of Carson City was made coadjudicator of the Diocese of Grass Valley (along with Bishop O'Connell) in 1880 and succeeded O'Connell in the position in 1884. Manogue moved the seat of the diocese to Sacramento. In 1887, Utah and southern Nevada were withdrawn from the Jurisdiction of San Francisco and placed under the Vicarate Apostolic of Utah, based in Salt Lake City. This Vicarate was run by Father Lawrence Scanlon, who had founded the parish in Pioche. Scanlon was consecrated as Bishop of this vicarate in June of 1887. The Vicarate was officially made a diocese on January 30, 1891, and contained the Nevada counties of Elko, Lander, Eureka, White Pine, Nye, Lincoln, and Clark (after its creation in 1909), as well as the State of Utah. This split jurisdiction continued until 1931, when Nevada was made a diocese in its own right (Gorman; Caviglia).

Due to the split jurisdiction, several bishops have guided the destiny of the institutional church in Nevada. Starting with Patrick Manogue (1884-1896) several bishops operated out the Diocese of Sacramento: Thomas Grace (1896-1921), Patrick Keane (1922-1928), and Robert J. Armstrong (1929-1931). From Salt Lake City, the line of succession was Lawrence Scanlan (1887-1915), Joseph S. Glass (1915-1926), and John J. Mitty (1926-1931) (Gorman). The earliest Bishops, particularly Bishop Scanlan, would face enormous difficulties in their territories at the beginning of the era due to the boom and bust nature of Nevada's mining industry.

The period between 1880 and 1900 is often called "the twenty year depression". The decision of the U.S. government to stop minting silver dollars in 1873 coincided with a general decline in silver prices worldwide and the playing out of the initial ore bodies that had fueled the first boom. When added to the fact that no major mining strikes were made in Nevada in the 1880s, a general population decline occurred throughout the state. Population declined from roughly 62,000 people in 1880 to close to 42,000 in 1890, a drop of over thirty percent (Hulse *Nevada Adventure*).

Parishes declined in size and in some instances in eastern Nevada were closed down altogether. Most of the stations mentioned earlier were closed, while St. Lawrence's Parish in Pioche and SS. Peter and Paul Parish in Hamilton were downgraded to missions in 1973. They were both abandoned completely in the early 1900s. Two other missions, St. Patrick's at Belmont and Cherry Creek were also abandoned in the early 1900s (WPA; Olson).

There were two major exceptions to this trend. The Delamar gold strike in Lincoln County in 1891 brought in thousands of miners, many of whom were Catholic. Nativity Parish was established by Bishop Scanlan of Salt Lake in 1895, which serviced a station at Hiko and St. Lawrence parish in Pioche. As elsewhere, the ore soon played out and Nativity parish was downgraded to a mission in 1906, while St. Lawrence's was abandoned altogether in 1904 (Olson).

Elko County also proved to be an exception to this trend. Based on the region's significance as an agricultural and grazing area, and the presence of the Central Pacific railroad, mining discoveries in the 1860s and 1870s helped create a mini-boom. Areas such as Battle Mountain, Carlin, and Elko became supply centers and population discharge points for miners entering the region. Cattle and sheep became a natural industry for the grassland zones, creating the opportunities for stable populations, and thus stable Catholic communities. Elko became a station of Eureka in 1887, and in the 1890s Eureka Parish serviced stations in many parts of Elko County. Sacred Heart Parish of Battle Mountain and Carlin was established in 1897, as was St. Thomas Aquinas Parish at Wells (Fries; WPA; Olson).

As in the previous era the majority of priests and religious in Nevada were Irish nationals or Americans of Irish descent. Some were holdovers from the previous era: Joseph Phelan, William Moloney, James Callan, D. Meagher, and John Nulty (other holdovers were Dominic Monteverde, of Italian extraction; and John Mevel, a Frenchman). Other Celts included Michael Kiely, John B. Ruddy, M. A. Kennedy, James M. Butler, Lawrence Kiernan, Patrick Maguire, M. Walsh, Patrick Sheridan, James B. Dermody, F. A. Reynolds, and Andrew O'Connell. However a few more non-Irish names began cropping up: E. M. Nattini, John Philip Bandanelli, Timothy Pacelli, and L. B. Demers (Gorman; WPA). The trend towards more non-Irish priests and Catholics in Nevada accelerated after 1900 but the nature of the change in the institutional church and ethnic makeup of the Catholic population actually began in the last decade of the nineteenth century.

By 1890, Italians comprised three percent of the state's population, twice the percentage of any other state west of the Mississippi River. They became miners, farmers, ranchers, businessmen, and continued as *carbonari* in the Eureka area. Carson City and environs, Reno, Austin, Dayton, and Paradise valley in western Nevada all developed substantial Italian communities, and Reno had its own "Little Italy" in the early years of the twentieth century (Earl; Cofone, "Reno's Little Italy"; Shepperson "Immigrant Themes").

These immigrants brought a different attitude towards Catholicism and the institutionalized church. Italians tended to be anti-clerical. distrustful of the church and its organization, and thus their lives revolved around the parishes much less than did the Irish. Their veneration of cults of the saints was also much different and more intense than that practiced by the Irish. This led to severe tension between the two groups wherever they were in proximity to one another (Cofone; Olson).

Slavic peoples entered Nevada in larger numbers in the 1890s, particularly those who can now be identified as Yugoslavians. The copper strikes in the McGill-Ruth-Ely area in the late 1890s and early 1900s drew many Slavs and Croatians (often called Austrians) who were Roman Catholic. They separated into ethnic enclaves, as did the Serbians, Japanese, and other immigrants, away from the "Americans" in the area. However they attended the local Catholic churches and mingled with Americans more often, beginning the process of assimilation more quickly than did earlier groups. Parents in these groups stressed learning English and getting an education as a way towards social advancement, leading these groups to get higher paying jobs than other ethnic groups in the area acquired. They also formed or joined unions, such as the Lane City Miner's Union, the International Mine, Mill, and Smelterman's Union (AFL), and other groups to secure and protect their rights as Americans. They became well integrated into the communities that they lived in, becoming a force for social and political stability and change (when necessary)(Kosso).

Basques also began entering Nevada in larger numbers at the end of the nineteenth century. They became shepherds, often running tramp sheep bands across the grasslands and mountains of northern Nevada. Individual male Basques would come into the United States first; they would then send money home to bring over brothers and nephews to help run the sheep as well as sisters and nieces to run the small Basque hotels that developed in the state. They became prominent in places like Ely, Elko, Winnemucca, and Reno, and later became prominent in local and state politics (Laxalt; Douglass, "The Basques of the American West").

The trend of new waves of immigration became more pronounced in the early twentieth century, with the Goldfield-Tonopah booms and the continued importance of copper mines in the northeastern portion of the state. Catholics came into the state from all over the country and the world, and often left established mining camps and towns elsewhere for the Tonopah ore fields. St. Brendan's Parish of Eureka had most of its parishioners move to Tonopah, so the pastor of the parish, Fr. James Butler, received permission from Bishop Scanlan of Salt Lake City to follow them. He established St. Patrick's Parish at Tonopah in 1905, plus a station at Beatty and a mission in Rhyolite (both south of Tonopah) in 1906. In addition the abandoned Catholic chapel at Belmont was physically moved to Manhattan in 1908 to form the nucleus of the Sacred Heart mission (WPA; Hulse, *The Nevada Adventure*; Olson).

The townsite of Las Vegas was established in 1905, an event that was to have major political, demographic, economic, and religious repercussions on the state later in the twentieth century. Fr. E.V. Reynolds established St. Joan of Arc's parish in 1908 under the authority of the Diocese of Salt Lake City. This parish, the mother parish of almost all Catholic parishes in southern Nevada up until the 1960s, served several stations and missions as well: Rhyolite, Delamar, Caliente, Pioche, Springdale, Searchlight, Arden, Goodsprings, Moapa, Milford (Utah), Ryan (California), and Kingman (Arizona). It remained the only Catholic parish in Las Vegas until the modern era and the establishment of Boulder City (St. Joan of Arc; Olson).

An examination of the earliest parish records of St. Joan of Arc reveals not only a variety of nationalities, but also the names of some of the earliest movers and shakers of the Las Vegas area. These include the Von Tobel family (lumber yards), the Harmons, John Graglia, Ernie Cragin (insurance), Mrs. Edna Borshack, Samual Mikulich, the Lorenzi family, the Foleys (politics and law), the Mendozas (law), and surnames that reveal ethnic origins from around the world. It appears that the Catholics of Las Vegas, either out of choice or necessity, did not form ethnic enclaves like those that occurred in other Nevada towns, but mingled rather freely in the one parish that existed at the end of this era.

However, particular ethnic groups with a heavy Catholic membership contributed significantly to the development and success of the Las Vegas region. Italians came first to Las Vegas to work on the railroad or in the local mines. They soon expanded their entrepreneurial horizons. For example, an individual named Dominic Pecetto opened a liquor store in 1905, and by the second decade of the century had expanded his businesses into a hotel, a bar, and rental cabins. He was in a partnership with his brother-in-law, Joe Graglia of the St. Joan of Arc Graglias, in several ventures (Balboni).

Another major contributor to the early success of Las Vegas was D.G. Lorenzi. He operated several businesses, most importantly the Twin Lakes Resort that he created from artesian wells. This was the most popular local resort in the 1920s and 1930s, and became the nucleus for Lorenzi Park, which is presently owned and operated by the City of Las Vegas (Balboni).

Hispanics also entered the region in some numbers in the early twentieth century, mostly to work on the railroads. There was a small Mexican enclave in Las Vegas, and in the Tonopah region as well. It was not until more recent times that the

Hispanic population in Nevada grew to significant numbers and began to have a serious influence on the course of events in the state. Hispanics have moved into politics, businesses, gaming, and numerous other endeavors that have a direct impact on the course of development in the southern part of the state (Shepperson "Restless Strangers"; Rodriguez; Balboni).

Catholics have had a serious impact on politics and business throughout the state. In the north, Theodore Martinez established an electrical wiring business in Reno in 1904 which expanded with many branches in many locations in the state. J. Emmett Walsh was District Attorney of Ormsby County from 1898-1900, and Deputy District Attorney and later District Attorney of Goldfield from 1905-1913. Clarence Hungerford Mackay, John W. Mackay's son, contributed heavily to higher education in Nevada. He donated the Mackay School of Mines Building and Training Center at University of Nevada-Reno, along with equipment and a $150,000 endowment. In 1925-1931, he contributed to enlarge the School of Mines and the athletic stadium, and donated the Mackay Science Hall for Chemistry and Physics (Davis).

In the realm of politics, two of Nevada's earliest twentieth century governors were Catholic. Emmett Derby Boyle (1915-1922), the first native-born Nevadan to become governor, was Irish Catholic in background. He pushed heavily for women's suffrage and prohibition, reconstructed the tax machinery of the state, and created the Nevada Department of Highways. Fred Balzar (1927-1934) was of Italian heritage and a native of Virginia City. He served as state Senator and Assemblyman, as sheriff, and as an assessor before he became governor. He signed the bill in 1931 that relegalized gambling in Nevada. He died in office in 1934 (Myles; Hulse, *The Nevada Adventure*; James).

In addition, an Irishman, William Woodburn, was a Congressman from Nevada between 1885 and 1889. He played on his ethnic background and the heavily Irish Catholic population of the state to place him in congress. As an avowed Irish nationalist, he was quite likely Catholic, given the identification of Catholicism and Irish nationalism in the nineteenth century (James).

The Modern Era: 1931-Present

For Catholics and the Roman Catholic Church, the focus of history shifts south from Reno to the Las Vegas/Southern Nevada region. From 1930-1939, the federal government pumped $23 million into the Las Vegas area as a result of the building of Hoover Dam and other depression-era projects. This brought thousands of jobs into the Las Vegas region with people looking for work in both the construction and gaming industry, which had been relegalized in 1931. The federal government also created Boulder City. The advent of World War II led to the establishment of the Basic Titanium plant and Nellis Air Force Base and the Gunnery Range. The Cold War of the 1950s and 1960s led to the creation of the Nevada Test Site. All of these contributed to the phenomenal growth of southern Nevada, a growth that continues to this day. However it is conceded that gaming and tourism, the lifeblood of Nevada's economy, have been the main driving forces behind this growth (Roske; Moehring).

It is ironic that, with the growth of gaming, there came changes in the institutional makeup of the Roman Catholic Church in Nevada. Nevada was granted separate diocesan status by Pope Pius XI on March 27, 1931, with Bishop Thomas Gorman being named the first Bishop of the Diocese of Reno (1931-1952). St. Thomas Aquinas Church in Reno was named the cathedral church of the diocese. At the time there were an estimate 8,500 Catholics among Nevada's 91,058 citizens, with only a handful of priests to serve them. Parishes existed in Carson City, Las Vegas, and Reno, as well as Sparks, Elko, Ely, Tonopah, Fallon, Lovelock, Hawthorne, Sparks, Virginia City, Winnemucca, and Yerington. There were missions in the Battle Mountain/Carlin area, Wells, McGill, Caliente, Manhattan, and Ruth, and a number of stations: Round Mountain, Searchlight, Beatty, Deeth, Halleck, Montello, Bullion, South Fork, Beowawe, Huntington Valley, Starr Valley, Lamoille, and Palisade (Gorman; WPA; Olson). The number of Catholic centers had grown ever larger until by 1980, Nevada had forty full-time parishes, ten missions, and thirteen Catholic schools (Roske).

Following Bishop Gorman, there has been a succession of bishops of the Diocese of Reno: Robert J. Dwyer (1952-1966), Joseph Green (1966-1974), Norman McFarland (1974-

1987), and Daniel F. Walsh (1987-1994). Each has brought his own unique strengths and weaknesses to the position, but all strove to improve and strengthen the structure of the Roman Catholic Church within Nevada.

With the expansion of population statewide, the parochial Celtic nature of the Catholic Church in Nevada has also changed. Nevada has become a magnet for populations from all over the country and the world, which is reflected in the ethnic makeup of people comprising the population of the church. Filipinos, Asians, Hispanics, and other non-European groups make up a larger percentage of the church membership than ever before. For example, in 1950 there were 205 Hispanics in Clark County, mostly in Las Vegas. In 1970, there were 9,927, and in 1980 there were approximately 35,000 in Clark County. The Filipino population demonstrates similar trends. From statistical negligence, the Filipino population of Las Vegas numbered 2,743 (Rodriguez; Roske; Moehring). A number of these groups, particularly Hispanics, have organized social and fraternal organizations to press for greater economic and political participation for their people in the Las Vegas area, and throughout the state. One group, the Nevada Association of Latin Americans, is at the forefront of the fight for improved social conditions for Hispanics throughout the Silver State.

African-Americans have also begun to comprise a larger percentage of the Catholic population of the state. Their importance as a group grew in the 1940s with the development of the Las Vegas region and Clark County during and after World War II. The Basic Magnesium Plant, gaming, and the general growth of the Nevada economy in the years 1940-1996 has seen a massive increase in the African-American population of the state. A number of this group are Catholic, and a Catholic parish, St. James the Apostle in North Las Vegas, is within the predominantly African-American westside area of Las Vegas. Many African-American Catholics are actively involved in the struggle for civil rights, increased political power, and improved economic conditions for their group throughout the state through organizations such as the National Association for the Advancement of Colored People (Coray).

This increased representation of minority groups in the Catholic Church of Nevada is bringing unforeseen and unforeseeable changes to the church in Nevada. The next few decades could be very interesting in terms of the church hierarchy and the composition of Catholic institutions and populations of Nevada.

This growth spurt has led to the establishment of many new parishes in the southern Nevada region since the 1930s. St. Andrew's in Boulder City was established in 1932. St. James the Apostle was begun as a mission in North Las Vegas in 1937, and was upgraded to a parish in the 1940s. The parishes of Our Lady of Las Vegas, St. Anne's, St. Christopher's, St. Bridget's, and St. Viator's were established in the 1940s and 1950s, all beginning as missions of St. Joan of Arc's parish in Las Vegas (St. Joan of Arc). St. Peter's in Henderson (1943) and St. John the Evangelist in Overton (1959) were also founded in this time period. In the 1960s Guardian Angel Cathedral was built, and St. Francis de Sales Parish was established. The 1970s saw the founding of the parishes of Holy Family and Christ the King, while the 1980s and early 1990s saw explosive growth: St. Joseph's, St. Mary the Virgin, Our Lady of Victory, Prince of Peace, St. Thomas Moore, and St. Elizabeth Ann Seton were all founded in Las Vegas in the last fifteen years, as was Our Lady of the Valley in Pahrump, and Guardian Angel Cathedral was also made the center of its own parish. Missions exist in Laughlin (St. John the Baptist), Bunkerville (La Virgen de Guadalupe), and Amargosa Valleys (Christ of the Desert Church), serviced by parishes in Las Vegas (Diocese of Las Vegas). Given the explosive population growth of the last two decades, new parishes will need to be established in southern Nevada, and probably in the Reno/Sparks region as well.

The growth of the Catholic Church in Nevada necessitated larger institutional change. In 1976, the Diocese of Reno was renamed the Diocese of Reno-Las Vegas, recognizing the growing importance of the Catholic population in southern Nevada. On June 28, 1995, the Diocese of Reno-Las Vegas was divided into two dioceses: the Diocese of Reno, covering northern Nevada and headed by Bishop Phillip Straling, and the Diocese of Las Vegas, covering five southern counties of Nevada (Clark, Lincoln, Nye, Esmeralda, and White Pine) and headed by Bishop Daniel F. Walsh (Diocese of Las Vegas). This change was a belated recognition of the size and strength of the Catholic community in southern Nevada and the need to administer this explosive growth of the church from the focus of that growth, Las Vegas.

Along with a growth in total numbers, individual Catholics and larger Catholic families have had a major impact on the economy and politics of the state, and on social movements that have had a statewide and national impact. In the economy of Las Vegas of the 1930s and 1940s, the Ronzone, Cornero, and Silvagni families (Italian Catholics) all were important. The Ronzones were active in retailing and in community service. Richard Ronzone served as the first president of the Las Vegas Chamber of Commerce, and served on the Clark County School Board, the University of Nevada Board of Regents, the Clark County Commission, and in the Nevada State Assembly (Balboni 1989).

The Cornero family, including brothers Frank, Louis, and Tony, were prominent in some of the early gaming ventures in the 1930s and 1940s. They had been forced out of southern California, where they had been involved in illegal gambling and bootlegging, by reform-minded local governments. They opened Las Vegas' first legal hotel/casino, the Meadows, helping to set the tone for future efforts in this area. They were joined in this endeavor by Guy McAfee, a corrupt former Los Angeles vice squad commander, who ran several illegal casinos in southern California. He bought the Pair-O-Dice Club south of the city of Las Vegas on what is now called "The Strip," renamed it the 91 Club, and enjoyed modest success. It is McAfee who is purported to have named the Las Vegas Highway "the strip" after the Sunset Strip area in Los Angeles from which he had been driven (Roske; Moehring; Balboni).

The Silvagni family entered the hotel business in Las Vegas with the construction of Boulder Dam. Pietro Silvagni built the Apache Hotel on Second and Fremont Streets in downtown Las Vegas, the first Las Vegas hotel with elevators and air conditioning. He brought in family members to help him run the hotel, including his sister, Philomena Mirabelli. The Mirabellis became prominent in Las Vegas politics, with two sons of Philomena achieving success. Philip Mirabelli was a Las Vegas City Commissioner, and Mike Mirabelli was Nevada State Treasurer from 1963-1968 (Balboni).

Gaming attracted other Catholics to the Las Vegas area in the 1940s and 1950s. Sam Boyd was attracted to the town and acquired gaming experience prior to purchasing a share in the Club Bingo in 1948, and later in the Sahara Hotel. Before his death he had owned the Union Plaza, the Nevada Hotel, the Eldorado Club, the California Hotel and Casino, Sam's Town, and the Fremont and Stardust Hotels. Benny Binion was also attracted to the area, opening the Horseshoe Hotel and casino in 1951. He purchased the Mint Hotel in downtown Las Vegas in 1988, and expanded the Horseshoe into the property (Moehring).

Many Catholics continue to be engaged in the gaming industry, both as owners, managers, and workers. Without Catholics, who are estimated to comprise nearly thirty percent of the state's population, the situation in Nevada may have been much different.

Catholics have been actively engaged in other areas of the state as well. There are twenty thousand Nevadans of Italian heritage in the greater Reno area who have played major roles in the development of northern Nevada and the state. There is, for example, Louis Lombardi, a University of Nevada Regent for thirty years; John Gabrielli, a Washoe County District Judge; Ernie Martinelli, who in 1988 was Chairman of Security Bank of Nevada; and numerous other Catholics who have achieved prominence and importance in the northern portions of the state (Mellon).

Catholics have been extremely active politically in the modern era. Possibly the most prominent Catholic politician of the modern era was Patrick A. McCarran, United States Senator from 1932 until his death in 1954. He dominated politics in the Silver State for many years. He served as a Nevada State Supreme Court Justice from 1913-1918, and was elected to the U.S. Senate on the Roosevelt political wave in 1932. While in the Senate he sponsored the Civil Aeronautics Act (1938) and helped sponsor legislation that stripped Federal agencies of their power to act as both judge and prosecutor in alleged violations of Federal rules (the Administrative Procedures Act of 1946) (Laxalt).

Unfortunately he was also involved in several less than honorable ventures. He was the main sponsor of the McCarran-Walter Immigration Act, an act that denies individuals the right to immigrate to the United States solely because of their political views. On this, he was admonished even by the Vatican, but held fast to his position and achieved passage of the act (Laxalt).

In addition he was involved in a major First Amendment dispute with the *Las Vegas Sun* newspaper in the early 1950s. Stung by criticism of himself and his association with Senator Joseph McCarthy by the Las Vegas Sun, he pressured Las Vegas casinos to withdraw advertising from the newspaper, nearly bankrupting the *Sun*. The publisher, Hank Greenspun, sued the Senator and the casinos for anti-trust violations and won (Edwards, "Patrick A. McCarran," "The Sun and the Senator," "Nevada Power Broker"; Whited).

Other prominent Catholic politicians of the modern era include five governors: Edward Peter Carville (1939-1945); Paul Laxalt (1967-1970); Donal Neil (Mike) O'Callahan (1971-1978); Richard Bryan (1982-1988); and the current governor, Robert Miller (1988-present) (Myles).

A number of Catholics from Nevada also achieved national political prominence. Paul Laxalt and Richard Bryant both went on to serve in the United States Senate, where Bryant is presently serving. Paul Laxalt became a prominent political advisor to President Ronald Reagan, helping to shape national policy behind the scenes at the White House. Other Catholics in Congress include recently retired Barbara Vucanovich and James H. Bilbray, who was defeated in 1994 in a reelection bid. These individuals have had a major role in helping to shape the course of politics in both Nevada and on the national level.

Catholics have been prominent in social movements of the modern era. The Catholic Church helped to lead the fight against legalized prostitution in Clark County, which was banned in 1955. The church continues to oppose the practice statewide. The church also runs Catholic Community Services, which is involved in adoptions; migration and refugee services; day care; senior citizen programs; St. Vincent's dining rooms, shelters, and thrift stores; and various other social services. The Catholic Church runs numerous elementary schools and several high schools in the state, and the Dominican Sisters run St. Rose de Lima Hospital in Henderson, Nevada.

Individual Catholics are involved in movements such as the Catholic Worker, an outreach program to the working poor; the Nevada Peace Test/Nevada Lenten experience, which stages protests at the Nevada Test Site for nuclear disarmament; and were on both sides of the abortion referendum, Question 7, that was defeated in November, 1990.

There are numerous clubs and organizations that Catholics belong to, some of which are ethnically oriented, and some of which are generally Catholic in outlook. These include the Filipino American Association, Nevada Association of Latin Americans, National Conference of Christians and Jews, the Knights of Columbus, the Italian-American Club, and the German-American Social Club. Catholics belong to labor unions, fraternal and political organizations, and other interest groups that have had a hand in shaping the politics and social agenda of Nevada in the late twentieth century. As a general statement the influence of the Catholic Church as an institution and Catholics as a group can be seen as having been essentially helpful and progressive in shaping the nature of the Silver State.

There are those, however, who see the role of the Catholic Church in social issues as being less than benign. Hulse, writing in his book *Forty Years in the Wilderness*, rails against the "corrupt" influence of gambling on Nevada, and in particular the lack of religious opposition to gambling. He states:

> A number of churches have taken the stand that there is nothing inherently evil in gambling, and therefore its legality is not to be questioned. It seems often to follow from this position that, like Pontius Pilate, the religious institutions can wash their hands of any responsibility for the social consequences. (117)

He goes on, singling out the Catholic Church for individual abuse on this subject. He declares that the Catholic Church has been "a non-entity in terms of any moral force" concerning the social abuses that accompany gaming because it considers gambling as a non-sinful activity except when indulgence interferes with one's duties. He castigates the Catholic Church for not considering the questions of Christian morality that surround gambling (Hulse *Forty Years in the Wilderness*).

In fairness, he also criticizes the Mormon Church in Nevada (the State's second-largest religious denomination) for its shortcomings in this area, but with nowhere near the vitriolic or passion with which he attacks the Catholic Church. He also tempers that criticism with several pages of glowing reviews concerning the Mormon Church and calls it "one of the potentially formidable moral forces in the state" (Hulse "Forty Years in the Wilderness"). This stance by Hulse demonstrates that Catholics and the Catholic Church still generate much passion in regard to the positions they stake out, particularly when these positions are viewed by and commented on by non-Catholics. This is quite similar to the anti-Catholic views expressed by many people in the second half of the nineteenth century.

Like the Catholics of the nineteenth century, the Catholic Church and Catholics of today face many challenges. One is handling the explosive growth of the Catholic population of the southern portion of the state. While the laity is expanding, the pool of available priests is shrinking. Fewer men are entering the priesthood from Nevada and as a consequence the number of diocesan priests (those ordained specifically for service in a particular diocese) has remained stagnant and even shrunk in relationship to the Catholic population. Priests have had to be imported from other dioceses in the United States, and a percentage of the priests in southern Nevada come from the Philippines. In this regard the situation resembles that of Nevada of the late nineteenth century, when the majority of priests were imported from Ireland to serve an expanding flock.

A second set of issues involves the changing composition and dynamics of the Catholic population of Nevada. Increasing numbers of Catholics are Hispanic and African-American in origin, and bring different sets of behaviors and cultural expectations to the church (Coray). The American Catholic Church has not been famous for its sensitivity to the needs of non-Europeans in the church and as a result church membership among the traditionally Catholic groups (most specifically Hispanics) has been slipping. How the institutional church handles this particular challenge will provide a stern test of the health and efficacy of the Catholic Church in the state.

A third set of concerns involves social issues, particularly those involving the poor and women. The National Conference of Catholic Bishops has issued two draft statements in the past few years, one dealing with the role of women in the church and one dealing with issues of economic justice. The pastoral letter on women reiterated the traditional Catholic view on women, that they are important aspects of the church but, for historical and biblical reasons, cannot be ordained as priests. Additionally the Catholic Church adamantly opposes abortion which is seen by many women, including many Catholics, as being their "constitutional right". These stances vis-a-vis women represent a particular challenge to the Catholic Church in Nevada, the majority of whose membership is women. How will the Catholic Church, in light of the shortage of priests and the marginalization of women, maintain the allegiance of women and thus its internal health as an institution? How the Catholic Church deals with these issues is crucial to the health of the institution in the years to come.

The draft letter on economic justice also tends to run contrary to the general mode of thinking on economic issues in the United States. It calls for a much more equitable distribution of wealth in the United States, a position that some construe as socialistic. It also opposes rapid or drastic cuts in the current welfare system which again runs contrary to much current political thought, even among its followers. These positions represent yet another challenge to the overall health of the institutional Catholic Church and its ability to influence social issues.

With these problems and challenges the best that can be predicted is that the history of the Catholic Church in Nevada should prove to be an interesting and exciting one in the next few decades.

NOTE

[1]Individuals professing faith in the Roman Catholic Church had a major impact on the development of the Silver State in areas such as exploration, mining, farming, gambling, and politics, an impact that continues to this day. The earliest histories of Nevada—including Angel, Bancroft, Wren, and Davis—discussed various religious denominations in Nevada, but focused on such matters as the dates of the construction of buildings, the establishment of parishes or congregations, and the names and personalities of the founders of each church. At best these discussions are found within the context of other historical developments within the state (Angel; Bancroft; Wren; Davis). The one document to focus exclusively on religion,

Trout's *Religious Development in Nevada* focuses on dates and places, although she did undertake some analyses of the impacts of the process of mining booms and busts on the rise and fall of various congregations of the separate religions throughout the state.

Even this treatment is vastly superior to the treatment religion receives in the more modern historical tomes. Religion and its impact on Nevada is either not discussed, or it is given cursory treatment almost as if it was an historical oddity not worthy of closer analysis (Hulse *The Nevada Adventure*; Shepperson "Immigrant Themes," *Restless Strangers*; Fletcher; Paher; Roske; Moehring). This paper does not entirely redress these shortcomings. It was designed to discuss one specific Christian denomination, Roman Catholicism, in broad strokes and to touch upon areas requiring further research. I believe that the history of the Roman Catholic Church is at least as important and its impact of Nevada's historical development at least as significant as that of the Church of Jesus Christ of Latter Day Saints, the religion usually discussed when Nevada's history is dealt with. Given the broad topic I can only hope to begin the process of analyzing the role this institution and its adherents played in the history of Nevada.

ACKNOWLEDGEMENTS

An earlier version of this paper was written for the *Nevada Comprehensive Preservation Plan* published by the Nevada State Historic Preservation Office located in Carson City, Nevada, whose encouragement and support he gratefully acknowledges.

REFERENCES

Angel, Myron, ed. *History of Nevada.* Oakland: Thompson and West Publishers, 1881.

Balboni, Alan. "From Banana Sellers to Successful Entrepreneurs: Italian Americans in Southern Nevada, 1905-1947." Paper Presented at the Second Nevada History Conference, Reno. 1989.

Bancroft, Hubert Howe. *History of Nevada, Colorado and Wyoming, 1540-1888.* San Francisco: The History Company Publishers, 1890.

Caviglia, Caesar. *Nevada's Catholic Heritage.* Reno: Diocese Of Reno-Las Vegas, 1976.

Cofone, Albin J. "Themes in the Italian Settlement of Nevada." *Nevada Historical Society Quarterly* 25.2 (1982): 116-130.

———. "Reno's Little Italy: Italian Entrepreneurship and Culture in Northern Nevada." *Nevada Historical Society Quarterly* 26.2 (1983): 97-110.

Coray, Michael. "Blacks in Nevada." Chapter 31. *Nevada Compre-*

hensive Preservation Plan. Eds Richard A. Bernstein and Ronald James. Carson City: Division of Historic Preservation and Archaeology, 1989.

Davis, Samuel P. *The History of Nevada.* Reno: Elms Publishing Company, 1913.

Diocese of Las Vegas. *The Official Directory of the Diocese of Las Vegas, 1996-1997.* Las Vegas: Diocese of Las Vegas, 1997.

Douglass, William A. "The Basques of the American West: Preliminary Historical Perspectives." *Nevada Historical Society Quarterly* 13.4 (1970): 12-25.

———. "The Basques of Nevada." *Nevada Official Bicentennial Book.* Ed. Stanley W. Paher. Las Vegas: Nevada Publications. 430-431.

Dwyer, John T. *Condemned to the Mines: The Life of Eugene O'Connell, 1815-1891, Pioneer Bishop of Northern California and Nevada.* New York, Vantage Press, 1976.

Earl, Philip I. "Nevada's Italian War." *Nevada Historical Society Quarterly* 12.2 (1969): 47-87.

Edwards, Jerome. "Patrick A. McCarran, His Years on the Nevada Supreme Court." *Nevada Historical Society Quarterly* 17.4 (1975): 185-200.

———. "The Sun and the Senator." *Nevada Historical Society Quarterly* 24.1 (1981): 3-16.

———."Nevada Power Broker: Pat McCarran and His Political Machine." *Nevada Historical Society Quarterly* 27.3 (1984): 182-198.

Eterovich, Adam. *Yugoslavs in Nevada, 1859-1900.* San Francisco: R & E Research Associates, 1973.

Fletcher, F. N. *Early Nevada: The Period of Exploration, 1776-1848.* Reno: U of Nevada P, 1980.

Fries, Louis J. *One Hundred Years of Catholicity In Utah.* Salt Lake City: Intermountain Catholic Press, 1926.

Gorman, Thomas K. *Seventy-Five Years of Catholic Life in Nevada.* Reno: The Journal Press, 1935.

Hafen, Leroy, and Ann W. Hafen. "The Old Spanish Trail." *The Far West and Rockies Historical Series, 1820-1875*, Vol. 1. Glendale, CA: The Arthur Clark Company, 1954.

Hulse, James. *The Nevada Adventure: A History.* 5th ed. .Reno: U of Nevada P, 1981.

———. *Forty Years in the Wilderness: Impressions of Nevada, 1940-1980.* Reno: U of Nevada P, Reno, 1986.

James, Ronald M. "British and Irish." *Nevada Comprehensive Preservation Plan.* Vol. I, Ch. 37. Ed. Richard A. Bernstein and Ronald M. James. Carson City: Nevada Division of Historic Preservation and Archaeology. 1989.

Kosso, Leonore M. "Yugoslavs In Nevada After 1900: The White Pine Community." *Nevada Historical Society Quarterly* 28.3 (1985):

158-174.

Laxalt, Robert. *Nevada: A Bicentennial History.* New York: W.W. Norton and Company, Inc., 1977.

Lincoln, Francis Church. "An Outline of the Mining History of the State of Nevada." *Nevada Newsletter* 19.3 (1924): 1-2.

Lord, Eliot. *Comstock Miners and Mining.* Washington, DC: U.S. Government   General Printing Office. 1883.

McAvoy, Thomas T. *A History of the Catholic Church in the United States.* South Bend, IN: U of Notre Dame P,1969.

McGloin, John Bernard. "Patrick Manogue, Gold Miner and Bishop, and His "Cathedral on the Comstock" *Nevada Historical Society Quarterly* 14.2 (1971): 25-32.

Mellon, Rollan. *Nevadans.* Reno: U of Nevada P,1988.

Moehring, Eugene. *Resort City in the Sunbelt: Las Vegas, 1930-1970.* Reno: U of Nevada P, 1989.

Myles, Myrtle Tate. *Nevada's Governors, From Territorial Days to the Present, 1861-1971.* Sparks, NV: Western Printing and Publishing Company, 1972.

Olson, James S. "Pioneer Catholicism in Eastern and Southern Nevada, 1864-1931." *Nevada Historical Society Quarterly* 26.3 (1983): 159-171.

Paher, Stanley. *Las Vegas: As It Began—As It Grew.* Las Vegas: Nevada Publications, 1971.

Riggs, John L. "Reign of Violence in El Dorado Canyon." *Third Biennial Report of the Nevada Historical Society.* Carson City: Nevada State Printing Office, 1913.

Rodriguez, Thomas. *A Profile of Hispanics in Nevada: An Agenda For Action.* Las Vegas: Latin Chamber of Commerce,1984.

Roske, Ralph. *Las Vegas: A Desert Paradise.* Tulsa, OK: Continental Heritage Press, 1986.

Salpointe, Jean Baptiste. *Soldiers of the Cross: Notes on the Ecclesiastical History of New Mexico, Arizona, and Colorado.* Albuquerque: Calvin Horn Publishers,1967.

St. Joan of Arc Parish. *St. Joan of Arc Parish, Las Vegas, Nevada: 1909-1959- Fifty Years of Catholic Life in Southern Nevada.* Las Vegas: St. Joan of Arc Parish,1959.

Scrugham, James G., ed. *Nevada: A Narrative of the Conquest of a Frontier Land.* Chicago: American Historical Society.1935.

Shepperson, Wilbur. "Immigrant Themes in Nevada Newspapers." *Nevada Historical Society Quarterly* 12.2 (1969): 3-46.

———. *Restless Strangers: Nevada's Immigrants and Their Interpreters.* Reno: U of Nevada P, 1970.

Townley, John M. "Early Development of El Dorado Canyon and Searchlight Mining Districts." *Nevada Historical Society Quarterly* 11.1(1968): 1-25.

Trut, Alice Francis. "Religious Development in Nevada." *Nevada Historical Society Papers 1913-1916.* Carson City: State Printing Office, 1917. 143-167.

Walsh, Henry J. *Hallowed Were the Gold Dust Trails: The Story of the Pioneer Priests of Northern California.* Santa Clara, CA: U of Santa Clara P, 1946.

Warren, Elizabeth von Till. "Armijo's Trace Revisited: A New Interpretation of the Impact of the Antonio Armijo Route of 1829-1830 on the Development of the Old Spanish Trail." Master's Thesis. University of Nevada, Las Vegas. 1974.

Weir, Jeanne Elizabeth. "Mementos of Nevada's Olden Days and the Work of the Nevada Historical Society, Trustee of the State of Nevada." *Nevada Historical Society Papers, 1913-1916.* Carson City: Nevada State Publishing Office, 1917.

Whited, Fred E. "Senator McCarran: Orator From Nevada." *Nevada Historical Society Quarterly* 17.4 (1974): 181-202.

Works Progress Administration. *Inventory of the Church Archives of Nevada-Roman Catholic Church.* Reno: Nevada Historical Records Survey,1939.

Wren, Thomas, ed. *A History of the State of Nevada.* New York: Lewis Publishing Company,1904.

Zeier, Charles D. "Archaeological Data Recovery Associated With The Mt. Hope Project, Eureka County, Nevada." *Cultural Resource Series* No. 8. Reno: Bureau of Land Management, Nevada State Office, 1985.

The Age of Institutions
Basques in the United States

CARMELO URZA

Communities come in many forms and guises. Some are identifiable through the geographic unity provided by a town or valley. Others, particularly those of ethnic groups, exist as a concept, in the mind, rather than on the landscape. This is the case with the Basque community. It exists in Nevada and in the West primarily as a mental construct which ties together ranches, clubs, and boarding houses. This kind of community also has a history, an evolution, and a living present, each with its own characteristics.

There exist seeming contradictions in the pattern of the Basque presence in the American West. The motives and opportunities for Basque immigration have long since disappeared, and indeed the last wave of traditional immigration ended nearly forty years ago. Today the first generations, those who embodied the original culture, have become the exception among Basque-Americans, and the norm are second through fifth generation Basque-Americans. Logic or some law of the social sciences would lead us to believe that the ethnic characteristics maintained by ever more diffused generations of Basque-Americans would become ever more simplified with ever fewer ethnic markers and that these should be characterized by increasing symbolism and ritualized manifestation. This phenomenon did, in fact, take place in the decade of the 1960s, 1970s and part of the 1980s and, at a certain popular level, remains true today.

Carmelo Urza was born in the Basque Country of northern Spain and grew up in Idaho. He received his Ph.D. from the University of Iowa. The author of over thirty articles and two monographs, he founded and has been director of the University Studies Abroad Consortium at the University of Nevada, Reno, since 1982.

And yet, on another level, the public image of the Basques has never been higher than that of today; nor has the knowledge that Basque-Americans have of themselves been as sophisticated as it is today. I want to examine these two antithetical tangents within the framework of the evolution of the Basque presence in the American West.

The Historical Period (1848-1948)

Although there remain many specific topics to be researched, the historical patterns of Basque settlement during its first one hundred years have been well documented in *Amerikanuak: Basques in the New World*. In it William Douglass and Jon Bilbao document the character of the Basques which, when combined with mthe attractive opportunities provided by the European colonization of the Americas and the inheritance patterns of old world Basques and European wars and famine, flushed thousands of Basques to the New World. They record how the discovery of gold in California in 1848 became the catalyst for the first wave of U.S. dateline immigration and the subsequent Basque capitalization of business opportunities provided by the vast, largely unclaimed, expanses of the West and the needs of a burgeoning population. Basques moved into many areas of economic activity but nowhere was their impact as great as in the sheep industry. Hundreds and perhaps thousands of Basques became entrepreneurs or worked as employees of sheep outfits for nearly a century. Most of the activity ended in 1934, when the Taylor Grazing Act restricted access to public lands. Basque sheepmen were forced to sell their herds and return to the Basque Country, to establish ranch based operations or to seek employment with established operators or in urban centers. Those who remained formed the backbone for the permanent Basque settlement in the United States.

Throughout this period, the unpopularity of the Basque itinerant sheepmen who competed for the open range with established livestockmen, the low social status of the herder, and the sparseness of Basque settlements meant that the Basques, as a whole, maintained a very low public profile. Their only ethnic haven was the private or semi-private Basque boarding houses which lodged, fed and tended to the needs of the largely single male population when they were between jobs or in town to visit the doctor, banker, or immigration official or were simply on vacation. (Figure 1.) These boarding houses also served as the meeting place for the wider local Basque population for purposes of celebrating weddings, funerals or other occasions. They held dances to the sounds of

Figure 1. A Basque boarding house. Photo courtesy of the University of Nevada, Reno Basque Studies Program.

the then universally popular accordion, though rarely would folk dances as such be enacted. Many boarding houses had a version of the handball court and, since the clientele tended to be strong, young, rural males, the courts were widely used. Other forms of Basque rural sports were generally not manifested, although there was no shortage of extemporaneous tests of strength and endurance.

This first historical period may be characterized as an immigration stocked with predominantly single male sojourners with little formal education who were scattered lightly around the ranching communities of at least seven Western states. There were no large scale gatherings of Basques and no true organizations. When viewed from the perspective of the larger American population, there was a generalized derogatory image of the Basques, although on an individual basis, they were viewed as honest and hard working. There were few if any Basques in positions of prestige; very few newspapers or magazine articles were written about them and when they were, they were usually negative. There existed no books published in English about the Basques. Basques were generally isolated as a group, kept to their own kind and no one knew nor cared to know much about them.

The Modern Period (1948-1967)

In the 1940s and '50s, labor shortages in the sheep industry caused by World War II and by the post-war economic boom brought another influx of Basques into the sheep industry, and many of those were also to remain in the United States. However, during this period the sheep industry as a whole was in decline. Competition from foreign countries, from synthetic fibers and a tightening up of grazing on the public domain all contributed to the decline. Further, the economic situation in the Old World improved immensely and the youth of the area were able to secure well-paying employment at home, which was more attractive than the low paying and lonely job of herding sheep in the U.S. The decade of the 50's was to mark the end of large scale Basque immigration to the U.S.

Most important, an enormous change in the group image of the Basques took place. The much hated itinerant Basque herder was now history, and those who arrived during the

labor shortage were hailed as heroes come to save an industry in crisis. Further, America itself had changed into an urban and suburban population living in planned tracts, with
shopping in chain stores located in cloned malls. Being different began to be valued, and few groups were more mysterious than the Basques. The remaining herders, found by the
media in the desolate wilderness, were represented as exotic,
romantic and colorful figures living in close communion with
nature. Americans were also in the midst of the *Roots* phenomenon, and having a unique ethnicity was now highly desirable. Finally, the nature of the Basque population had
matured as well. No longer were most of the Basques living
on the range or in boarding houses; rather they had settled
down, gotten married, purchased property, and become citizens.

After the last spurt of immigration had run its course, the
private or semi-private Basque boarding houses had lost much
of their traditional clientele and had to find new forms of economic viability. Many couldn't make the transition and closed
their doors. Others, however, shifted their attention to their
dining facilities and opened their doors to the public. They
soon won over the customers with generous portions of sometimes slightly exotic fare, generally served family style in which
customers sit at long commonly-shared tables. The cuisine
was usually the Americanized version of Basque soups, beans,
chicken and beef. If the food usually did not represent authentic old world cuisine, it was at least prepared and served
by authentic Basque immigrants.

Warmed by the new friendly environment for ethnicities,
Basques began to band together and to display their culture.
The Boise, Idaho Basques built the Basque center in 1948,
and it serves as the dateline for this period. In 1959, the first
large scale Basque picnic was organized in Sparks, Nevada,
and was attended by approximately five thousand Basques
from throughout the United States. As William Douglass has
discussed in "Inventing an Ethnic Identity: The First Basque
Festival," this festival served to reinvent Basque-American
culture in a way which was part old-world but also distinctly
new-world, coming to define the concept of a Basque festival:
the Catholic mass, the picnic fare, folk dances, and many of
the rural sports that would come to be considered stock

Basque in the U.S.: weight lifting and carrying, log chopping, and so on.

The visiting Basques at the Sparks festival returned to their communities and, almost spontaneously, created their own Basque clubs and festivals, modeled to varying degrees on the Sparks archetype. An array of activities were spawned during this period. Communities sought to tout their unusual ethnic groups, the public was interested in the unique, mysterious Basques, and the Basques were eager to show and tell. Nearly two dozen clubs were created in the following decade.

The Boise Basques created a folk dance group in 1960 that became very popular and which was replicated in other communities of the West. The folkdance costumes, put together hastily for the Sparks festival, composed of white pants and shirts with red sash and beret, were to become widely adopted, and the folk dances themselves were generally limited to a manageable group of three to six, usually the same ones at each club. Furthermore, in 1959 Robert Laxalt published the highly acclaimed *Sweet Promised Land*, a book about his immigrant Basque father. The Basques now had a literary spokesman and were the topic of discussion among the well-educated.

The modern historical period may be characterized by the recognition, acceptance and, indeed, high desirability of the differences represented in the Basques. The private boarding house, if it survived, became a public restaurant where everyone was invited to enter the realm of immigrant Basque-Americans. The Basques organized themselves into clubs and proudly displayed their culture. If handball, the most popular Basque sport, was largely lost with the private boarding house, the public demonstration of other rural sports, music and folk dances compensated for it (Urza, *Historia*). As a group of immigrants with a distant and narrowly based memory of their land, the Basques interpreted their culture through widely reproduced symbols and ritualized manifestations. The media tended to play upon obvious elements such as the mysterious origins. It was a period of discovery, an introduction at once to old world origins and new world adaptations.

Scenes from a contemporary Basque festival. Photographs by Richard Lane.

The Age of Institutions
(1969 - present)

To be sure, the activities described thus far have continued to the present day. Festivals continue to flourish, as do Basque clubs, and new centers have been constructed in Elko, Nevada and in San Francisco, Chino, and Bakersfield, California. The rustic Basque boarding houses which had been converted into restaurants continue to flourish. Many other new restaurants have also been established, imitating those of the boarding houses but on an upscale model, oftentimes owned and operated by second or third generation Basques. Basque culture in the new restaurants is highlighted in a much more studied and systematic way: through cultural icons, photographs of the old world, folk music, and waitresses dressed in folk costumes. Oftentimes, Basque history and culture is described on the menus or walls. Basque rural sports continued to be displayed at festivals, but, since the immigrant population is aging, sports tend to become a demonstration rather than actual competition. The sheep industry and Basque involvement in it continues to decline.

All of this activity during the modern 1948-1967 period had had a cumulative impact upon the image of the Basques. Many thousands of people had been exposed to Basqueness through club organized festivals and through the popular Basque restaurants. But these activities tended to imprint a mythical structure on the events or activities, producing ritualized repetition, but adding little new. The question to be answered was no longer "Who are the Basques?" but rather "What do any of us really know about the Basques?"

If the modern period was characterized by the emergence of Basques from the privacy of sheep camps and boarding houses into high public visibility and approval, the post-modern period is characterized by the creation of institutions, particularly educational institutions. These differ from Basque clubs and centers in several ways. First, clubs and centers are run by volunteers who donate their free time sporadically to help realize usually short-term objectives. Institutions are primarily staffed by professionals who have a clearly stated short or long-term mission. As a result, their activities tend to be more complex and permanent than those based on a volunteer structure. Institutional projects may be long-term and may be involved in more diverse activities such as the arts, research, publishing, student exchanges, and museum projects. These projects require both the funding and the professionalism brought in from other fields and applied to Basque-related activities.

Institutional Basque-related projects are funded through grants or on-going funding that tend to be supported by permanent governmental entities, creating an economic source and stability rarely enjoyed by social clubs that are interminably involved in labor-intensive fundraising. Finally, the activities of institutions involved in Basque activities oftentimes are subjugated to the larger mission of the funding source: libraries, universities, museums, grants awarding agencies or governmental institutions. They tend to rely less on the effectiveness of the individuals and more on the soundness of the mission, enjoying a much more stable base upon which to build their projects.

Some Representative Basque Institutions

Basque Museum and Cultural Center

The historic Uberuaga boarding house is located in Boise, Idaho, on Grove Street, next door to the Basque Center. It had been virtually abandoned when Adelia Simplot bought it in 1983 with the intent of preserving it. Two years later, the Basque Museum and Cultural Center of Idaho, Inc. was created to reconvert it into a boarding house museum. Subsequently, this organization has purchased the building to the East, converting it into their headquarters. The historic *pelota fronton* (handball court) to the east of that bulding was then purchased by two Basque individuals and retrofitted into its original form. Finally, the building on the corner which houses the Basque Bar Gernika was purchased by the Basque Museum and Cultural Center. Today, the entire southern block of Grove Street is completely dedicated to Basque activities, a concentration probably unparalleled outside of the Basque Country itself.

In addition to managing the boarding house museum, the Museum and Cultural Center of Idaho houses a library, archives, gift shop, classroom, and an exhibit area. Its own activities include the teaching of the Basque language, organizing exhibits and conferences, and it also handles the over-flow of children learning Basque dancing from the Basque Center. In September of 1997, it began to house an *Ikastola*, a school for children in which subjects are taught, at least partly, in Basque. The children are taught by a teacher sent from Europe by the Basque Government. Over the last three years, the center has enjoyed approximately ten thousand visitors annually.

Educational Institutions

Boise State University was the first United States university in which the Basque language was taught—in the 1940s. It was the first to organize an academic year-long study abroad program in the Basque Country. It continues to offer Basque at its campus on occasion, has been involved in faculty ex-changes with the University of the Basque Country and par-ticipates very actively in the University Studies Abroad Con-sortium, and has held numerous art exhibits, film festivals, and academic conferences.

The University of California, Santa Barbara received a grant in 1994 from the Basque Government to establish a Chair in Basque Studies. It has, subsequently, offered several courses on Basque topics and organized several conferences.

The University of Iowa has developed an interesting collection of Basque-related materials, occasionally offers Basque-related courses, has been involved in faculty exchanges with the University of the Basque Country, and actively participates in the University Studies Abroad Consortium.

The University of Idaho has also collected a strong core of Basque books, participates actively in the University Studies Abroad Consortium, and has been involved in several faculty exchanges with the University of the Basque Country.

The Basque Educational Organization forms a part of the San Francisco Basque Cultural Center. There it houses a modest collection of publications and occasionally organizes confer-ences and other educational activities.

The Basque Studies Program at the University of Nevada, Reno.
The creation of the Basque Studies Program in 1967 represents the beginning of serious involvement of American intelligentsia in studying the Basques and the emergence of educational entities as major participants in Basque-American
ethnicity. I may be accused of bias toward my home institution, but I think scholars are generally agreed that the UNR
Basque Studies Program has had the greatest impact and the
greatest diversity of activities.

It was the BSP that addressed the void of scholarly publications about the Basques in the English language in 1969
with the publication of *A Book of the Basques* by Rodney
Gallup, and the creation of the Basque Book Series at the
University of Nevada Press (Gallup). To date the BSP has published thirty-eight books within this series as well as four
more through a BSP Occasional Paper Series. The editorial
board has approved an additional eight titles for publication.
These monographs analyze the history, politics, sociology,
culture, literature, cuisine and other topics related to both
old and new world Basques. Among its more important contributions was the original research and subsequent publication of *Amerikanuak*, which documented Basque immigration to, and settlement in, the Americas, particularly in the
West (Douglass). The BSP also developed, over a period of
more than a decade, the first *English-Basque Dictionary* and
a self-taught Basque language text for English speakers
(Aulestia). In addition to scholarly works, the BSP publishes
literature, both traditional in translation, and original works,
including all of Robert Laxalt's Basque-related books. This
series has definitively transformed the body of knowledge
available to the English speaking world on the Basques.

The Basque Studies Program has also had an impact on
the popular culture of Basque Clubs. While engaged in research for *Amerikanuak*, Douglass and Bilbao discovered the
FEVA—(The Federation of Basque Centers in Argentina) and
organized a meeting of western Basque clubs in Reno. The
result was the formation of The North American Basque Organizations, Inc. (NABO) which will be discussed below. Since
NABO does not have a permanent locale of its own, the BSP
still displays NABO's artifacts.

The Basque Studies Program has introduced Basque art
into the United States. Working in collaboration with the So-

ciety for Basque Studies in America, the BSP was instrumental in the realization of the National Basque Monument, a $400,000 sculpture complex located in Reno. It has also worked with the City of Reno to produce a major sculpture by Basque artist Mikel Lertxundi and with the University of Nevada, Reno to attain a major art piece by Basque artist Nestor Basterretxea which dominates the entrance of Getchell Library. It has collaborated in arranging for exhibits in Reno by both of these artists, as well as by José Luís Cuevas and Andrés Nagel. The BSP is currently planning future projects in the areas of the arts and museology.

The Basque Studies Program has developed one of the most extensive collections of Basque-related publications in the world. This collection is supported by the main library of the University of Nevada, Reno, and stays current with new materials. As a result, it has become an almost obligatory Mecca for anyone seriously involved in Basque research. The Basque Studies Program offers an undergraduate minor and a Ph.D. in Basque Studies, thus assuring continued research and future scholars.

Another of the seeds planted by the BSP has been the creation of university-level Basque Studies in the Old World itself. It organized the first summer program in 1969 and assisted Boise State University in developing the short lived Oñate Program. Subsequently, the BSP worked with Boise State University to create the University Studies Abroad Consortium which is discussed below.

University Studies Abroad Consortium (USAC). USAC was created in 1982 by the Basque Studies Program of the University of Nevada, Reno and by Boise State University as a way of joining scarce resources to enhance the stability and continuity of the study abroad initiatives undertaken previously by both entities. USAC offers U.S. students the opportunity to engage in accredited university courses on four campuses in or near the Basque Country, studying the Basque, Spanish and French languages as well as political science, anthropology, history, art history, sociology, economics, education and even cuisine and dance. There are now ten United States universities with USAC membership who send approximately three hundred students annually to its Basque-related campuses in San Sebastian (Gipuzkoa), Bilbao (Bizkaia), and Pau (France). An additional contingent of European and international students also study on USAC Basque-related campuses each year. The use of a consortium structure has allowed USAC the ability to develop the economies of scale necessary for viable study abroad programs. It allows other institutions, their students and faculty, to participate without the expense of organizing their own programs. Since the programs can be accessed by students from throughout the U.S., USAC thus fulfills a national need. Students from other parts of the world can also access the Basque Country academically, thus relieving the Basque entities from having to create their own programs.

Further, USAC facilitates several faculty exchanges each year between faculty of the public University of the Basque Country, which hosts USAC programs, and member universities of the Consortium. USAC also provides the avenue for study for several dozen students and faculty from the Basque Country at member United States universities. USAC and the Basque Studies Program collaborate with the Ministry of Education of the Basque government and with the University of Nevada to secure funding for a visiting Basque scholar and for graduate students to do research and graduate study at the University of Nevada, Reno.

The objective of all of these educational entities is to educate the larger society as well as the Basque community itself. Some of these institutions are more interested in introducing the neophyte to Basque culture and thus contribute to their goals of ethnic maintenance. But even those designed to address the esoteric needs of the intelligentsia indirectly strengthen the very social fabric of the ethnic community they study.

Cultural Institutions

The North American Basque Organizations, Inc. (NABO) was established in 1974. It is the federation responsible for coordinating the activities of the clubs, and for sponsoring intra-club activities such as the annual *mus* (card game) tournaments. It represents the interests of the clubs to other institutions such as the Basque Government and facilitates common projects. NABO provides important institutional stability to the nearly thirty member clubs.

The Basque National Monument. Rancho San Rafael is a 560 acre regional public park in Reno, Nevada. It provides the setting for the National Basque Monument. In offering this role, it views the representation of the Basque people, through its monument, as that of one of the groups which had historical significance in the development of the Great Basin. In addition to the Basques, Rancho San Rafael park displays exhibits which represent the native American Indians, the Miners and the Cowboys.

The monument complex also works as an integral part of other community-wide interests. The Monument Committee sought and received the support of the Washoe County School District, the Girl Scouts of America, the Sierra Club, the Audubon Society and others who had hoped to create a series of nature trails at the monument site that would be used to teach country schoolchildren about the environment of the valley. The monument location, paralleling the natural setting of the Basque herder, underscored the need to maintain the natural habitat of the area while adding another element to the educational value of the site. The yearly visits of hundreds, perhaps thousands, of schoolchildren to the setting advances the goals of all of the entities involved. Rancho San Rafael is also providing space and funding to develop a Basque museum in the near future, in collaboration with the Basque Studies Program at UNR.

The High Desert Museum of Bend, Oregon has developed exhibits on several of the people who have had historical impact on the high desert. The first was on the Chinese immigrants followed by a recent exhibit on Basques. In the museum's words: "With its contemporary photographs, artifacts, historic images, quotes and text, *Amerikanuak* addresses a wide variety of significant aspects of Basque culture in the region, previously interpreted only in books and scholarly research. Among the themes explored are the immigration of Basques to the Americas from their homelands in France and Spain; their role in the livestock industry and other businesses in the High Desert; the success of the Basques in maintaining their distinctive culture and lifestyle; traditional music, dance, sports and games; and the experiences of Basque women and families." The exhibit was developed with

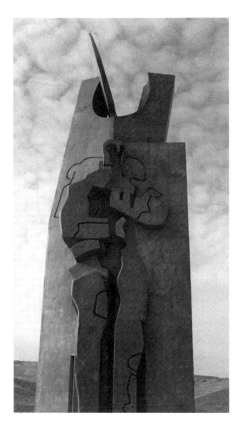

Basque Monument at Rancho San Rafael Park, Reno, Nevada. Courtesy of Basque Studies Program.

the cooperation of numerous Basque scholars, including NABO and the BSP. After a year-long exhibit in Bend, it is on a tour which will last at least three years, which includes the Boise, Idaho Basque Museum and Cultural Center, the Herrett Center for Arts and Sciences in Twin Falls, Idaho, the Redding (California) Museum of Art and History, and the Nevada State Museum in Carson City. The Smithsonian and a European museum have expressed interest as well. By all accounts, the *Amerikanuak* exhibit represents a highly professional and accurate depiction of the Basques in the West.

The Society for Basque Studies in America is a blend of academic and popular activities. It publishes a *Journal of the*

*Oreaga, a sculpture by Basque artist Nestor Basterretxea
that graces the entrance of the main library at the University
of Nevada, Reno*

Society of Basque Studies in America, which is distributed bi-
annually. It was the institutional sponsor of the National
Basque Monument. The Society is the sponsor of an annual
Basque Hall of Fame ceremony, at which it inducts Basques
of note and their significant fellow travellers from various parts
of the country and, most recently, Mexico.

The Basque American Foundation sporadically published the
Journal of Basque Studies, and, during the early part of this
decade, received funding from the Treaty of Cooperation between Spain and the U.S. to translate and publish several
Basque literary works. It also played a role in acquiring a

grant from the Minister of Education of the Basque Government to fund the Chair in Basque Studies at the University of
California, Santa Barbara. This society has not been active in
recent years, having published its last *Journal* in 1993.

Cities Carrying on Basque Community Traditions

Two western cities have developed Sister Cities Relationships
with Basque Cities: Reno, Nevada has been twinned with San
Sebastian (Gipuzkoa) since 1987, and Boise, Idaho is twinned
with Gernika (Bizkaia) since 1992. The relationships were
developed to help promote cultural and economic exchange
between the Sister Cities. To date, the relationships have
mostly produced the exchange of official delegations, but there
are hopes that they will lead to the exchange of musical, dance,
and other cultural groups. Indeed, in the summers of 1997
and 1998, the Silver Wings girls soccer team from Reno, Nevada participated in the Donosti Cup tournament hosted by
Sister City San Sebastian. The team of 16-19 year olds enjoyed the active support of both cities and of other Basque
entities. Also, at the invitation of San Sebastian, Reno Mayor
Jeff Griffin participated in the Governability and Citizen Participation in Local Administration conference held in San
Sebastian in May of 1997.

These relationships provide the potential for cultural en-
richment and, inevitably, an equal amount of frustration due
to a vastly different attitude towards the concept by both sides.
Indeed, the issue has deeper roots since, fundamentally, it
has to do with a vastly different notion of what government
should fund and in the value of culture per se. For example,
the American mayors have viewed the purpose of Sister Cities Relationships primarily as an avenue to open *economic*
links abroad. European cities, while not devoid of economic
interests, view the Sister Cities relationships as a way to fo-
ment primarily *cultural* exchanges.

To underscore these different approaches one should note
that San Sebastian, roughly the same size as Reno, has a
budget of well over a million dollars for cultural activities,
approximately $93,000 of that dedicated exclusively to its
Sister Cities relationships. Reno has a budget of approximately
$155,000 for cultural activities, with zero dollars dedicated
to Sister Cities relationships. Consequently, when Reno mayor

Pete Sferrazza visited San Sebastian for the twinning ceremony, he personally paid for his airfare. Similarly, when Boise
Mayor Dirk Kempthorne made a trip, it was sponsored by the
American Basque Foundation. Both Reno and Boise view Sister Cities as a volunteer staffed and funded activity. The European cities twinned with them view this activity as part of
their cultural patrimony, staffed and funded by professional
employees of the city. The resulting lack of equilibrium creates the perception on the part of the European partner that
the U.S. partner does not value the relationship since they
are unwilling to fund, and thus create, cultural exchanges.

State Governments

The States of Idaho, and Nevada, eager to provide the tourist
with a unique dimension, oftentimes display Basque images
as part of each state's attraction. Photographs of Basques
dressed in colorful traditional costumes regularly grace these
states' airports and tourism related publications. That is,
Basques have come to be viewed as an integral part of the
state's unique makeup and not as a unique people who came
from the Basque Country. Today, they come from, and reside
in, Nevada and Idaho.

The Basque Government

With the death of Spanish dictator Franco in 1975, and the
reestablishment of a democracy on the Iberian peninsula,
there emerged a highly autonomous government which in-
corporates the Basque Provinces of Bizkaia, Gipuzkoa and
Araba. The Basque Government controls virtually all aspects
of its territories except for the armed forces, border control
and foreign relations. In addition to the enormous impact it
has had within its territories, it has also initiated activities
directly in the Basque diaspora, as well as indirectly through
other of its dependent institutions.

Its activities abroad through the Basque diaspora are, in
part, the result of one of the competencies it is denied by the
Spanish government—that of foreign relations. While it cannot have formal foreign representatives abroad, it can engage
in cultural and economic missions. It is then in its interest to
collaborate with Basque cultural centers abroad, and through

them to promote its cultural, economic, and perhaps even political interests. In 1978, for example, on the pretext of visiting the Basque diaspora, Jose Antonio Ardanza, the Lehendakari or President of the Autonomous Basque Government, visited several Basque communities in the U.S. Along the way he met with the governors and representatives of several states, as well as with President Reagan himself.

The Government has also established an unofficial lobbying group in Washington, D.C., and has developed close institutional links with Basque centers in North and South America. In 1982 and in 1995, the Basque Government organized a Congress of Basque Centers in the homeland with over a hundred representatives from many parts of the world. One result of the last congress was the recent government purchase of computers for each of the centers abroad through which the government can keep them informed of the most recent events in the homeland. It has funded research, translations, publications, the construction of centers abroad, the visit of dignitaries and students to the Basque Country, the performance abroad of its best cultural representatives in the form of dance groups, rural sports figures, students, academics, artists, politicians and others. It has not only linked Basque Centers vertically, from the government to the center abroad, but also horizontally —center to center. For example, during the fall of 1997 William Douglass, Director of the BSP at UNR, joined other scholars on a touring lecture of centers in Latin-America. Furthermore, the government sponsored Basque television has, during the last decade, filmed documentaries of Basques in the diaspora. Not only does it give these and other video series to Basque centers in the diaspora, but it will soon begin transmission of its television channel in Latin American and, eventually, perhaps the American West. Today, the Basque government collaborates and contributes in some degree, directly or indirectly, to virtually every Basque-related entity in the U.S.

Thus, I hope it is clear that there has been a natural progression in the evolution of the Basque presence in the American West, and our knowledge of it. The first period, encompassing a century, was played out by a large group of immigrant farmers who stuck to their own kind at the margins of American society, and who left scant traces of their presence.

The second period of only twenty years represents the renaissance of Basque culture in the U.S. and the exuberance of having their ethnic differences not only become acceptable but, indeed, laudable.

The contemporary period strayed away from performance based activities to academically based ones. It tended to study Basques rather than to promote Basque identity, although of course they did this as a by-product.

If the modern period tended to be manned by volunteers, the current age is characterized by professionals in the fields of academia, government, politics, literature and the arts. In this sense, involvement in the Basque-related activities has become a livelihood for many. Their jobs depend upon accomplishing established objectives, and upon professional knowledge subjugated to that of the wider interests of the libraries, universities, and local, state, and national governments who fund them.

If the activities of the former are intended for mass consumption, the age of institutions tends to be intended for a highly motivated minority.

While distinct and separate, these two periods do not exist in isolation. Not only do they coexist, but indeed, there is considerable cross-pollination between the two worlds. For example, one young resident of Oregon first became interested in the Basques through her participation in the Oinkari Basque Dancers of Boise, Idaho. She then participated on a study abroad program in the Basque Country organized by the University Studies Abroad Consortium and studied dance with Juan Antonio Urbeltz, one of the foremost authorities of traditional Basque music and dance. She then moved to Reno, Nevada, to continue her studies with the Basque Studies Program. While in Reno, she started her own Basque dance group and, as a result of the influence of Urbeltz and her continued study of dance, made the group singular in the United States through its recreation of authentic and vastly diverse costumes, dance and music. This in turn has spurred similar changes among other dance groups. The result is a profoundly richer representation of this Basque art form and through it a much deeper appreciation of the diversity existent within the Basques themselves. She is now working on her Ph.D. in Basque Studies/History at the University of Nevada, Reno.

The resulting effect from the last three decades of institutional involvement has been to provide depth and breadth to the body of knowledge available in the English language on the Basques. The traditional way of revitalizing culture through continued immigration is a thing of the past. And yet, in the American West, this loss has not given way to cultural amnesia; rather, to a great extent, it has been compensated for by institutions who offer young Basque-Americans the knowledge and opportunity to revitalize their ethnicity in a more profound way than was available to their forefathers. The effect of these institutions has been to create an important and significant corpus of people who possess this level of knowledge, and who, in turn, are passing on to others the full richness and complexity of a unique ethnic group.

References

Aulestia, Gorka. *Basque-English Dictionary*. Reno: U of Nevada P, 1989.

Douglass, William A., and Jon Bilbao. *Amerikanuak: Basques in the New World*. Reno: U of Nevada P, 1975.

———. "Inventing an Ethnic Identity: The First Basque Festival. *Halcyon: A Journal of the Humanities* (1980): 115-130.

Gallup, Rodney. *A Book of the Basques*. Reno: U of Nevada P, 1970.

High Desert Museum. News Release. November 23, 1994.

Laxalt, Robert. *Sweet Promised Land*. New York: Harper, 1957.

Urza, Carmelo, ed. *Historia de la Pelota Vasca en Las Americas*. Donostia, Spain: Elkar, 1994.

———. *Solitude: Art and Symbolism in the National Basque Monument*. Reno: U of Nevada P, 1993.

Evolving Communities

Are You Sure You Belong?

KEVIN HEARLE

Stumbling into the bathroom at three in the morning after my twenty-year high school reunion, I heard my mother call groggily from her bedroom, "How was it?"

"It was okay." And with that I knew she would be able to gauge enough of my feelings to hold her until—over orange juice and carrot cake—we would inevitably compare reunion stories. But at breakfast, I kept circling around the notion that it had been "okay." I knew that my mother, who loved her reunions, had no problem hearing the disappointment in my voice at 3 a.m. What I wasn't sure I understood myself, however, was that my disappointment was perfectly understandable. It only makes sense that because my mother and I grew up in different worlds, we would go back to different reunions.

She was born in 1931 in a rural town of just over thirty thousand people in Southern California. Raised in the house her great-grandfather had built among the orchards he had had planted, she attended the same Southern Methodist church that the family had attended for three generations before her. When she graduated from the high school, twenty-one out of the other twenty-four members of her kindergarten class graduated with her. Later, she lived at home while she attended the nearest state college. When she got married, my father—although older—had also grown up in the

Kevin Hearle is the author of Each Thing We Know Is Changed Because We Know It, and Other Poems *and revision editor of* The Grapes of Wrath: Text and Criticism. *He is on the editorial board of* Steinbeck Newsletter, *and has taught at the University of California, Santa Cruz; San Jose State University; and California State University, Los Angeles.*

town and graduated from the same schools. In sixty-five years, she has never lived more than twenty miles from where she was born.

I was born in 1958 in a city of about one hundred thousand people which was also the county seat of the fastest growing county in the nation. The only two names I can remember from my kindergarten class are those of my then best friend and his twin sister, and I haven't seen either of them in thirty years. From my birth until I was fifteen, we lived in three houses in that city, and each one was newer and further from the decaying downtown than the one before it had been. Finally, as I entered high school, we moved to the adjacent "planned community" of Irvine. From there, I went off to a college four hundred miles away, to graduate school a thousand miles further away still, and then I married a woman from Connecticut and settled again four hundred miles from "home."

The odd thing is my mother and I were born and raised in the same hometown. Her Santa Ana was populated with innumerable maiden aunts, great-uncles, and cousins who lived just around the corner or down the block which carried the ancestral name. In her Santa Ana, people knew and at least pretended to care that her great-grandfather had been the town's first doctor. The children of her mother's schoolhood friends were her friends. It was the kind of town in which a new girl moving into her third grade class was so surprising that almost fifty years later my mother would remember her as "Suzanne from Ketchikan" and look her up on a trip to Alaska.

My Santa Ana was instead the county seat of Disneyland, and when I graduated from elementary school there was no one in my class whom I had known for more than two years. I had one schoolmate then who cared deeply about history, but, rather than being someone who would have felt comfortable in my mother's or grandmother's Santa Ana, Rodney McCaslin was a character out of Faulkner. On the playgrounds and cul-de-sacs of 1960s Orange County, Rodney would call—in a voice no more of Dixie than my own—for the glorious Confederacy to rise again in triumph, for Robert E. Lee and Stonewall Jackson to redeem their nation's promise. My family's past, which made no claims on his peculiar brand of history, was to him, as it had already proven to be for the rest of my friends, a matter of no consequence. For my classmates and the kids in the neighborhood, those transplants from other suburbs or from states whose men had won the Revolution, history was always something that had happened someplace else.

And everything around us conspired to approve their shortsightedness. When I had started school, Santa Ana had been a separate city. By the time I started junior high school only the street signs marked where one city ended and the next began in our corner of greater Los Angeles. The bean fields that had separated us from Costa Mesa and Fountain Valley became shopping malls. The orange groves that had separated us from Orange and Anaheim and Tustin gave way to housing developments. And we lived in those new houses on newly mapped streets, and spent our days in schools so new the teachers would get lost between classrooms. Every few months, a different line of eucalyptus trees would, without warning, disappear from the horizon. Then, as they had come for my family's trees not too many years before my birth, the bulldozers would come to scrape another orange grove flat, and—no longer needing fear the farmer's shotgun loaded with rock salt—we would prowl the site, trying to gauge from the wooden forms or the foundations what sort of structures were going to be built.

What we always knew, without having to say it or even think it, was that these new buildings were being built for white, middle-class people like ourselves. My mother's Santa Ana had been almost 90 percent white; my hometown was simultaneously both less and more white than my mother's had been. My Santa Ana was 30 percent African American and Chicano, but as the population grew, whites and white money increasingly fled the downtown and hastened its decay. My family was no exception. When school boundaries were redrawn in 1965, our neighborhood, which had been the one block west of Bristol to fall within the almost exclusively white Wilson Elementary zone, was shifted to the zone for a predominantly black elementary school. The summer before that redistricting became effective my parents sold our wonderful house to a black preacher and his family.

For years now, I have wondered if I was the deciding factor. Our friends on that block stayed there for a year or two before deciding to make the same move, but my schoolteacher parents—who would themselves teach for many years in just such schools—hadn't even been willing to give an integrated school a chance with their sons. I, being both large for my age and so awkward that a school psychologist would later declare me the most uncoordinated kid he had ever tested, had been constantly a source of amusement for white bullies, so I am grateful to my parents for having done their best to protect me from what they must have assumed would have been further abuse as a token white boy. Still, I have never been proud of what that decision to move away said about the kind of community we were a part of building.

Whatever the deciding factor was in the decision, we left a sprawling home with beautiful wood floors, a six car garage, and a huge yard with a grape arbor and mature plum and apricot trees for the scraped earth of a two story stucco house in a new housing development. From a house within a five-year-old's walking distance of the downtown library, we moved into what had not long before been that margin of agriculture which had helped to give Santa Ana its insular quality. For a child as different and as accustomed to retreating from the taunts of his peers as I was, that first backyard had been a haven. The new yard threw me and my brothers first out into the street and later over the back fence into the new schoolyard to play. And that was only appropriate. We hadn't moved because of the quality of the two houses. We had moved because of the quality of the two schools.

It seemed then that, other than the city park in Orange (across the new scar of the Garden Grove Freeway), Fairhaven Cemetery was the only place exempt from the chamber of commerce impulse to wipe the earth clean. At different times that exemption seemed to me to be a blessing or a curse, because, being the last branch of the family in town, we were the keepers of the graves and the hosts upon whose table each funeral feast was spread. I learned my family history while trimming grass away from the graves of my grandmother's parents and sisters and brothers. And so, for me, the past of Santa Ana, which had everywhere else been scraped clean of me and mine, will always be buried in that cemetery. Although I can no longer find them among the rows of headstones, I know that my mother's family names live on there in the old plots. And, as my family did for generations before me, I have stood at the fresh graves of my own great aunts and great uncles and grandmother. There are only two gravesites left. One is for my mother's older cousin. The last one will be my mother's. That is only fitting; they each will belong there in ways I never have and never will.

So I approached my high school reunion much differently than my mother has approached each one of hers. Not only has she attended her reunion every five years, she has been on the organizing committee. In fact, the week before my twentieth reunion, my mother had been to a potluck to plan for her class fifty-year reunion, which was still three years off.

For me, the twenty year reunion was my first. It wasn't that I had been indifferent to my past before; there were good reasons I hadn't seen these people in twenty years. I had lived elsewhere and been in school for much of the time. Also, no one in the class had organized a five- or a fifteen-year reunion, and the ten-year had fallen on a date when I had already been obliged to be out East.

Still, when presented with the opportunity, I had not displayed my mother's zeal for organizing. In December, as the twenty-year anniversary approached, I had called University High School in Irvine and asked for information on a reunion. No one there had known of any plans for anything. For my mother, that would have been a call to action. I waited a month and called back. In January, the school gave me the first name—Cindy—and phone number of a woman in Nevada who had appointed herself to head the committee. Cindy's response to my call was to allow as how she didn't recognize my name and then to ask if I was sure I had been in the class. A man more like my mother would have responded, "Yes, I was student body president." I merely admitted that I didn't recognize her name either and assured her that I had been a member of the class. When she tested me by saying surely, though, I remembered her brother-in-law who had been voted class clown, I agreed that I remembered Greg.

And yet for me, high school had been more about forgetting than it had been about remembering. When I entered University High School in September of 1973, knowing there only my younger brother and a few girls I had met at the pool, I began to understand for the first time the powerful attraction of a life in which the past is private. No one at my new high school had ever pitied me or mocked me as the neighborhood freak. No one could have remembered me as the second grader whose hands had been so unruly he couldn't tie his shoes. No one there had seen me at the eighth-grade dance, managing only to move either my hands or my feet to the music but never both together. No one there knew that at fifteen-and-a-half I had never kissed a girl, had a girlfriend, or even held a girl's hand. And none of the teachers in that only three-year-old school knew my older brother, the brilliant and arrogant screw-up, who had preceded me through every other grade. It was appropriate that as I approached my reunion I was once again a stranger; after all, the most important lesson I had learned in high school was how to remake myself.

From the preparations alone I knew my reunion was going to be different than my mother's had always been. The days around her reunions had always been marked with a festivity akin to New Year's Eve. One or another of her old classmates would arrive with their families a day early or stay a day late, and my brothers and I would either finally get to meet these mythic characters or perhaps renew our acquaintance. At the reunions themselves, my mother would work the registration table and almost never have to ask anyone's name.

I approached my reunion with something resembling a sickening fascination. Twenty years before, I had been voted "the boy most likely to succeed," and now the head of the reunion committee didn't recognize my name. On the other hand, knowing even in high school that I wanted to be a writer, I had voted that Jeff Hassett would be the successful one. As the date grew nearer, my dread became more palpable. Cindy, whom even after looking at the yearbook I still didn't remember, had ceded control to a company that specialized in arranging reunions. Their questionnaires were inane, and the prices were outrageous. More importantly, none of the three friends from my class with whom I had always kept in touch was going to be there. Jon Mark had to be in New Orleans for a committee of emergency physicians. Trent had made his own reunions earlier in the year when he and Pat had driven down from Seattle to take the kids to Disneyland. And John had simply decided that at

$80 per person he wasn't interested. Who, I wondered, would I see?

I was right to have gone. It turned out not to be the out-of-body experience of my worst imagining, but it wasn't the perfect resolution of anything either. It was merely, as I had anticipated in my more reasonable moments, disappointing. There was no one there I was sorry to see again, and there were a number of people it was pleasant to catch up with; however, only Juliette made me feel that the years of absence from each others' lives had been perhaps regrettable.

Mostly, I felt a sense of absence. The odd friends I had treasured because they had never tried to fit in, stayed away. The neighborhood girls who had thrown me a surprise party for my sixteenth birthday weren't there. My first girlfriend, the girl who had taught me love only to break my heart and then avoid me for nineteen years, didn't show. But I had expected those absences. The surprising absence was the one I felt as I spoke with the people who were there.

Maybe I would have had a better time had I gone to my mother's last reunion rather than to my own twenty- year festivities. With my mother's classmates, at least, I share a past which lasted longer than high school. I have either known them or their stories all my life. I have been to their family weddings. One of them taught me to ski and stayed with us over the years while her mother slowly died. The daughter of another was the first woman to take me to bed. I have learned about myself and my family by how we have lived with these people, and so they are at least as much a part of my family as are the dead in their graves at Fairhaven.

And yet, I went to the right reunion. Because—in my own way—I grew up there, I already know most of the lessons my mother's reunion had to offer. Because I could have walked into one of her Santa Ana High School class of '49 reunions and had my name and heritage recognized, the temptation for me is to pretend that my mother's hometown was a better place than mine was. I know better than that, though. I know that on the morning of May 25, 1906, the Santa Ana city council voted to evict approximately two hundred Chinese and to burn down Chinatown. I have read the newspaper account which states that one thousand townspeople turned out that same evening in the rain to cheer the fire. And I also know that the parents of Marie Chan, my mother's friend from kindergarten through high school, never told her why they were the only Chinese-American family in town. In my own home, I remember all too well my grandmother's diatribes against Catholics for rating Mary with Jesus and God. I know that I would not have wanted to be conspicuously different in my mother's hometown. And I know that as first a child born with congenital defects that would then have been beyond correction, and later as a poet, a liberal Democrat, and an agnostic, I would have been both conspicuous and different.

Yet that doesn't do Santa Ana or my grandmother justice. Having been a hunchback from the age of three, my grandmother understood something about prejudice, but my mother, having been friends all her life with Harold who was gay and with Marie Chan, didn't understand prejudice well at all. When her sorority rejected affiliation with the national organization because they would have had to kick out all but the white girls, my mother was shocked by the controversy. She told her mother she didn't understand how people could be bigots, and, to my mother's astonishment, grandmother replied, "I'm a bigot, but I never wanted you to be."

So, if my mother's reunions are about the importance of memory to knowing who you are, they are also about acceptance and love. Those are worthy causes for celebration, and I will continue to welcome the stories they generate every five years. I, on the other hand, expect that in the future I will side with the odd friends and fellow exiles I treasured back in high school because they were so tenaciously themselves.

That's not fair either. Unlike me, most of the people at the reunion had never left Southern California after high school, and many of them had stayed in touch with one another. Perhaps over the years they have developed a shared sense of values that I never knew, or that—in my rush to leave behind Orange County and my crumbling family—I abandoned twenty years ago. Perhaps their children will go from kindergarten through high school with the same twenty other kids. Perhaps they and their children will feel about the removal of a favorite restaurant or store the way my family and I once did about the disappearing orange groves. I don't know, but it is their place now rather than mine. The only fair judgment I can make about us is that, if we were friends or even something more once, we are strangers now. If there is any blame for that, it's mine. I am the one who left.

And, if my mother's Santa Ana has taught me anything, it's that communities need to be grounded in both place and history. I, on the other hand, have grown accustomed to rarely seeing most of my closest friends. It's been over two years since Re and Glenn moved back to Colorado. Dozier and I have commiserated exclusively by mail over the pains of life and art for six years now. And it has been seven years since Rafa was last out from Spain. Trading letters a couple of times a year or talking on the phone for an hour is not the same as being together and annoying each other or fighting but staying friends anyway. Perhaps Cindy was right to ask if I had been a member of the class.

Erika, my love, I miss you and will probably always wish you all the best. More importantly, though, I think I now understand the years of silence. Good-bye. Inger Shiffler, Patty Commerford, Pat Collentine, Lauren Mayer and all the rest of the individualists of my memory, wherever you are, whoever you are now, feel free to call whenever. Five years would be too long. Juliette, I'm glad you were there. Let's keep in touch. The rest of you, I wish you well. Just don't expect to see me.

Four Poems
on Southwestern Cities

STEVEN SCHROEDER

Dallas

*Borger and Phillips were boom towns built on the oil
economy in the Texas Panhandle, unbuilt when the
economy failed. A shadow of Borger remains, nothing
of Phillips.*

Yeah, I've seen Dallas
from the air
edgewise, from the ground,
and from the middle
on a tightrope curb stretched alongside
an endless Mary Kay Cosmetics plant.
Lights or no, it ain't a pretty sight.

When the man said Dallas was made of God and oil,
He was just short of half right.
Dallas is made of money.
The city of God and oil
Is between Borger clinging to life
And the absence where Phillips was.

---

*Steve Schroeder is Associate Professor of Religion and Phi-
losophy at Capital University in Ohio. A native of the Texas
Panhandle, he now divides his time between Chicago and
Capital's Dayton Center.*

Mockingbird

After visiting Austin for the first time
a friend of mine recalled a car alarm
set off by wind that set off a mockingbird
who sang a mock alarm in real time
a mockingbird who sang
a culture made of mirrors
and a disturbing song

Austin is better as a figment
of imagination
than as a city
and Texas as a state
of mind.
Both in memory
sing music
seldom heard
in places out of mind
and neither in memory
is composed of August heat
that cultures yoghurt on the back porch
breeds rangers rednecks George W cockroaches
to make you expecting a human presence
answer the door
and the cat faint
when they scrabble against it.
Exile and memory
make the place
a dip in a cold spring
a drink with friends
a mockingbird
that sings visions
not mirrors
like Dallas
of infinite regression
and car alarms.

San Antonio

Two streams meander under a city with no center,
Parallel. I make a third with a faster current
And almost overlook the stone friar
Standing at a river bend,
Amused by this encounter
With another ghost out of time,
Hand raised in blessing
Equally bestowed on the two streams flowing,
The third I make, still, and a mall
That is no place at his left hand—
A shrine to sameness for pilgrims on holiday.

In the guidebook history begins
With a stream of Europeans
Who remember the Alamo,
Forget the Payaya, and know
Not the river, but the day they came upon it,
Who build fortresses and call them missions
In the name of the hammer of heretics.

Coming up from the river of pilgrims below the street,
I am startled by the light and a man in uniform
Trained to smile at tourists and speak a word of greeting
In the language of this place: *haaidee.*
The alamo is smaller than the myth and smaller still than
    the memory.
North along a deserted street in occupied territory
At the edge of power a man who has found something
meets me
Outside a museum. In another language, he says,
    unfolding it,
I don't expect no free ticket, but I found this. . . .
I look like the power is mine
But point to people in uniform at the desk inside.
Talk to them? he says.
I slip past and see him stumble out a moment later.
A man who is looking for something crosses the street.

Hey big man. Hey big man.
I look like the power is mine.
Hey big man, you got a quarter?
Sorry.
Smoke?
Don't smoke.
Keep walking
Back to the center
Look like the power is mine.
The alamo is smaller still than the memory.

Elk City Dialogue

Old man tells me he don't get no chance in Oklahoma
So he takes his chances in Texas, two a week.
Gettin' hot agin he says and puts his chances in the register
As I shut the door on pavement-melting heat.
He's been fingering them, filling long intervals between
　　customers with hope.
Looks like it I say *Think you come out ahead?*
Naw. But they's always a chance: twenty million this time.
I say *Guess that's what keeps people goin'.*
And he says *Man I knowed played the same number*
Ever' week for fi'teen years.
Figgered he had to hit it sometime.
Missed a week.
Number come up.
Put a gun in his mouth.
Bet on a sure thang.

"A Child Goes Forth"

A community project by members of the
Unnamed Writers' Group:
Chuck Alvey, Jennifer Baumer, Kay Fahey, Wilda Garber, Cindie Geddes, Diane Glazman, Diane Green, Heidi Hart, Kelli Nicolato, Paula Riley, and Carol Waldren

There was a child went forth every day,
And the first object he looked upon and received with
  wonder or pity or love or dread, that object he became,
And that object became part of him for the day or a
  certain part of the day . . . or for many years
  or stretching cycles of years.

Walt Whitman, 1855

The idea behind this project was simple—to let the children of homeless families tell their stories. We listened to the children tell us what it is like to grow up in a family whose place of residence may be a car, a shelter, a relative's apartment, or temporary housing. We asked them to tell us about their dreams, their fears, their favorite toys, their last birthday, their parents, their teachers, their pets. Most important, we wanted them to share their stories with the public in their own words.

The Unnamed Writers' Group was founded in the fall of 1995 by Kay Fahey, Cindie Geddes, and Carol Davis Luce. The mission of the group is to help published and pre-published writers to write better and to be more successful. Presently the group has roughly two hundred members throughout northern Nevada and the Sierra. The group not only sponsors writers' workshops and critique groups, but is engaged in community projects as well.

Carolyn, David, and Calvin
Interviews by Wilda Garber and Heidi Hart
Photographs by Diane Glazman

Carolyn, David, and Calvin live with their mother in a small subsidized home in Stead. Boxes and clothes filled the living-room; a friend of the family was moving in. We interviewed the children one at a time on the front porch. Large bees circled empty pizza boxes on the porch. Several broken bicycles lay on the grass.

Carolyn (transcript by Heidi Hart), age twelve, sat on a plastic stool in front of us and didn't make eye contact at first. Sometimes she turned to scold her brothers, who had just come back from sliding on a friend's mattress down the street and kept interrupting her. When we asked Carolyn to describe her idea of "home," she shrugged and said, "I don't know, a place to stay." When asked to describe herself, she said, "Long eyelashes."

> I'm in seventh grade. I don't really know yet what my favorite class is, but I like reading and math. I like my science teacher, he's kind of funny, but I don't like science. We just do measurements and stuff like that. I did like this class I took called "Being Your Best," that gives you tips on how to do your hair and makeup and what colors look good on you. I haven't found out yet what colors look good on me. So far we've just been taking personality tests, and one of the things that I found out was what would be a good job for me . . . a legal secretary, or a doctor, or a physician. I'd like to be a doctor or a lawyer someday.
>
> After school I like to call my friends, go play with my friends, ride my bike, and baby-sit. I have two best friends right now, Lisa and Ofelia. Ofelia is a Mexican name. We like to play games, talk, watch TV. I like to go roller-blading at the skating rink, the one over there when you're on I-80 or whatever, there's a Best West hotel or something like that, and it's back

Carolyn.

in by that. It's called King Skate. I like to get books from the school library, too. I like mysteries, and all kinds of scary books, like the Goosebumps books, and there's some other ones, like "Fear Street."

I baby-sit after school, too. There's a girl that works as a janitor at the school, the elementary school, so Monday and Tuesday her dad baby-sits her kids, and Wednesday her husband's off, so I baby-sit Thursday and Friday. They have two kids, a boy and a girl. The boy just turned three not too long ago and the girl's, like, seven months.

For my last birthday, we stayed home, we didn't really have a party or anything. I just had one friend come over, and we had ice cream and cake. I got money instead of presents, and I used the money to take a baby-sitting class. They didn't really teach us CPR, but I already know CPR pretty well because of my brother Calvin . . . We had to learn it because he was having heart problems. At the baby-sitting class they did teach us the Heimlich, and how to clear the airway, and they gave us this binder that has like, all these papers in it, in case you don't know what to do if something happens to the baby or whatever. And they gave us some papers for the kids to color, and some activities for them to do.

I like kittens. That's the biggest cat that we have, right there. That's J.C. And then we have two that are about the same age. One's black, and one's Siamese. Our dog just had puppies, but I don't know where they are, we don't have them no more. I don't know what my mom did with them because I was in California.

Before this I lived in Ridgecrest, California. I still like Sacramento and San Diego, because it's green. I get to go to California to see my aunt in the summer, and I like that because we go school shopping and swimming. We just had a family reunion in August, no, July, and we went to San Luis Obispo. We also got to go to San Francisco to take Calvin to the Shriners' Hospital, because my dad's girlfriend, she works for Social Services, and so she told my mom to get him into Shriners', just for an appointment to see if everything was okay. He was three months early, and he had surgery, but he still walks on his tippy-toes sometimes.

I don't know where my real dad lives, but my stepdad lives in Reno. Me and my mom have moved around, but only two or three times. Right now my mom's friend is moving in with us. I don't have to share a room, but this guy who's staying with us, he puts his stuff in my room, and sometimes, like when I get up for school, he gets home from work, so he goes in my room and takes a nap. So I'm kind of sharing a room.

If I could have anything in the world . . . I don't know, a new car or a new house, I guess. If I could go on vacation anywhere, it would be . . . Disneyworld.

David (transcript by Jennifer Baumer), age seven, talked of his favorite things at school:

Recess. I play at recess. Chase my friend Josh's friends off. He has girls that chases him. This one girl, his [points to his brother] old girlfriend, when you go RARR! she'll go [pulls arms in and makes a face.] She's always scared.

David's favorite subject:

We do pudding math. You write! With your fingers, with pudding. It's fun. Our teacher is the funnest teacher in the school. Yeah, this year we had chocolate and last year vanilla. When you make a letter, when you get one right, you get to eat with your finger, your whole finger.

David's favorite food . . . besides pudding:

Pizza. They got this . . . they got this, um, rectangu-
lar pizza. It's good. I like pepperoni.

David's favorite pet:

Cat and dog. [My dog's name is] Duchess. And my
cat's name is Buddy. He grabs your hair. He chases
you around because he likes hair. All the cats sleep
on my bed 'cause my bed's the highest bed in the
house. I got a bunk bed. [I share a room with] two
brothers. My sister gets her own room. But when we
move into a bigger house out in the country, I'm
going to have my own bedroom.

When are you going to move into a bigger house in the country?

I don't know! My dad's going to. And I'm going to
have my own bedroom, and Tom's going to have his
own bedroom, and Calvin's just going to have his
stuff in his bedroom . . . toys for Dad's, toys for
Mom's house . . .

David's dad:

He lives at Shamrock (trailer park). [I see him] every
other weekend. Um, we like, go swimming, we go to
Circus Circus sometimes, we go to the Silver Legacy
sometimes, and then sometimes we might even go to
see his friend . . . He has quail, not the kind with
those things on their head, the kind that doesn't.
And he has quail that pecks on the birds' heads and
the fur comes off . . . and he has other animals. He
has geese, he has chickens, he has . . . he used to
have pigs, but he killed his pigs. He always eats the
pigs. But he don't got no more. He lives out in the
desert, out over there. His name's Art.

David's favorite things to do in the summer:

[I like to ride my bike] . . . a whole bunch. But the
tire's broke. I skidded on it.

What David wants to be when he grows up:

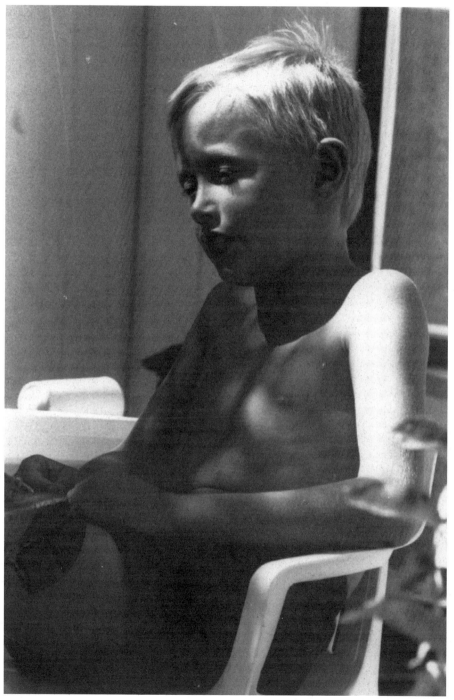

David.

I haven't thought about that . . . maybe . . . a police officer.

David's favorite things to do:

There's too much [to talk about]. There's like a hundred and one. A motorcycle is my first one, and bike racing is my second favorite. There's a new kid down there, he . . . his two younger brothers, they all bike race, his one brother, Josh, is the meanest. And they all three race. And Josh, he always messes up his bikes. He popped a wheelie, about this high, and his tire popped. I got a GT. And Jacob wants my GT Net. I got a skateboard I like to ride. Better than a bicycle! 'Cause you don't even have to jump, you don't even have to pull up, you just fly.

Sports David plays:

I play baseball. T-ball. I got my trophy in my house. I'm playing for the Dodgers. My friend, Johnny, he has a trampoline, and I go about this high, I go like this . . . and . . . .BOOM! I jump as high as four people.

David's friends in the area:

My friend, Tyler, he's the only friend I got around here. Except Johnny, when Johnny's home I can play with him, and Jacob, and Jason. I don't play with Josh 'cause he's mean! [Tyler is a good friend] 'cause he always plays what I want to play . . . and he plays . . . I play what he wants to play. When I first met him, this girl moved out of the house and Tyler moved in, and I saw Tyler and I asked him what's your name and he said, "Tyler" and from then on when we were both six — my birthday's before him, and I went to his birthday party — and we have sleepovers and he . . . and I invited him to my birthday but he never came. I got a truck from Jacob and Josh and Jason, but I didn't really want Josh to go. 'Cause my mom didn't let us . . . October 13th was my birthday. Calvin's is before me. He'll be six and I'll be eight.

Calvin with his bike

Do you like each other? You get along?

> Not that often.

It's kind of hard to have brothers sometimes, isn't it?

> He's the nicest brother I got, Jeffrey is.

Calvin (transcript by Wilda Garber), age five:

> I'm Calvin, can I talk too?

> I'm going to be six, September, um September 17. My name's Calvin. I don't know how long we've been living here [Reno]. I been going visiting my Dad. I like to go swimming and go ride my bike. Only now I can't 'cause it got ran over [by the lady who lives here with us]. It's all scratched up. Sometimes I get to ride my brother's bike, but not right now 'cause he's gone up the street.

> I like to climb stuff, too. I always climb the monkey bars and I'm in first grade. I do lots of papers and

homework in school. No, I don't take any home, I just do them at school and I color. We get to go on recess and I swing. I can go high and I'm the fastest runner.

My favorite food is chicken, roasted chicken.

The dog is my favorite pet 'cause she saves us. Yeah, 'cause every night we see guys that come up to our window and the dog bites 'em. Her name is Duchess. This one guy, he was climbing over the fence, and my dog bit him. On the arm. He went away real fast. He was afraid of my dog. Thought it was a [Rotweiler], and it ain't.

I didn't have a birthday party, but I had a whole bunch of presents. Last year, I got a new bike, the one that's broke.

Yeah, I like my brother, but not that much because he always hits me. He's down the street.

From right: Jeffrey, Calvin, and David.

I'm going to kill the bee [running after it with a tennis ball]. I play pitcher and first baseman for the Dodgers team, and sometimes catcher, too. I keep catching the balls. I keep getting out, and out, and out [Calvin runs with mitt and ball] and oh! lost the ball. . . .

Joey, Kristopher, Ronny
Interviews by Cindie Geddes and Kay Fahey
Photographs by Carol Waldren

It was a beautiful, sunny day, but Ronny and Kristopher wanted to sit inside their apartment where they could color and snack on veggies and ham and crackers while we sipped our lemonade. Sitting across from each other at the big kitchen table, they each talked to an interviewer, occasionally interjecting comments into each other's stories. Throughout the hours we spent with the young cousins we were introduced to Dudley the Dragon, a doll who'd lost his name, several toy cars, a live iguana, two birds, a cat, and the two women the boys live with—their aunt Ginger and Kristopher and Joey's mother, Sandy—all were quite friendly and polite except Dudley who insisted on trying to eat the tape recorder.

Next we went outside with Kristopher's older brother, Joey (eleven), who showed us his prized skateboard and perched high on a cement staircase as we interviewed him while his friends watched in envy.

Joey (transcript by Kay Fahey), age eleven, told us:

I moved here from Colorado. I like Colorado a little better because there's no drive-bys. The Fourth of July I jumped on the floor because of firecrackers. I thought it was gunshots. I was sleeping on the couch and I woke up to it. All of them went up at one time, it was like bambambambam and I go, "Aaaghh. Hit the floor! I heard gunshots!" My aunt looks outside and there's a bunch of firecrackers shooting off in the air. Everybody's up there on the third floor watching them.

We keep hearing drive-bys, but we never see anybody. We just hear people fighting and then all of a
sudden there's gunshots. Sometimes you'll hear
gunshots and then cars driving off really fast. One
time we heard one of them, it sounded like it
crashed going around that corner. It takes at least
five seconds if you're going fast to get around that
corner. I did it on my bike, and I almost killed
myself because I had no brakes and I went down a
big old huge hill.

All my friends usually ride their bikes around the
lake. There's only one thing I hate. I had a really
nice bike that I got from Colorado that I was fixing
up. It had brakes so I could pedal backwards and it
had hubcaps for a bike. It had everything on it that
a kid could want, and it got stolen.

I know for one thing Ronny's uncle will steal my
cards and sell them for drugs. That's why my aunt
doesn't like him, because he's a thief and a liar
and a drug user. She doesn't really care about the
drugs, because he barely does them. He went
through my dresser and stole a lot of socks. He
doesn't have any socks. Another reason I don't
like staying with my aunt: she washes her dishes
with dirty socks. And I didn't like staying over at
her house because she always threw a bunch of
stuff on us while we were sleeping. She'd go to bed
really late. She'd have towels and laundry on her
bed and she'd take it all and throw it everywhere. It
was a disaster in there.

And Ronny's afraid of the dark and he's scared of
having the bedroom door shut because his Mom
would shut the door and lock him in there, lock him
in his bedroom and keep the light off. She actually
broke off the light switch to keep it off. They got in
trouble from their manager by doing that.

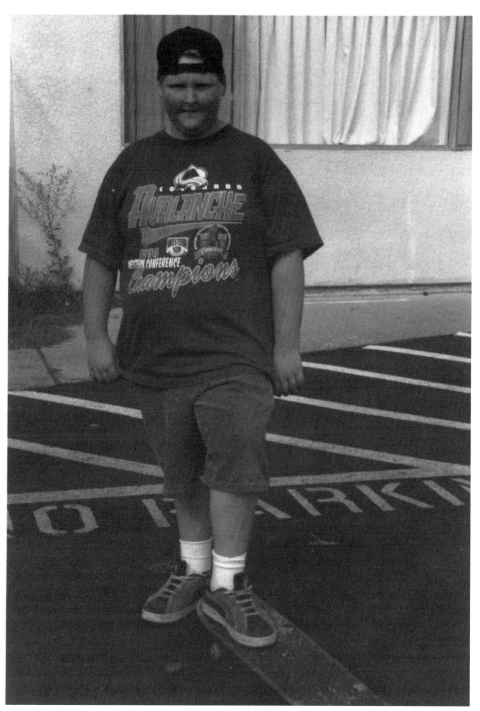

Joey.

What do you want to be?

> Marine biologist. Because I like whales and the sea
> and sea animals. Or an auto mechanic, because my
> Grandpa's got his own shop and if I study it, he
> could leave it to me.

> I like year-round school better because you get
> shorter breaks, which I sorta like because you don't
> forget as much. You barely forget anything. But on a
> three month's vacation, you forget everything you
> learned and they spend most of the school year
> teaching us it again. While here they get the idea to
> us, and then we start with new things. And all the
> teachers are nice except for last year's teacher,
> which I'm glad retired. All the kids did celebrate
> when he retired at the end of the year. He was just
> really mean. I got bad grades all last year and now
> this year I'm getting really, really good grades com-
> pared to last year. Now I'm showing my teacher in
> sixth grade that it was just him and not me.

> I like it down here because . . . there's one reason.
> Because all my friends live around me. I like a
> seventh grader. She used to live right across the
> hallway from me. I used to get beat up at school by
> these kids in her class. I told her to talk to them and
> she did. She told them if they didn't stop that she'd
> come over to their house and personally beat them
> up in front of their Mom. So everybody in her class
> liked her.

> One of the reasons we moved is my aunt died there.
> Grandma says if she loses one more child she's
> gonna die herself, because this is like the third
> death she's had. My Mom's Mom, my cousin's Mom
> and she lost her husband, my Grandpa. I miss him.
> And I miss my Grandma because she always gave
> me football cards and baseball cards. She had
> stacks and stacks of them. Now I'm collecting comic
> books and cards, which are better, because they're

Ronny.

worth more. I have lots of them. I have one that was made in 1988, so I think it's old.

I'm Grandma's little boy. I lived a block away from her. I'd sneak out of my house really early, go over there. She'd make me breakfast—pancakes, eggs. She'd make omelets with cheese in them, sometimes cheese and ham. It was fun. I miss my other Grandma, too, who lives in California. She made big old huge breakfasts. She had a pig down there that got slaughtered while we were down there. But that's what they're raised for. And she gets all the meat free. One day we had bacon, one day we had sausage.

My Grandma was always out with our aunt. Gambling. You know what's funny? She said she had a secret. She'd put quarters in the refrigerator or the freezer and she'd take them and put them in a slot machine. She goes, "Cold quarters rigs the machines." She said if you dropped a cold quarter in it would mess up the machine and make you win.

Do you think that's true?

Nah.

Or your Grandma would be rich?

She sorta is. She has her own house.

Kristopher (transcript by Kay Fahey), age six, asks:

Guess what I like? Giraffes. Because at the Denver Zoo, guess what? They have a white giraffe named Lu the Giraffe and he's my best giraffe in the whole wide world now and I miss him. I lived in the Denver, but I moved out here now.

Which do you like better?

Denver. Because the baby giraffe is over there and my Grandma's over there. You know why I like giraffes? You know what brontosaurus is? They eat

Kristopher.

leaves. Well, I like brontosaurus because they eat leaves and giraffes eat leaves.

My grandpa lives in California. In the jungle. He lives in the jungle on a farm. You know my Mom's Mom died? So my Grandpa married someone else named Grandma Kay. Guess what? He has a pig bigger than me. Two big pigs, like four hundred pounds, live outside. One's black and white and one's pink. You can lock up all the animals, but the two big pigs stay out. One pig would bite our trailer. Guess what? The black and white pig was trying to get out and put his nose under the fence and lifting the fence. I'll tell you what her feet look like. It's like big pig's feet. They stepped on your feet it would hurt them bad.

At my Grandpa's house they wouldn't let us watch 911. We had to stay in the kitchen eating ice cream. Before dinner we always eat ice cream.

You know what school I go to? Anderson. It's just right down the street from us. Everyone is my friend at school, even in my big brother's class before school. My teacher's name is Ms. Oliveria. I have a lunch ticket.

What do you like for lunch?

Pizza. With meat on it. And chocolate milk. We get to pick all what we want.

They have a little playground there. The kindergartens had to stay in the little one and I get to play baseball in the big kid's playground. They have a big slide that makes you go fast. You hold on right on the edge and go whooo and it makes you go fast.

Some people chase me and I chase them. I like it. And guess who chases me? Salvador. It's fun. He growls like a lion. He's six and he's a lot bigger than me but I run faster than him.

It's fun at recess time. Everybody go out and play for like, until the bell rings. After lunch recess you get two bells. When the first bell rings you can still play. If the second bell rings you get to go back in.

Guess what there was in the swimming pool? You know those eels that look like eels, but they shock you? In the water by the deep end I saw an eel shock. I got out of there. In the deep end, I can swim in it. It's seven foot. I can go to the bottom.

How did you learn to swim?

My Mom just threw me in. So I tried to swim and I did. I just learned easy. I can swim from the middle to the deep end. Guess what? I pushed my brother in the water.

You know those other apartments over there? They don't have a swimming pool so they come over here to our apartment's swimming pool. Our manager tells them to get out and go back to your house. That's what he says. That will make them learn to stay out of these apartments. Because we live in these apartments. I think we're going to win Megabucks and guess what? We're going to buy a big house with our own swimming pool and at night we can go swimming.

Is your brother a good brother?

Sometimes. But he throws fits, sometimes. He kicks the door. I sleep out here in the living room. Because they put everything on my bed, all their stuff and my stuff. They move my stuff. I can't sleep on my bed.

Whoever is beating up my big brother, I'm going to beat 'em. Then they get hurt. You know why? I'm more bigger and I'm more tougher. Guess what? He grabbed my foot and hit my nose. Because we were practicing fighting. Then I got really mad.

I'm six. He's eleven. When I'm five birthdays, I'm going to be eleven.

What will you do when you're eleven?

Go to park every day. They have basketball court and swing and slide. They have a lot. And there's tunnels to go through a tunnel slide. You have to crawl through the little tunnels. One goes in and one goes out. My Mom taught me how to pump. You know how they pump the swings to get high?

My Mom works at graveyard. At night, at WalMart. She unloads boxes. My aunt works at pizza at night. So at my Mom's day off, my aunt goes out. Ginger's day off, my Mom works. Every time she goes to work at night I sneak in her bed and sleep there and she comes home and she snuggles me. . . .

Ronny (transcript by Cindie Geddes), age five, when asked about his mother:

Shelly(?). She don't live nowhere. She's in a car somewhere. But she has a little baby with her that's my little brother. Sometimes he bites. But I don't do nothing. He's one. But he's getting a lot of teeth. When he's biting me I don't feel no teeth. I only feel gums. I can draw m-o-m.

Where he lived before Reno:

My mom. Texas. But I do not like Texas. Big dog. But he does not like the back yard. We stick our head in there and he runs after. And a gate. But every time when we look in there, he runs after the gate. Actually we stood him. But this man who lives

Kristopher and Ronny at a "getting to know you" picnic.

next door, he says come pet him if he's out in the front yard. He likes that, but he don't bite.

I went to the ocean once and it scared me. I used to live in California too. But I do not want to go to the ocean again. Sweeping waves. You know what they do? They pull us back in where the sharks eat us and the whales. Only if we have a gun that you can kill whales or sharks. That's when we can go in. I can ride in the sand if someone else is riding close to the sweeping waves.

Know why we went there? To see our little pig. We had him there but Grandma and Grandpa took it. We get eggs at Grandma and Grandpa's. Easter Bunny brings us.

But I do not like Halloween. 'Cause a man in a mask had a werewolf. But it was a mask. For Halloween, I'm gonna be a drackyla. You know, how they suck

blood? I been watch all old movies about it. I watch
one vampire threw a cape over him and bite a
woman. There's this stuff, what my mom put on,
even I was a fake drackyla, then I like suck it in. It
had red stuff in it. You know what this thing is? (he
draws a Dracula) Gotta make those cape. Don't
know how to make a bat. This is the big old cape.
'Cause he has big cape. Know why? So no one can
look what they're doing. The people.

Even I like Christmas. I like the elves best. Santa.
But he don't bring no presents. I think the dogs do.
He has elves. Where they build all the toys. In the
sky. Reindeer. They fly. And they land on the roof.
Did you know in the middle of the night, I woke, I
heard some bells on the reindeer. I seen, first I
rested, then I went up and got up on the roof.
Santa, he sent me up to help him. I took fast toys
and throw down the chimney and come back up. It
was just a dream.

What he would want if he could have one wish, while drawing
a shark:

I don't know. That's a shark thing. The thing on the
back. This is what a ocean look like. We sat on a big
rock. I'll make it. Grandma, Grandpa. This is this.
Sandy. Joey. I'm gonna draw him in the water.

We have a lizard. Over there. That tank. But that's a
mean one. He whacks his tail. With his short nose
he whips out a stick. Herman. Got him from these
people.

See the fish. That one. We had two, but one died.
He's Big Eye and the other one was Little Eye. That's
what we named them. There's another one. But I do
not like sharks. But I like Free Willies. 'Cause
they're nice. But in the ocean, they do bite. Only if

you have a gun they don't bite. They just swim
away. That's only for a movie. Not real. If its real.
Did you know me and Kris saw a whale jump? In
the water. You know, like Free Willy does? In the
ocean.

I can draw a shark's thing where they stick up and
you know where the shark is. Does it look like it?
Yeah? I really saw the shark. But I can swim. In the
swimming pool. Even I can act like a Free Willy.
Without fins. I can swim in the six foot and the five
foot and the three foot. But I always go at the bottom. To get the keys. Dive for the keys. That's what
they told. Gin threw us in. That's when we started to
swim.

When asked what his favorite animal is, as he begins to draw
a lion:

A hairy lion. 'Cause they're mean. I would like to be
mean. It's hard, but he's grown on, and he's kinda
hairy. I used to know how to make one. Because
they attack. This one's gonna be hard. (Explains his
new drawing) Can't tell. You have to find out. Pretend this one's on the back, okay? 'Cause you don't
know what it is! Where's black. Stripe, stripe, stripe,
stripe, stripe, stripe. Now you know what it is?
Starts with this. A zebra! I made a z. Like that, that,
that.

When asked what his favorite thing about school is:

Uh. Eat lunch. Mmm, but we have to wait 'til lunch
is ready. They have chocolate milk and white milk.
They have three pitchers, one is chocolate, one is
blue, one is red. I like chocolate.

I don't like someone in my class because one said a
bad word and they went to talk to the office to talk
to him. Even Allison Huffaker said shut up to Sam
on the bus. He went to the office. I never say bad
words.

(He begins to draw) Okay. It's gonna be very tricky. Guess what that is. It's an angel bringing an x down (he scribbles very hard across the page). Ground. Where they put the children. Which I don't like the bad ones.

About his favorite toy, Dudley the Dragon:

Dudley. Want me to go get it? It needs to be here, where it can show (puts recorder in Dudley's hand). See his teeth (pointing to the stuffed dragon)? And spines. 1, 2, 3, 4, 5, 6, 7, 8, 9, 10, 11, 12, 13, 14, 15, 16, 17, 18. He just sleeps with me. Dudley watches out after me 'cause the cat tries to wake me up. His name is Cricket. He just sits down and watches. But, but you can't come in our room. It's messy. This make our room at night and in the morning it gets a mess. We think it's a mess monster. You know, they pull all the stuff on the floor. But I watched them. One was green with polka dots. They're little. I think they're littler than Chuckie. Do you know if I bring one into Chuckie's shop, they could bite him. I don't think it's the mess monsters. I think it's Cricket. I think it's her.

When I scratch his back, he likes it? (He puts Dudley in his lap and rubs the dragon's back scales.) He likes that. Sometimes I tickles him. (Puts Dudley next to the recorder) "Hello." Dudley! He likes one of those. Hey, what's up doc? (he asks Dudley). "A butthole." (Dudley replies). I said a butthole. Do you swim by your feet (he asks Dudley). "No" (Dudley replies). He does swim by his feet. MMMM, ow! (Dudley bites the recorder.) Ahhhhh (Dudley keeps biting the recorder). Do you see his little back bottom teeth? See this one disappear? (showing Dudley's teeth, tucking one under, showing it again).

I have a different teeth. My teeth. It's cool. Doctors put it in. Did you know there was a drill? It hurted. Because I had cavities. It hurted! I brush my teeth.

"I have two" (Dudley says). I brush them for him. Because he can't reach his arm up to his mouth. Only to right here. I can reach the teeth. We can, sometimes I put toothpaste and his tummy doesn't shake. Sometimes it does this. Sometimes I hurt him for that. When . . . I talk . . . I punish him. Ummmm. "Settle down". "I'm gonna put you to bed." That's what I say.

Alan, Amber, Robert
Interviews by Chuck Alvey and Kelli Nicolato
Photographs by Paula Riley

Alan, Amber and Robert were staying at the Salvation Army Family Emergency Shelter on Galetti Way when we visited. They were waiting for the shelter to open for the night. Their father, Mark, was looking for work. Their mother, Kim, was working housekeeping jobs.

We sat on the grass and talked, drawing stick-figure pictures of each child to get things started. Amber was the last interview and she came to us shivering and soaked from a swim with Alan in the Truckee. The river is in the "park at their house."

Alan (transcript by Chuck Alvey), age seven, began:

I'm never scared in a fight. I have been in one fight. He didn't beat me up, I beat him up. He was eight, I was seven, um, six. First he had a wide sword. I had a little sword about that short. He had a long sword from here to here (demonstrates with hands.) His name was Jesus. He was eight. I was seven, actually. He was actually twice . . . twice bigger than me, but I still beat him up. First he pushed right here (motions to neck) and then he made me mad and then I got him. I'm never scared in a fight. I'm not even scared of a pit bull. The pit bull is the meanest. I'm not even scared of the pit bull. What he was doing was just growling or barking. Just grrrr, trying to catch me. He also bit me and I didn't even feel it. (holds out arms) This is a monkey bite. I got it at a picnic. Yep, I didn't do anything to him, he just bit me. First he scratched me right here and then on my arm, he bit me.

Once I had a toy spider. Robert lifted it. I asked him nicely to give it back and he wouldn't. He lost it. He told me he threw it, he said he, he said he threw it in the bushes but he won't tell me which bush he threw it in.

I seen a rodeo in real life. First part that I like about the rodeo is, um, seeing the bulls. I'm glad they have the clowns there or them cowboys would be dead.

I got a real football in storage. I had a . . . I got a black, uh, a really black cowboy hat in storage, too. And I've got cowboy jeans. I got, um, boots, cowboy boots. It's with the other stuff that I got. I haven't went to the storage yet.

Amber (transcript by Kelli Nicolato), age six, informed us:

I'm six. I'm the middlest. My brother has a girlfriend (laughs.) Robert has a girlfriend, too. She's four. I don't have a boyfriend. I hate boys. I have a friend named Jessica. She lives here in the shelter. We play cards and they also have a play area in there. One time, I made a snowman out of mud. I have a doll, but it's in my room. My room is number five. My Dad and my brothers' room is number six.

I had a dog named Chico but he got lost. He's still a dog.

I like being in parks 'cause they have swings and slides and ladders. But my favorite thing to do is color. Want to see how I write my name? This is how I spell it.

I want to be a teacher and a cop when I grew up. I'd put grown-ups in jail 'cause they do drugs and if I was a teacher, I'd put the kids in time out.

Alan.

Amber.

Robert.

I wanna be hair on me (rubbing his closely shave head).

You got dogs? I like dogs. I got a teeger one time. I ate it. I chew it up and drinked it all. Knock my head off (laughs.)

I live here at the park. Do you have a park at your house?

I swim in the river water. Yeah and it got deep. It got, I found deep, deep, deep place. I wasn't scared. Nope. And we were sinking. Frogs in the water, too. Little ones. Mom, our mom, almost catch one. Alan got one for me and I put it in my pocket and zip pocket and . . . didn't fall out. Sit with it and I didn't kill it. I do still have it. Next time you'll see it at my . . . at our park. My frog jumped higher, higher in the sky. I still have that frog. I take it in my toat [coat]. I still have my toat.

I fight Alan. And I push Alan. Amber pushed Alan in the nose and he bleed. Her hit it and it bleed everywhere, on this place.

My birthday's far away . . . far away at my friends. You make me waff (laughs). . . .

Night at the West Edge of Grand Forks, North Dakota

BILL STOBB

There are only three buildings now, but I can imagine
a day when there will be ten or more of these unlikely,
secretive atriums called Centers for Aerospace Science,
where people can look west out black glass windows
at the absolute expanse of the wild prairie while being taught
how to fly planes and rockets.
                        The interstate will have to be moved,
I suppose, as it borders closely this west edge, restricting
development like a belt holding the fat stomach of town
with red and white lights moving at speeds
some would consider fantastic.
                        And this little convenience store,
hidden like a small bulb under those dark staircases
    of architecture,
what will become of it? Where, on any given night
you can walk by, look in from some distance and see
the blonde hair of the woman behind the counter,
so bright it lights even that fluorescent space.

In 1994, Bill Stobb earned an M.A. from the University of North Dakota. He is the recipient of an Academy of American Poets Prize, the winner of the Black Rock Press Poetry Broadside Competition, and a recent nominee for the Pushcart Prize. His interviews with Nevada authors have aired on KUNR, northern Nevada public radio.

Prisons and Economic Diversification

Panacea or Bitter Pill for Rural Communities?

MARIE I. BOUTTÉ

We thought a state institution would serve well in giving us a secure position with the state in terms of assistance. Rural communities are often felt to be left out in terms of state assistance and state resources. The state doesn't generally look out well for rural communities—not generally looked at for state institutions. Nevada has a different pattern in that state institutions are not dispersed throughout the state. We looked at other rural communities throughout the country with successful diversification and there were more direct ties to state facilities than with the private sector.

Comment by a member of the Economic Diversification Council of White Pine County, Nevada

In many areas of the American West, the foundation of rural economies rests on one primary resource, and in many communities these resources are rapidly being depleted. Mining, for example, has historically been one of the predominant resources for rural communities in the state of Nevada. In White Pine County the economy has been directly linked to the fortunes of the mining industry since the 1800s, and the community has historically experienced "boom and bust" cycles. Like other rural communities of Nevada, White Pine has sought different economic alternatives for stability and

Marie I. Boutté is a cultural/medical anthropologist on faculty at the University of Nevada, Reno. Her research interests are cultural and medical ethnographies of rural communites, including issues of economic diversification and environmental health.

growth over the years; among such alternatives has been the solicitation of state prisons.

The increasing demand for prisons in Nevada and other states raises questions about what such an industry means to persons living in the communities that host these institutions, especially small and remote communities. I will explore the impact prison industry and prison culture had on the mining community of White Pine County, especially the county seat of Ely, during the first years of operation of the Ely State Prison. I will argue that the prison industry has added to the economic base of the county, but not to the extent expected by county residents, and that perceptions concerning prison culture have helped to shape ideas about the economics of the prison industry.

My data are largely ethnographic, collected while living in Ely for three months (February-April 1991) and during four return trips to the community for several days or weeks; the last visit was for three weeks in the summer of 1994. My initial project in White Pine County was a study of community perceptions of health problems, but ideas and comments about the newly constructed prison kept surfacing in interviews and in general conversations during periods of participant-observation. I thus began collecting data on the relationship between the prison and the community, in addition to that on health problems. Data were collected primarily through interviews with key informants such as the County Commissioners; members of the diverse committees on economic diversification, especially those involved in seeking the prison; staff of most agencies and services in the infrastructure framework, including the prison wardens; and general members of the community, including wives of prison inmates. I also surveyed documents such as correspondence from county and city officials to state officials; minutes of relevant meetings; environmental assessment reports; local newspaper articles, including letters to the editor; and other archival data. I have not used the personal names of individuals in this paper in order to provide some sense of confidentiality. However, all written documents cited in the text are available in county records with appropriate names included.

The Community and the Prison

White Pine County in eastern Nevada is close to nine thousand square miles in area and is sparsely settled. The population density is around one person per square mile. The majority of the county's population lives in Ely, the county seat. It is the largest community in a two hundred mile radius. Within a few miles are the small communities of Ruth and McGill. This cluster of three communities sits at the end of what *Life* magazine in July 1986 designated as "The Loneliest Road in America."

White Pine County has essentially been a mining community since 1865, first with silver, then in 1904, with copper. McGill, Ruth, and Ely were run like company towns. Since 1983, the quest has been for gold. All have had cycles of boom and bust. As a response to these continuing cycles, White Pine County officials in the late 1960s began looking for ways to broaden the area's economic base. Over the years they sought, studied, and/or proposed a number of diverse economic projects such as a ski facility, a Pinion wood chips project, the White Pine Power Project, an industrial park, an MX missile site, the Nevada Northern Railway, and medium and maximum security prisons. In the late 1970s, when Kennecott Copper shut down mining operations and the county suffered unemployment rates as high as 23 percent, the county took further action to restore its economic prosperity by forming the White Pine Development Corporation, an Overall Economic Development Plan, and an Economic Diversification Program.

Most of White Pine's efforts for economic diversification have been unsuccessful. For example, county officials dropped their solicitation efforts in 1978 for a medium security prison when the Nevada State legislature located the prison in Clark County. In the mid-1980s, however, the county began vigorous solicitation for a maximum security men's prison as part of the Overall Economic Development Plan. A Prison Feasibility Study Committee was established in March 1985 by the Economic Diversification Council to research the pros and cons, as well as community attitudes, toward the prison locating. After much lobbying by county officials, the State Legislature Site Selection Committee in 1986 selected Ely as the location for the new maximum security prison. Construction of the facility took place during 1988-1989; it officially received its first inmates in August of 1989.

Ely State Prison (ESP) is the State of Nevada's only maximum security prison for men. Located nine miles north of the city of Ely in Smith Valley, it houses seven types of classified inmates: minimum custody, medium custody, maximum custody, death row, long-term segregation, long-term protective custody, and safekeepers from neighboring counties. According to an "Ely State Prison Fact Sheet," the facility housed 1,050 inmates in 1994. In terms of inmate statistics, the average age was 34.39 years (the largest age group was 30-34); 55 percent were in for violent offenses; in ethnic distribution, 55 percent were classified as White, 30 percent Black, 10 percent Hispanic; 69 percent were from Clark County, 17 percent from Washoe County, and 13 percent from other counties. The average stay at ESP was 4.27 years. The facility was budgeted for 386 employee positions, which included medical, business, administration, education, maintenance, recreation, training and custody personnel. The budget for fiscal year 1994 was over fourteen and a half million dollars, 82 percent of which was payroll (ESP Fact Sheet).

Community Concerns and Impacts

In prison impact studies a number of community concerns have been identified in regards to siting a prison. Maxim and Plecas for example, identified four factors of concern in their survey of the Fraser Valley region of British Columbia: concern for family safety, concern for general quality of life, concern for value of neighborhood, and concern for neighborhood instability. Rogers and Haimes pointed out that community concerns cited in the literature generally had to do with property values, security, impact on local institutions, psychological impacts, and economic impacts. Shichor, in his article on "Myths and Realities in Prison Siting," identified community concerns regarding: crime rates and fear of crime, release policies of departments of corrections, prisoner families, property values, general economic impact, general quality-of-life issues, and community prestige and efficacy. Katherine Carlson ("Prison Impacts"), an anthropologist who has studied the impact of prison siting on host communities for the U.S. National Institute of Justice, carried out an extensive review of the relevant literature and identified four categories of concerns or impacts: the economy, inmate escapes and inmate families, the criminal justice system, and community lifestyle. According to a Draft Environmental Assessment document prepared by the Bureau of Land Management (Rajala 28-30), some residents of White Pine County expressed concern about the siting of the Ely State Prison because of the danger of prisoners and the potential for their escape, the presence of "camp followers," the disruption of lifestyle and peace of mind, a reduction in the quality of life,. and relocation of ex-prisoners into the county. For purposes of summarizing my research on the concerns and impacts of the prison on White Pine County, I will use the four categories identified by Carlson since they include those expressed by county residents and those generally of other investigators. Although I will discuss each category separately, there is overlap among them. For example, facets of economic impacts are generally woven throughout all the categories.

Economic Impacts

According to Rogers and Haimes, towns most often lobby to get prisons sited in their areas if "the local economy is very depressed, unemployment rates are high, and prisons can serve as an economic stimulus for the local economy" (29). These were the major reasons for White Pine County officials soliciting the Ely State Prison. As noted earlier, the closure of the Kennecott copper facilities (the mine in 1978 and the smelter in 1983) had dire economic consequences for the county. According to a letter from the County Board of Commissioners to the District Manager of the Bureau of Land Management (BLM) dated April 25, 1986, the Kennecott closure resulted in the loss of an 18 million dollar annual payroll and the loss of tax revenues that "put the local government in a difficult situation, unable to meet the basic needs of its citizens" (3). The county unemployment rate in June 1985 was 14 percent ("Proposal for White Pine").

It was projected that the economic stimulus to the county would occur during both construction of the prison facility and during its operation. For example, it was estimated that the total gross income in the local economy, generated by subcontractors' construction activity, employment, and capital spending would be $5.7 million. It was expected that prison operations during Phase I would provide for two hundred employees and a gross income in the community of $6.3 million, and 325 employees during Phase II, along with additional millions in income (Rajala). As already mentioned, the prison budget for fiscal year 1994 was over 14.5 million dollars.

As in most small communities that have been successful in lobbying for prisons, White Pine County generally benefitted economically from the Ely State Prison in terms of jobs and additional revenue. Whether the county received the benefits that it initially expected was impossible to measure objectively, however, because mining began a comeback in the county and brought in additional revenue at the same time the prison began construction. The general consensus of the business community during the research period was that Ely and its surrounding smaller communities could not have survived without a stabilizing component in their local economy, and the Ely State Prison was viewed as that component. There were, however, many economic expectations that were not met. For example, the volume of procurement for the facility that was purchased from local vendors, use of local services, and retail sales did not come close to reaching levels expected by county officials and local businessmen. During one interview a member of the Economic Diversification Council expressed the sentiments of the business community in this way:

> The expectations have not been met with the business community. The prison is operated through state bidding and we don't get the bids. We have had workshops with businessmen on the bidding process. The prison has more lee-way in bidding so there is some cooperation with a few vendors, a few contracts, but they didn't meet the expectations.

This individual went on to say that:

> The main thing is stability. When mining drops we see more public employment. This community has a mining mentality. Whatever comes in will be a savior. With the prison 'You told us this was going to be a savior and now its not.' It's hard to come to grips with the reality of the prison.

In addition to receiving far fewer state bids than expected and losing retail sales when prison staff shopped out-of-town on their days off, there were also far fewer local hires by the prison than anticipated. Most staff were brought in from the outside, people who already had experience in the state correctional system. This situation would have raised more community ire had mining not been making a resurgence in the early phases of prison operations. The much higher salaries and familiarity with the industry drew many residents into mining who might have originally sought employment in the new prison facility.

In prison impact studies, the most often voiced negative in regard to economics is the decline of property values in prison communities (Shichor). Research has shown, however, that this does not necessarily occur. In fact, in many cases the opposite is true. One study, using both target areas near prison facilities and control areas, showed that property values in target areas were higher than those in control areas (Rogers and Haimes). In White Pine County, there was no evidence of concern about loss of property value, but during the period of solicitation, there was concern over whether or not there would be adequate housing, both in number and quality of units for construction and prison personnel. Rents in the area went up substantially because of a shortage of housing, but this was also due to increased mining operations bringing in more people. There was a problem initially of prison staff not qualifying for home loans because of their long employment probationary periods and their low salaries. Houses in a new sub-division were initially left vacant even though they had been built with prison employees as the target population.

Some of the negative economic impacts in the community were more subtle and indirect than others. For example, there were some personnel from local law enforcement, health care services, and other city and county offices that went to work in the prison. Even though the numbers were few, they were often trained or professional staff that were difficult to replace, especially given the remote and rural nature of the community. The small and simple county courthouse, built in 1916, had to initially have rudimentary renovations at the expense of the county for temporary holding cells and courtroom security. The prison brought in more revenue for the local hospital, but it created conflict among the volunteers who comprised the Emergency Medical Technical staff (EMTs) over transporting sick and injured inmates. When several EMTs refused to go to the prison, an outside mediator had to be brought in. There was little economic impact on the local schools, but there were perceptions by some teachers that "urban" students were bringing in "gang" ideology. The local community college benefitted in that faculty developed courses on Corrections and Developmental English and the prison employed a number of educational staff on both a part-time and full-time basis.

Inmate Escapes and Inmate Families

In terms of safety and security, many communities fear that crime will increase (Rogers and Haimes), and there is often a fear of escapees. These were not concerns generally expressed by White Pine residents, in part because the prison is one of maximum security. There were exceptions, however. One woman said that:

> There's a man who lives on the road to the prison and he says he's buying an extra car and leaving it in front with keys in the ignition so when someone breaks out they can just take the car and leave and not have to bother or harm him or his family for his getaway. There are concerns from the houses nearby, but the public tours of the prison helped a lot of people to relax.

One of the issues raised by the EMTs in their refusal to service the prison was their fear of attempted escapes, especially on the relatively isolated road leading to and from the prison.

In addition to the Ely State Prison, White Pine County also has an Honor Camp, built in 1985-1986, that houses about 150 inmates. My research did not show much concern by residents about escapes from this facility. One law enforcement official did say that at first there was concern over the Honor Camp, but once the prison was built, the discussion ended. He said there had been escapes from the Honor Camp, but that these inmates, in contrast to Ely Sate Prison inmates, were not perceived as very dangerous by the community because Honor Camp inmates have a high profile in the area. Under supervision, they do such things as shovel snow for the elderly, engage in construction projects around the cemetery, clean camp grounds, and participate in fire control. The general consensus of the community was that the Honor Camp had benefitted the community.

In White Pine County one of the biggest concerns was over safety during court proceedings held in the local courthouse. This concern was made apparent in a letter from the District Attorney to the Prison Warden about an unescorted inmate who entered one of the county offices. The District Attorney wrote that "Such a breach in security created a potentially dangerous situation needlessly subjecting Mrs. X to a frightening experience and a barrage of lewd language."

Research findings are inconsistent on the topic of increased crime in communities with prisons, but the issue of releasing inmates into the community came up in White Pine County as it has in other communities that host prisons. For example, the County District Attorney again wrote a letter of concern to the County Commissioners when she was notified by a Department of Prisons official that inmates would be released into the community. In this letter she said that:

> These individuals will be deposited at the airport or bus stop to await their departure without any further supervision by the Department of Corrections. This causes me great concern as this could possibly be hours and/or days before these individuals leave the county.

> As you recall, this is contrary to what the state "promised" White Pine County during negotiations for the maximum security prison

The County Commissioners in a follow-up letter to the State Director of Prisons, called attention to the fact that:

> Prior to a decision being made to locate the Maximum Security Prison in Ely, one of the main concerns expressed by the citizens of White Pine County was the release of prisoners into the community. This concern was voiced at a County Commission Meeting held September 12, 1985 . . . There were approximately 200 concerned residents in attendance at that meeting.

This same issue was addressed in the analysis prepared by the Department of Interior, Bureau of Land Management, Nevada State Office; and again, addressed in the draft Environmental Assessment prepared by the Ely District Office of the Bureau of Land Management.

In this same letter the Commission pointed out that the Prison Warden had assured them that the policy of the Department of Prisons was to return parolees and ex-prisoners back to the county of commitment. The letter asked that there not be a change in this policy. The general sentiments of the Commission were expressed in the following way:

> All the promises of assistance for White Pine County during the transition have been nullified and it seems that the community has been "hung out to dry." The comments have been made that "You asked for it, now live with it."

The Director of Prisons responded back in a letter to the County Commissioners that inmates were "not being released to roam the streets of Ely," but he said that public transportation would be used to get parolees to their release destinations and he pointed out that released inmates with expired sentences had no restrictions on their movements. Some inmates released from the Carson City prisons had remained in Carson City he stated, but "ex-offenders are not similarly attracted to Ely."

Inmate families and friends, often referred to as "camp followers" (See Millay) are often a concern, especially during the planning phase of prison projects. This was certainly the case for White Pine County as well. At a public meeting on the proposed prison in April 1986, one resident of McGill submitted in writing his views on this subject: "I am against the maximum prison being built at the Smith Valley prison site for many reasons. Having prisoners and their families to this area will cause many more problems for everyone and increase more welfare." Another individual from McGill who also submitted written comments objected to the prison siting because of the: "Presence of camp followers (such as) relatives and friends of inmates who may be a burden or threat to the community."

Prison impact studies, by and large, do not report that large numbers of inmate families move into communities (See

Shichor; Millay). According to Shichor, if there is any measurable movement of prisoner families or camp followers to host communities, it occurs in larger established urban areas, rather than in smaller isolated communities. The reasons are that in larger communities there are more opportunities for employment and it is easier for family members to blend into the general population and avoid the stigmatization and isolation often fostered on prisoner families. In addition, most inmates and their families are primarily from urban areas and are thus generally not attracted to isolated, chiefly rural communities (Millay).

Very few families of inmates moved into White Pine County once the prison opened. The majority of inmates were from urban Clark County, and employment opportunities for family members were limited in rural White Pine County. During my interviews with two wives of inmates, both expressed dismay over the long driving distance to Las Vegas, and both reported feelings of stigmatization by local county residents. In addition, the only work opportunities for these women were generally as motel maids or waitresses. This was due in part to the stigma attached to their identity and also to their need to have days off during the regular work week so they could visit their incarcerated husbands and work on their release or transfer from the Ely State Prison. Both of these wives lived in subsidized housing and this increased their stigmatization, because county residents saw this as part of the welfare system. This supported their previously held stereotype of prisoner families increasing the welfare rolls. Initially there had been concern in the school system about children from prisoner families interacting with children of correctional staff, but this did not present a problem as it was generally only a few inmate wives who moved into the community.

The Criminal Justice System

One of the biggest impacts on local institutions was on the court system in White Pine County. Personnel in the courthouse reported a big increase in the volume of paperwork and legal documents that needed processing. According to the County Clerk, the paperwork at least tripled and there was no increase in staff.

The District Judge wrote a letter to the Governor expressing his concern about impacts on the justice system during the period of prison solicitation. He wrote:

> I know that you are well aware of the difficult economic condition of White Pine and Lincoln Counties. It is because of that fact that I write this letter.

> I have all the work I can presently handle serving as one Judge for three Counties with two prison farms, and occasionally helping out in Elko. I am told that a prison would mean a substantially increased workload in terms of writs and crimes in prison to be tried in the local Court.

> If the increased workload is substantial, we will need a second District Judge for this area. The problem then will be to find another courtroom, court staff and additional library facilities.

At the time of my research in 1994, a second district judge had been added, but no new facilities had been constructed, except for the rudimentary renovations already mentioned, and no additional court staff had been hired. The first district judge said in an interview that:

> The State does pay cost of trials, but not all the costs. It's harder on a mining community. We've got to get a loan for $100,000 for the courtroom. When Carson City got a second courtroom, it got paid for because they are closer to the seat of power.

> I never anticipated the caseload. The paperwork is just physically impossible.

One impact in the criminal justice system that the county did not anticipate, but one that placed a very heavy burden on its citizens was jury duty. The small population of the county resulted in a small jury pool that was constantly called upon to sit on the multitude of cases brought to court. Several county residents said that they had been called to serve up to six times in one year. One woman who had been called six times in one year said, "We can't work or go out of town because we're always on jury duty. People run and hide from the summons server." Another woman was upset over jury duty because her husband was a driver for a local delivery service and there were no backup drivers. She said, "It is a great hardship on families, especially when economics are poor anyway for families." Everyone interviewed deplored being in the jury pool, especially those individuals who were self-employed. The district judge also pointed out the hidden costs in serving so frequently on jury duty, a job that paid $9 per day if called and $15 per day if served.

Community Life Style

White Pine County's character and identity have been linked historically to mining for well over a hundred years. During my stay in the community, residents often initiated conversations about changes in life style by making comparisons between mining culture and prison culture. For example, one woman said: "Miners are known even if they're from the outside. They make a living in a way that we're used to. Prisoners haven't done anything but something wrong." Another said: "Mining is a fluid community or industry, but it is also a 'closed' community. There is a line of acquaintances and a large network. With mining, people go from small town to small town; with prisons, they go from city to small town."

The consensus in the community was that the biggest change to life style did not come from the prisoners or their families as most people had anticipated. One person summed up general community sentiment when she said that "Prison employees have caused more trouble than the prisoners or their families."

It was the influx of correctional officers (COs) with an orientation toward urban living that created immediate conflict within the community regarding life style. One individual highlighted this issue when she said:

The COs got culture shock and saw only the negative side of rural living. They went out of town and did their shopping so we lost the revenue and they weren't here to participate in weekend community activities or the life of the community. These people have to learn a whole new approach to social life. We have to rely on volunteers for a lot of services and they don't get involved.

There were also other strains put on the community by correctional officers, created in part by the nature of their work. This was made apparent in a quote taken from a member of the Economic Diversification Council:

We expected single men or men with families. We got a high percent of females COs, a large number of them single parent, female-headed households. We had no daycare other than day time; they need 24 hour services. Daycare was limited anyway because many families in the community have extended family or neighborhood cooperation. It was a problem because the work site is so far out of town and it is shift work seven days a week. The households were newcomers, making low salaries. With mining you have long distances and shift work, but generally one person is at home. Sometimes both parents were hired by the prison and they were put on different shifts and this helped with child care, but it raised a different kind of stress because the parents never saw one another.

There was some community sentiment that the "flavor" of the community had changed in character and identity with the arrival of the prison. One informant said that there is "now a rougher edge to the community." One woman gave her perspective on the difference in the community since the opening of the prison:

We use to go to the local hotel before the prison was built to hear the music and to have a few drinks, but we had to quit going because the women got hassled so much. The guards didn't care if you were with someone or not. They just wouldn't take no for an answer and there were a lot of fights. We just quit going there. Wherever they hang out, none of us goes because they're always fighting and bothering the women.

Although it has not been a focus of study, prisons impacts may be different for women in this community than for men. Women, for example, expressed much more a sense of danger and unease in relationship to the prison. Several informants spoke of being exposed to lewd language and general harassment from both inmates and correctional officers. The previously cited example shows how women's activities were constrained by the behavior of COs in social settings. The following quote by a woman employed in the courthouse gives her perception of women's vulnerability in terms of prison inmates:

> The women in this community are trusting. They talk to people and are used to going out at night. They live by the rule that you treat others like you want to be treated. They don't know the con of these inmates and I have to try and limit contact with the women in the courthouse and these inmates. These men are like sonars; they're experts at getting information. You have to be especially careful if you have family in law enforcement. Women of Ely are not used to this level of manipulation. If you are in any position in the prison system, you are out of your element, especially in an all-male situation.

There was some concern in the community about becoming known as a "prison town". One individual said:

> Some people do feel that now there is a stigma of the community by having a maximum security prison here. There was a segment on television some time back that showed something about the prison and it showed Ely. Some people don't want Ely shown in this way. It has brought more publicity about the town because of the happenings at the prison. It highlights the community, but many don't think it's a good light.

Another man said:

> Some felt that the name 'Ely' State Prison stigmatizes the community. Some suggested 'Nevada State Maximum Security Prison' would be better. The prison was spotlighted on a cop T.V. show and people had a fit. However, when Masterlock used Ely prison in its Superbowl commercial, many thought it was grand.

Naming the institution the "Ely" State Prison raised some debate among residents, but not as much as it raised in

Clallam Bay, Washington, when the state prison there was given the town's name (Carlson, "Doing Good" 61). The name could have become a bigger issue in White Pine County if the county were promoting a particular image, such as Clallam Bay promoting itself as a tourist destination. Since the establishment of the Great Basin National Park, White Pine County is more and more promoting tourism so the community could become more image conscious over time and perhaps make a concerted effort to change the name of the prison.

The Overall Assessment

In assessing whether or not the Ely State Prison has been a panacea or a bitter pill for White Pine County, the argument would have to be made that it is both. For some segments of the community, such as those with commercial interests and the hospital, it is more a panacea or cure-all for the county's woes. For some areas in the infrastructure, such as the district court and the volunteers in the EMT program, it is more a bitter pill. The general consensus, however, is that overall the prison has brought a sense of economic stability to the community. But, there are attendant impacts that were overlooked in the intensive solicitation period. Much attention was given to the physical, environmental impacts on Smith Valley, on some aspects of the community infrastructure, and those arising from the inmate population. A totally neglected aspect was the impact of the correctional staff. This area needs further research. The community did not anticipate the influx of single-parent women who were hired as correction officers, nor consider the cultural differences of the prison staff and how such differences would articulate with rural culture.

McShane et al. point out the need for more methodological rigor, and the need to go beyond the level of exploratory research in the newly emerging field of prison impact studies. This study does not do that, but it does suggest some salient variables and significant questions for future research: How prisons impact differently on men and women in the community, and across the generations. My preliminary data suggest that the impacts, especially on lifestyle may be different for women than for men.

There is an overlooked variable in community research referred to as "density of acquaintanceship." This is defined as "the average proportion of the people in a community known by the community's inhabitants" (Freudenburg 30). Several variables can be expected to affect a community's density of acquaintanceship: a community's population, length of residence, anticipated length of residence, diversity, segregation (if different types of people have relatively little contact with one another), and expected consequences (interpersonal agreements/personal accommodation). With mining, even though "outsiders" historically moved into the communities of White Pine County, the density of acquaintanceship remained high because of cultural similarities; with outside prison employees, this is not the case. Data suggest that there is a move to lower density because of cultural differences. This needs further exploration because change in density may even occur after local employees become acculturated to the prison.

Studies are needed that differentiate "type" of facility and community impact. For example, issues of security may be manifest to a greater degree with minimum or medium security facilities in contrast to maximum security. Whether it is a prison for men or women may also give rise to different impacts and interactions. Prison impacts may differ depending on "type" of community as well. Research is beginning to show different impacts between urban and rural communities, but types of rural communities need to be differentiated. For example, this preliminary research used the case study of a mining community, but perhaps there are different impacts on an agricultural community, or one that has ranching as it primary industry and cultural orientation.

There is a need for longitudinal studies as prison and community accommodation may occur in stages. The three phases of prison siting, construction, and operations may carry different impacts, and there may be stages that can be identified once operations are established. Perhaps the framework of "culture shock" would be applicable to this situation given that two cultures—prison culture and rural culture—are brought into contact with one another.

It would seem that perceived impacts may be different if the prison is sought or if such a facility is imposed involuntarily on a community. Generally, correctional facilities are categorized as "LULUs", Locally Unwanted Land Use (See

Shichor). They are among "those projects or facilities that are needed by the community-at-large to solve a community problem, but are opposed by immediate neighbors who see them as a threat to property values, safety, or health" (Chambers 18). In my study the Ely State Prison does not meet the full criteria for a LULU, because the community-at-large was not opposed to the facility. It was viewed as a very manageable enterprise. This suggests that diverse frameworks may be useful in analyzing these types of facilities. For example, separating "standard effects" from "special effects" could offer some insight. (Standard effects are those expected from any type of large-scale project; special effects are those unique characteristics of a particular project). Prisons, in fact, may have unique characteristics, a unique culture, from other types of LULUs that give rise to "special effects." These need to be teased out.

Abrams suggests that a facility's impact on a community can be assessed in two ways. First, it can be assessed through subjective factors such as attitudes, opinions, beliefs, and perceptions; and second, through objective factors such as the facility's expenditure in the community, changes in the crime rates, and property values. However, as pointed out by Shichor (72), "Community attitudes are usually based on both objective and subjective factors," but arguments for seeking and siting a prison are usually based on objective factors. More research has been carried out on objective factors than subjective factors. This could lead to a skewed picture, as some of the more subtle and indirect impacts are captured through an investigation of subjective factors. An ethnographic approach is needed to fill in the missing gaps in prison impact studies.

ACKNOWLEDGEMENTS

The work for this paper was partially funded through a grant from First Interstate Bank, now Wells Fargo. Dr. Boutté acknowledges the Bank and the many people of White Pine County, Nevada, who assisted her in this research.

REFERENCES

Abrams, Kathleen. "Prisons as LULUs: A Sequel, Part 2." *Environmental and Urban Issues* 15 (1988): 24-27.
Carlson, Katherine A. "Prison Impacts: A Review of the Research." Unpublished manuscript from the U.S. Department of Jus-

tice, National Institute of Corrections Information Center, 1860 Industrial Circle, Suite A, Longmong, Colorado 80501, 1990.

———. "Doing Good and Looking Bad: A Case Study of Prison/Community Relations." *Crime and Delinquency* 381 (1992): 56-69.

Chambers, Marian. "Learning to Live with LULUs." *Environmental and Urban Issues* 16 (1989): 17-22.

Comment Form for Public Meeting. April 1, 1986.

Ely State Prison Fact Sheet. December 1, 1994.

Freudenburg, William. "The Density of Acquaintanceship: An Overlooked Variable in Community Research." *American Journal of Sociology* 92.1 (1986): 27-63.

Krause, Jerald D. "Community Opposition to Correctional Facility Siting: Beyond the 'NIMBY' Explanation." *Humboldt Journal of Social Relations* 17.1,2 (1991): 239-262.

Letter from County Commissioners to District Manager of BLM. April 25, 1986

Letter from District Attorney to Prison Warden. October 11, 1991.

Letter from District Attorney to County Commissioners. September 1992.

Letter from County Commissioners to Director of Prisons. September 23, 1992.

Letter from Director of Prisons to County Commissioners. October 5, 1992.

Letter from District Judge to state Governor. June 24, 1985.

Maxim, Paul, and Darryl Plecas. "Prisons and Their Perceived Impact on the Local Community: A Case Study." *Social Indicators Research* 13 (1983): 39-58.

McShane, Marilyn D., Frank P. Williams and Carl P. Wagoner. "Prison Impact Studies: Some Comments on Methodological Rigor." *Crime and Delinquency* 38.1 (1992): 105-120.

Millay, John R. "From Asylum to Penitentiary: The Social Impact of Eastern Oregon Correctional Institution Upon Pendleton." *Humboldt Journal of Social Relations* 17.1,2 (1991): 171-195.

"Proposal for White Pine County, Nevada as the Site for a Maximum Security Prison." Submitted by the White Pine Board of County Commissioners and White Pine County Prison Facilities Study Committee, August 1, 1985.

Rajala, Jake. "Draft Environmental Assessment for Smith Valley State of Nevada Maximum Security Prison." Bureau of Land Management, Ely District Office, Ely, Nevada. March 14, 1986.

Rogers, George O., and Marshall Haimes. "Local Impact of a Low-Security Federal Correctional Institution. *Federal Probation* 5.13 (1987): 28-34.

Sechrest, Dale K. "Locating Prisons: Open Versus Closed Approaches to Siting." *Crime and Delinquency* 38.1 (1992): 88-104.

Shichor, David. "Myths and Realities in Prison Siting." *Crime and Delinquency* 38.1 (1992): 70-87.

Two Poems
on Los Angeles

MARSHA ROGERS

Watering Los Angeles

the aqueduct
irrigates change
half a thousand
miles away
as it steals water
of northern deserts —
lakes of ancient origin
and wetlands
of traditional flyways
are abandoned,
left with no option
but death.

Marsha Rogers, an educator in rural Nevada, is a member of Ash Canyon Poets in Carson City and a founding member of Shadow Canyon Poets in Hawthorne, Nevada. Her poetry has been accepted for publication by Pegasus, Remembrance, Night Roses, Candlelight Poetry Journal, *and the anthologies* Drive, She Said *and* There's No Place Like Home for the Holidays.

I-5 at 3:30 P.M.

It's the most exciting
part of the day.
The inmates are released
from the factories and early
shifts. They are out to beat
the rush.

We weave intricate patterns
of carbon monoxide,
downshift, accelerate,
pass on left
and right,
let it glide to seventy-five mph
going down,
then power up.

Every nerve is alive,
adrenaline pumps.
We refuse to let the low rider
into line
and beat the truck
entering from the weigh station.

I have not forgot my skills;
nor have I lost my nerve
out in the wasteland—
I can still drive
like a true maniac.

Barthell Little Chief
Kiowa Visionary Artist

MICHAEL FLANIGAN

On September 17, 1874, near what is now Carnegie, Oklahoma, a large column of the U.S. Tenth Cavalry under the
command of Lieutenant Colonel John W. Davidson came upon
a lone Kiowa warrior named "Ket-Ty-Shun" or Little Chief.
The soldiers tried to disarm him; yet despite the overwhelming odds—over a hundred to one—Little Chief resisted and
fought—in the tradition of the Kiowa Koettsenko warrior society—until he was shot dead. Today his great-grandson
Barthell Little Chief, a well-known painter and sculptor, lives
less than twenty-five miles away from where his ancestor's
remains lay buried at Zodal-tone Peak. The closeness of his
great-grandfather's remains serves as one of many ties to his
Kiowa and Comanche heritage that have helped shape and
inspire his art, and his role in the present-day Kiowa community.

"A painting or sculpture for me isn't just what I see; it's
what my ancestors saw. It's me, my father, my grandfathers,
my great-grandfathers, my people; that's what I try to create.
My way of seeing comes from my experiences—but it also
comes from their experiences—the stories my grandfather and
father told me. It comes from the Native American Church;
from conversations with my elders; from the ancients and
their symbols, their myths, and their legends. What I create
flows from all those and through me onto the canvas or into

*Michael Flanigan is the Earl A. & Betty Galt Brown, Jr. Profes-
sor of Rhetoric and Composition and Director of Composition
at the University of Oklahoma. Living in Oklahoma the last
eighteen years has given him an opportunity to learn about
Native American art and culture thanks to his good friends
Barthell and Debbie Little Chief who have taken him under
their wings.*

shaping the stone. I believe the vision I shape is my people's vision."

Little Chief, who lives south of Anadarko, Oklahoma, on his father's original Kiowa allotment, creates dual visions of the Kiowas and Comanches in both stone and paint. In his sculptures he shapes traditional representational images of eagles, medicine men, and visionaries and fuses them with abstract visual impressions that create a flowing, moving art. For example, in *Medicine Song* (facing page) the bronze head of a Medicine Man, almost the color and texture of mahogany, meditates and seems to bring his visions to life as a waterbird flies and flow's through his hair. The waterbird's beak begins at the forehead of the Medicine Man and almost seems to swim as its wings and tail feathers move to complete the image trailing down the back of the head. It's as if the images of natural life that the visionary conjures up are made transparent for all to see. In other works, such as *Eagle Medicine* and *Eagle Vision* (following page), Little Chief's bronzes (which often look like wood, gold, bark, and even mottled greenish water) need to be viewed from every angle because their multidimentionality create diversity as the eye moves.

For example, a first glance at *Eagle Vision* shows an eagle looking proudly as if into an unclear future as it emerges from the head of a visionary. As the eye moves around the sculpture the visionary changes to a healer, a medicine man; the eagle and the man become almost one creating an energy that dynamically underscores their union and mutual destiny.

Little Chief has always concerned himself with the visionary and how best to represent the views of his people—his community—both present and past. For example, before he devoted himself full time to sculpture he used a meticulous, detailed, highly demanding traditional style that captures the mystic quality of Kiowa warriors, chiefs, medicine men, and prophets. His images stride and leap before the eye, their energy radiating in all directions. His warriors burst across the sky-plumes, spears, shields, horses manes, swirling toward the heavens as if they just materialized before us. In his modern mode, Little Chief creates bold solid half images and quarter images of Ghost Dancers, buffaloes, chiefs, and shields. These paintings combine the ancient and the modern. For example, in *The Native Americans* (page 237) the

Medicine Song, two views (1996)

Eagle Vision (1995)

The Native Americans (1991)

head of a large buffalo thrusts in profile, behind a partial half image of another chief (striped in red, white and blue, stars highlighting his face and body) who moves in tandem with the buffalo.

The chief holds a shield in his left hand and his right reaches forward, the index finger almost touching the canvas edge like a modern Adam seeking the god that will save him, his ancestors, and the buffalo from extinction.

At first it may be hard to believe that these creations flow from the same source, but common threads of concern, viewpoint, and spirit mark them as uniquely from Little Chief'ss hand and ancestral wellsprings. For example, in a traditional painting the *Owl Prophet* (following page) is suspended in the air, his magic swirling around him. And in another modern painting (page 328) he creates a partial image of a chief striped like an American flag, his eyes gone, stars on his cheekbones—a muted, stilled, silent figure.

In a recent sculpture, *Eagle Medicine* (page 331), the long, slim face of the medicine man emerges from the bronze in various tones of brown, tan, gold, and bronze that make it appear that the head is coming to life right before our eyes from the folded wings and body of an eagle. The union of the two is inseparable, yet they hold onto their distinct existence,

Owl Prophet, 1989.

American Indian II (1991)

separate yet together. So both the traditional and the abstract reflect Kiowa life as conjured up in the imagination. Both use color brilliantly, one to celebrate the magic of the past and hint at the fullness and lushness that only abstraction can capture and convey, the other to give pause and to remind us of the fragility of life and culture, and how much of the past has disappeared and been replaced by more form and less substance. In the modern painting, a single buffalo horn and some fur on a headpiece are the only remnants of a

flourishing culture that survives, except for the stoic and heroic stance stamped on the chiefs face (page 333). Little Chief seems to reserve the traditional style for his visions of a once thriving Kiowa community and culture; he uses the modern abstract style to focus on a fragmented culture, a community that strives to wrest its identity from the dominant American culture that would assimilate it, an attempt to preserve its shape and identity (following pages).

The roots for Little Chief's style come from his awareness that he is a product of his people, a person not only shaped by his ancestors, but also one who believes in the magic, mysticism, and the unity of nature that they believed in. However, he is also shaped by modern culture too, and he cannot ignore the erosion of the values he tries to preserve in his art and life. Such conflicts, tensions, and multiple visions are also a legacy of his people's past. Enrolled Kiowa tribal members number fewer than 6,300 today. The buffalo is virtually gone. The nomadic Kiowa are now settled on land allotments. The Sun Dance, once the most important unifying community tribal ceremony, last took place in the 1890s. The last battle to keep invading whites off the land took place in 1874 at the Battle of Adobe Walls in Texas. But even with such dramatic changes, Kiowa culture survives in communities throughout Oklahoma. Central values are passed from one generation to the next. The warriors, presented in Ton-kon-ko or Black Leggings Society, still hold an honorable and central place in Kiowa culture. Kiowa warriors from the First and Second World Wars and all other wars the United States has fought in this century gathered in the summer of 1991 to induct new members who had fought in the Persian Gulf. Equally central to the Kiowa community and culture are its artists. Early artists painted histories of battles, ceremonies, and special events on tipis and large buckskins. Ledger art,

Eagle Medicine, *1996*

Winter Hunter (1987)

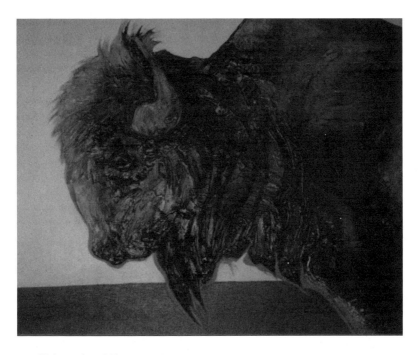

Buffalo II (1992)

which depicted Kiowa history and served as calendars to the tribe, made artists vital to Kiowa identity. And as early as 1891 Kiowa artists were doing commissioned work for international expositions. In the 1920s the famous "Kiowa Five" artists traveled throughout the world displaying and selling their works. One of the artists, James Auchiah, taught Little Chief in informal meetings at his house. He showed Little Chief the secrets of mixing paints, and like Kiowa artists before him, he left Little Chief part of the legacy that had been given to him.

However, Little Chief's love for art grew out of his first love—hot rods. "I used to pin stripe hot rods and paint pictures on the dashboards. I even wanted to do it professionally." But the influence of Auchiah, and "a few semesters" of education in art at the University of Oklahoma, plus the dedication and skill of his father, Tom Little Chief, a master beadworker, composer, and Headsman of the Kiowa tribe, all worked a different magic on Little Chief. In the '60s Little Chief traveled with a friend, Ray Darby, an artist and a descendant of Hunting Horse. Darby paid Little Chief five dollars a day for just tagging along.

However, to keep himself busy, Little Chief painted. A first work of a buffalo sold for twenty-five dollars, and subsequently almost anything that Little Chief painted people snatched up as quickly as the paint dried. Little Chief's paintings were selling better than Darby's, and they traveled to California and then to Nashville where he met Roy Orbison and Ray Price, who loved his work and bought art works Little Chief was painting in his hotel room at night.

After his travels, Little Chief returned to Oklahoma and his father introduced him to Woody Big Bow, a highly recognized Kiowa artist. At this point Little Chief underwent a kind of visionary conversion. Woody Big Bow, who was also a Kiowa elder, continued the education in Kiowa traditions, dances, and culture begun by Little Chief's father, grandfather and other tribal members who came in contact with him when he was a boy.

"Big Bow's stories about Kiowa life opened up the Kiowa cultural view—their way of seeing the world—that my father had started as far back as I can remember. Big Bow did not influence my artistic techniques, but he helped transform the way I saw the world around me. He, along with my father and grandfather, fundamentally changed my artistic soul."

The change that Little Chief experienced made him realize that as a Kiowa he saw the world differently than European-Americans, Algonquians, Hopis, Pawnees and other groups and tribes.

"I realized that my knowledge, my experiences which had shaped me were the result of peyote meetings I had attended; stories of the Koettsenko (the ten Kiowa elite warriors, one of whom was the first Little Chief); Saynday, the Kiowa trickster hero; stories of Tai-me and spiders; the Kiowa language (which told me I was a Kwuda—"a coming out"); and most of all my father, Tom Little Chief. My dad was an Indian when people hated Indians. He was proud to be a Kiowa. When I was a little boy in the 1940s it was still against the law to sell alcohol to an Indian. My father stopped in a bar for a beer. The bartender said, 'If you tell me you're Mexican, I'II give it to you.' My dad looked at him, turned and left."

Once Little Chief accepted who he was and reflected on how his ancestors, elders, and people had shaped him, he dedicated himself to preserving his community, and the heritage of his people through his art.

"What was odd was back in art school they told me traditional art was dead. They ridiculed it and contemptuously called it 'Bambi Art.' But I eventually came to see that my heroes were my people, the people I respect and emulate. They are in my art—heart and soul."

By fully embracing the culture that had formed him—and was him—Little Chief opened himself to experiences that might not have been possible otherwise. In 1969 he married, and shortly afterwards his wife, Debbie, came down with multiple sclerosis. After seeing numerous doctors who said they could do nothing, Debbie, blind in one eye, approached Little Chief's father and told him that modern medicine could do nothing. Tom Little Chief and his wife loved Debbie like a daughter, and he immediately contacted the top Medicine Man in the Kiowa tribe, Horace Dakai. A twenty-six foot tipi was erected and inside an alter with a carefully arranged pile of fire wood was in the center.

"At the time I didn't believe anything would happen. But when you're desperate you'll do most anything for those you love," Little Chief remarked.

When all was ready only twelve people showed up for the ceremony. At least fifty had been expected, and the slight was felt. But as things began, Horace, dressed in traditional Kiowa dress said, "Do not look for others to come. Those here are here because He fixed it that way. This is how He will work His will. Those here are here for their strength, their love, and their power as a unit."

The ceremony lasted all night long and shortly after one a.m., after various visions and many prayers inspired by the moment, a spectacular event occurred.

"Debbie lay on the ground next to the crescent shaped earthen alter as the medicine man performed his healing ritual. Suddenly a kind of static lightening, almost like a liquid, shot down the tipi poles and moved through all the people in the tipi, into Horace Dakai, and through him into Debbie. Horace leaned over her, working; pulling the sickness from her into himself and spit blood out of his mouth. At that moment Nelson Big Bow sang his 'morning songs,' and Horace sat Debbie up."

Debbie was cured. She could see out of her blind eye; and after checking her, other medical doctors could only say that the disease had mysteriously gone into remission so that all symptoms had vanished.

Visionary experiences seemed to grow after Debbie's cure. As Little Chief allowed himself to believe, he began to see. And his growing ability to see has made his art the dynamic blend of vision, tradition, brilliant color (which regrettably cannot be shown in this volume), and unique style it is today. To meet Barthell Little Chief and to talk with him and to hear the stories of his life, gives a person a sense that we must give back in some way what has been given to us. What strikes a person is that Little Chief's great grandfather, who fought and died like a Koettsenko Warrior, lives riding on the backs of the *Sky Pony* (below), like an Eagle Vision in the mystic world he and his progeny inspired in his great-grandson. Almost reluctantly over his lifetime Little Chief has been pulled toward the visions that are at the center of his art.

Reference

Nye, W. S. *Carbine and the Lance* . Norman,OK: U of Oklahoma P, 1937.

Sky Pony, 1992.

The Strange Career of the American Hobo
Masculinity, Myth, and Community, 1890-1940

TODD A. DePastino

Throughout his career, Wallace Stegner depicted the American hobo as embodying everything that "hampered the development of stable, rooted communities" in the West: acquisitive individualism, footloose mobility, and the reckless pursuit of quick wealth (*Bluebird* xvi). But the hobo of Stegner's *Big Rock Candy Mountain* and assorted essays was but a variant of a larger myth which had inscribed upon the hobo the entropic and alienating qualities perceived as endemic to the post-frontier West. "The hobo," argued University of Chicago sociologist Robert E. Park in 1925, is "merely a belated frontiersman." Unlike the pioneer, who had brought civilization and stability to a howling wilderness, the migrating hobo founded no settlements and formed no communities, preferring instead to move from job to job and place to place according to individual whim. "The hobo," Park continued, "who begins his career by breaking the local ties that bound him to his family and his neighborhood, has ended by breaking all other associations. He is not only a 'homeless man,' but a man without a cause and without a country" (159-160).

Beneath the surface of this widespread myth, which alternately romanticized and demonized the hobo's individualism, lies a fascinating and hidden history of hobo subculture in the West. The history of the western hobo, subsequently

---

Todd A. DePastino is a historian of twentieth-century American social and cultural history. He has recently completed his Ph.D. dissertation, "From Hobohemia to Skid Row: Homelessness and American Culture, 1870-1950," in the history department at Yale University.

repressed and transformed into myth in the 1920s and 1930s, reveals much about the social and cultural processes of community formation among marginal groups. Through distinctive social networks, rituals, and institutions, migratory hobo workers of the West resisted marginalization as individual "homeless men" and forged vibrant single-sex communities. Headquartered in urban lodging house neighborhoods and extending along railroad lines and into the mines, forests, lakes, harvest fields, and countless other sites where hoboes pursued casual and seasonal labor, these communities drew upon shared experiences of class and peculiar constructions of masculinity. Forging a community of footloose migrants was also a social and cultural project pursued by organizations like the Industrial Workers of the World which, through its propaganda and organizing efforts, mobilized the hobo identity for the purposes of "labor's emancipation." In the eyes of a dominant culture which viewed feminine domesticity as necessary for true community, however, the hobo could only gain legitimacy, or at least recognition, as a rugged individualist or romantic dreamer personifying, in Wallace Stegner's words, "the indigenous optimism of the West" (*Bluebird* xxi). This myth of hobo individualism eclipsed the history of hobo community at just the moment when the hobo's distinctive patterns of lodging, labor, and migration had begun to pass away.

Etymologically obscure, the word "hobo" first appeared in print in the 1890s. According to one observer, the term "originated in the West [to designate] the many who, failing of their first hopes, were forced to the necessity of tramping from community to community in quest of employment" (Bailey 218). By the turn of the century, "hobo" denoted especially the hundreds of thousands of transient workers who circulated in the relatively new agricultural and extractive sectors of the West. Hobo workers harvested wheat on the Great Plains; picked fruit and felled trees in California, Oregon, and Washington; cut ice on the Great Lakes; mined iron, coal, and copper in Minnesota, Colorado, and Montana; and constructed the railroads, towns, and cities that comprised the very infrastructure of the industrial West.

The experience of homeless migration, of course, was not peculiar to the West of the 1890s. In the economic depression of 1873 to 1878, the "tramp" emerged as a category of widespread concern and moral panic when unprecedented numbers of jobless workers across the nation took to the road in search of work. The tramp crisis itself had been decades in the making as the American working class saw its shelters against unemployment and geographic drift eroded by an ever-increasing dependence upon wage labor. Premier among these waning protections was the household as a patriarchal domain and site of productive activity that allowed families to subsist during jobless periods. With the final disappearance of non-market-oriented artisans, farmers, and other producers in the late nineteenth century, many would-be household patriarchs found themselves as "tramps" and "hoboes," moving about in pursuit of wage jobs which were almost always irregular and whose geographic distribution was uneven. But not all unemployed working people enjoyed the privileges of homeless migration. Social convention, the law, and extra-legal violence prohibited most women, African Americans, and eastern and southern European immigrants from striking out on their own in search of work. What would come to be known as "hoboing," then, was but one way to experience the insecurity and poverty endemic to wage labor, a response reserved almost exclusively for white, male, and English-speaking workers.

Although joblessness and homelessness were national phenomena, turn-of-the-century western workers rapidly gained reputations for being especially footloose. As one social worker put in 1903, "[t]ramps are made in the West" (Spence, "Knights of the Tie" 5). The extraordinary volatility of western labor markets, heightened not only by boom-bust cycles, but also by the largely seasonal nature of much of the labor, made unemployment a routine feature of what Carlos Schwantes has called the "wageworker's frontier." (*Pacific*) Moreover, as many work sites were geographically isolated at points of extraction or were located in smaller towns and cities where labor markets were homogenous, losing one's job almost always entailed migration, quite often of long distances. To facilitate such extreme transiency, western laborers perfected the dangerous art of "train flipping" to an extent unrealized by their eastern counterparts. "Now it is notorious," remarked Jack London in 1902, "that Eastern tramps do not know how to 'railroad.'" Indeed, those whom London dismissed as "the lesser local tramps" of the East traveled in regions where work sites were relatively concentrated and often accessible by foot (*Jack London* 89, 94). With passenger rates high and employers often unwilling to pay transportation expenses, stealing rides on freights was often the only option for western job seekers. Suppressing such trespassing when labor demand was low, railroads also often subsidized the transportation costs of labor by disregarding ride-stealing hoboes when labor was scarce or when employers wished to depress wages, such as during harvest seasons.

While railroads provided cheap transportation, urban lodging-house neighborhoods supplied inexpensive food, shelter, clothing, and other services to the migratory worker. These "main stem" or "slave market" neighborhoods first appeared in western cities and towns in the 1890s as new metropolitan economies absorbed surrounding hinterland markets and productive regions. The lodging house and its satellite businesses served the needs of hinterland employers, who benefitted from these neighborhoods' ability to reproduce and deploy a cheap and highly flexible labor force. Located adjacent to towering new central business districts and within walking distance of railroad yards, rivers, and major thoroughfares, these neighborhoods included an array of commercial services such as second-hand stores, saloons, cheap restaurants, burlesque and prostitution houses, and employment agencies. Seattle's "Skid Road," San Francisco's "South of Market," Minneapolis's "Gateway," and Omaha's Douglas Street all functioned as resorts and clearinghouses for hobo labor, feeding harvest fields, mines, forests, and construction sites throughout their hinterlands and receiving a steady inflow of migrants back to their districts when jobs ended. Dwarfing even these was Chicago's vast "hobohemia" which encircled the Loop and extended at least one-half mile in each direction. According to one habitué, this neighborhood hosted an "hourly exodus from West Madison Street to the far reaches of the West" (DeCaux, *Labor* 55). With over fifty employment agencies, three-hundred lodging houses, and forty separate railroads radiating outward from the city center, Chicago rightfully claimed the dubious title, "Hobo Capital of America" ("Chicago").

Lodging-house neighborhoods like Chicago's West Madison street not only served as centers for the circulation of hobo labor, but also provided the physical landscape in which the hobo identity and community flourished. Visitors to these neighborhoods quickly noticed the presence of a distinctly independent, aggressive, and flamboyant persona. "There was an atmosphere of recklessness and daring about these fellows," recalled Charles Ashleigh of Minneapolis's Gateway in the years before the First World War (*Rambling*, 92). In 1927, William Edge similarly described the western hobo as resistant to any label, such as "homeless," which connoted disaffiliation, resignation, or victimization. "In Chicago," Edge wrote, "the hobo is self-conscious":

> In New York, Pittsburgh, Cleveland, Baltimore, the hobo was an adventitious migratory. He went dumbly from job to job, impelled by the relentless forces of modern capitalism. He was simply a man beaten by an economic system. In Chicago, the hobo seemed to be a hobo by choice. The men were large, strong, conscious of their disinheritance. They seemed not to be victims of circumstances; they came to Chicago of their own free will, to 'get by' during the winter. They knew what they were about. They had definite standards. They did not allow themselves to be kicked about from job to job. They had worked on the wheat all summer, or on war jobs. Now that winter was coming, they had left for Chicago. The hegira was not accidental; it was as conscious as the migrations to Palm Beach or the Riviera. (202)

The Chicago hobo, Edge suggested, achieved his margin of autonomy and independence through the shared codes, standards, and practices transmitted and reinforced by West Madison's subculture.

Undergirding this subcultural autonomy was an ethic of reciprocity and mutualism which informed virtually every aspect of hobo community. While on the road, migrants often improvised makeshift hobo "jungles" strategically located outside the purview of local officials and residents but close to running water and railroad division points. The jungle constituted, in one observer's words, a "marvel of cooperation" where migrants pooled resources and split the necessary tasks of scavenging, begging, and wage labor (Kemp 1270). Frederick Mills, an investigator of migratory labor for the California Commission of Immigration and Housing in 1914, also remarked on the "hearty camaraderie in these jungles." "If you have nothing to eat," he explained, "you are usually hailed and asked to join the group (Woirol 79). What Mills called the "code of hobo ethics" also governed hoboes' interactions in cities. "I gave money to several fellows [in Fargo]," recorded Powers Hapgood in his journal as he hoboed from St. Paul to the West coast in 1920. "It's the way the floaters do. When one has money he gives it to the man who needs it, and when he is broke he asks the price of a meal from the man who has it" (Journal, 16 Oct. 1920).

Much of the reciprocity which characterized hobo subculture took the form of treating others to drinks, a prevailing custom in the working-class saloon culture of the late nineteenth and early twentieth centuries. The saloon ritual of treating, so central to the everyday affirmation of working-class solidarity, took exaggerated form in the hobo world which alternated periods of intense labor at isolated worksites with those of relative leisure, albeit unemployed leisure, in densely populated urban centers. Arrival on the main stem thus often involved, as Frederick Mills put it, "a period of more or less riotous living" (Floating 67). Hoboes landing in Minneapolis's Gateway, recalled Charles Ashleigh:

> spent their money royally. After working for a couple months or more in a construction camp, where they slept in wooden bunks, or in a lumber camp, they would come into town with their pockets full of money; and then there would be a prodigious celebration! Everybody was welcome to share in the 'stiff's' prosperity; and everyone did! (*Rambling*, 92).

This practice of accumulating wages and then spending them in convivial surroundings not only affirmed and drew upon practices of reciprocity, it also represented a sharp rebuke to the ethic of individual acquistivism. Indeed, the uncompromising rejection of this bourgeois ethic was one of the strongest and most striking aspects of hobo subculture. Most investigators recognized this lack of a drive to accumulate savings and acquire property to be the hobo's most glaring "maladjustment," one which explained more than any other the problems of labor discipline and "homelessness." "It seems that when a laborer has earned a sum which road tradition has fixed as affluence, he quits," wrote Carleton Parker of

California's migratory workers in 1915. "This sum," Parker explained:

> is known as a "jungle stake," and once it is earned the hobo discipline calls upon the casual to resort to a camp under a railroad bridge or along some stream, a "jungle," as the vernacular terms it, and live upon this 'stake' till it is gone. (78-79)

The rejection of acquisitivism was also the root of the hobo's noted independence and volatility on the job. "Hobos are easily piqued," commented sociologist Nels Anderson in 1923, "and they will 'walk off' the job on the slightest pretext, even when they have the best jobs and living conditions are relatively good" (*Hobo* 74).

These privileges of mobility, nurtured and sustained by hobo subculture, accrued almost exclusively to men. While gender determined eligibility for membership, the subculture, in turn, fostered a group identity and relations which were highly gendered. Hoboes delimited their world through an absence not only of women, but of feminine manners, morals, and domesticity. One hobo, describing a group of fellow workers in 1919, emphasized the subculture's distinctly masculine and "uncivilized" characteristics:

> Youths, rough and rude, but all the more manly for that, other men blasted and seared in countenance— all conversing in a language which, in another sphere, would be accounted blasphemy—but in their estimation only emphatic—with their own moral code (it may not be yours), but in their case the one most suitable to their mode of life. (Quirke 4).

Hoboes considered the absence of the "other sphere" as a necessary condition of their independence and superiority. Even the proximity to women through domesticity compromised one's masculinity. The hoboes of West Madison street, recalled Elizabeth Gurley Flynn from her first visit there, "regarded the city workers as stay-at-home softies—'scissorbills.' They referred to a wife as 'the ball and chain'" (*Rebel Girl* 103).

The distinct gender ideologies at work in hobo subculture were manifest in the hobo's sexual practices which frequently included, even centered upon, sex with men. "Sufficient to say," commented one observer of hobo life, "that sodomy is more often the rule than the exception" (Nylander 230). Numerous other investigators reached similar conclusions. "Every hobo in the United States knows what 'unnatural intercourse' means," stated Josiah Flynt in 1899, "talking of it freely, and, according to my finding, every tenth man practices it, and defends his conduct" (360). "All studies indicate," concurred Anderson in 1923 after reviewing previous research, "that homosexual practices among homeless men are widespread" (*Hobo* 144). The hobo world certainly provided the period's largest and most important single-sex environment bringing together young working-class men from vast geographic areas. Like the military, hoboing freed young men from family, neighborhood, and small-town supervision and granted many their first opportunities for sexual experience. Life on the road also required that men share close quarters, whether they be bunkhouses, jungles, park benches, or lodging houses which achieved the extremes of lodging density. Hoboes in transit also huddled together, "often body to body," as former hobo Len DeCaux described it. "Stretched on the floor in the dark," DeCaux explained, "I didn't mind bodies rolled against mine by the jolting. I didn't like stealthy fingers." These fingers searched not only for money, but also for erotic encounter. "Once I awoke," recalled DeCaux, "after a crawly nightmare, to find my fly-buttons undone and my private parts exposed to public view" (*Labor* 59).

Not all such encounters were unwanted or unsolicited, and the mere opportunity for sexual relations does not explain or guarantee motivation. Hobo life, entailing as it did material deprivation and frequent migration, bred close, if temporary, friendships. On the main stem or on the road, men frequently coupled off for reasons of safety, frugality, and company. Sharing rooms, beds, boxcars, and other resources for extended periods was not unusual, and most such relationships were not sexual. Edge, for example, hoboed for over one year with his friend Slim, sleeping in the same beds, working the same jobs, and enjoying the same saloons between 1917 and 1918. Edge never indicated, however, an erotic dimension to their bond. In fact, after he and Slim parted company, Edge rejected another potential companion after discovering this hobo to be a "fairy" who entertained erotic interests in men (125-26). Edge's disgust with his companion's homosexuality attested to the homophobia which existed in hobohemia, as well as in the culture at large. But Edge's rejected mate also bore witness to the prominent role that sexuality could play in the bonds between hoboes. While Anderson assessed most homosexual relations in Chicago's hobohemia as emotionally barren and of short duration, he noted some "attachments between men and between men and boys 'that surpass the love of woman.'" "Many of these are not more than a few days' duration," continued Anderson, "but while they last they are very intense and sentimental" ("Juvenile" 306).

Initiation into hobo subculture also often included a sexual component. Most prevalent, and certainly most widely discussed and lampooned among hoboes and non-hoboes alike, were the relationships between older hoboes, or "jockers," and young initiates, or "punks." Coercing, cajoling, or enticing punks into sex, jockers offered in exchange protection, money, or general instruction in the skills of begging, freight-hopping, and securing food and shelter. Jockers commonly approached punks on the road, in jungles, parks, lodging houses or even on the streets. "One need not be in the [hobo] class long before he learns of the existence of the practice," testified Nels Anderson, "and any boy who has been on the road long without having been approached many times is an exception" ("Juvenile" 301). The jocker-punk relationship pervaded the various literatures of and about hobo life, from social welfare and police reports to autobiographical accounts of initiation and even popular hobo folklore. Indeed, before popular singers and folklorists in the 1920s bowdlerized "The Big Rock Candy Mountain," this most famous of hobo folksongs originally recounted in sardonic fashion the luring of a boy into a jocker's lair through promises of "cigarette trees," "lemonade springs," and "soda water fountains" (Greenway 203-204).

The sexual bonds between older and younger hoboes comprised one part of a larger erotic system which, as George Chauncey has recently demonstrated, was widespread among not only hobo laborers, but also among seamen, sailors, prisoners, and other male working-class groups disengaged from family and home neighborhoods. Jockers generally abided by the conventions of predatory masculinity, refusing to be penetrated, not taking feminine nicknames, and otherwise, in the words of Anderson, "substitut[ing] the boy for the woman" ("Juvenile" 302). Many inside and outside the subculture regarded involvement with a jocker as a sign of weakness or "femininity" rather than of homosexual tendencies or "queerness." Consequently, young hoboes often considered the evasion of predatory jockers as crucial to preserving their manhood. Mac McClintock, author of "The Big Rock Candy Mountain," rated his boyhood battles with jockers as the most strenuous aspect of his initiation into the hobo world at the turn of the century. "There were times when I fought like a wildcat or ran like a deer," recalled McClintock, "to preserve my independence and my virginity" (Spence 55).

Hobo sexual practices, especially the jocker-punk system, must be understood in the context of more general working-class defintions of masculinity or "manliness." Whereas early-twentieth-century middle-class culture increasingly equated manliness with heterosexuality, working-class culture, as Chauncey argues, "regarded manhood as a hard-won accomplishment, not a given," and as something "confirmed by other men and in relation to other men, not by women" (80). As members of an almost uniformly homosocial subculture, hoboes especially constituted, challenged, and reaffirmed their manhood daily through rituals and performances of solidarity and competition. These included the sexual domination of women and other "non-men" like "fairies" and "punks." The fragility of the hobo's gender status, in the face of predatory jockers and other ritual challenges to manhood, explains both the vigilance with which many hoboes defended their masculinity and the lengths to which some might go in demonstrating manliness.

If this emphasis on the performativity of manliness illuminates the place of the jocker in the hobo community's gender system, then the subculture's extreme homosociability also sheds light on the more reciprocal and mutually-constituted homosexual relationships among hoboes. These relationships in many ways merely extended into the sexual realm the bonds that all hoboes shared with each other as men. Describing an evening at a migratory workers' saloon, for example, Edge captured both the erotic extremes to which some hoboes took their homosociability and the limits which others, like Edge, placed on theirs. "Two workers whom I knew by sight," commented a disapproving but unsurprised Edge, "were dancing in a disgustingly homosexual manner." At the same time, Edge expressed frustration at his own inability to converse or connect in any way with the available women at the bar: "how I wish these girls were men. I could talk to the men. . . . But these girls!" (119, 127). Others expressed similar uneasiness with female companionship and anxiety at the prospects of a settled heterosexual relationship. In 1921, Anderson reported that many of the hoboes he interviewed attributed their homosexual interest simply to the values, attitudes, and general sociability they shared with other men, but not women. These hoboes claimed "that in the homosexual relations there is the absense of the eternal complications in which one becomes involved with women" (*Hobo* 149).

In addition to informal sexual practices, gender ideologies, and rituals of reciprocity and anti-acquisitivism, hobo subculture also nurtured formal organizations that fostered communal ties and a sense of larger purpose among its members. The famous "Industrial Armies of the Unemployed" established an important and spectacular precedent for these organizations in 1894 as they recruited marchers from western lodging-house neighborhoods for their cross-country "petition in boots." Of more profound and lasting importance for the hobo community was the Industrial Workers of the World (IWW), founded in 1905 and headquartered on Chicago's West Madison street. IWW halls on West Madison street and elsewhere provided those things most desired by hoboes: food, shelter, employment information, and a sense of community. Wobbly halls, wrote Parker, "are not so much places for executive direction of the union as much as gregarious centers where the lodging house inhabitant or the hobo with his blanket can find a light, a stove, and companionship. In the prohibition states of the West, the I.W.W. hall has been the only social substitute for the saloon to these people" (115-16). By virtue of its unqualified commitment after 1908 to direct economic action, the union also organized hoboes in the field, winning higher wages, shorter hours, and improved sleeping and working conditions for migratory workers throughout the West.

Although meeting hoboes' basic needs remained a fundamental mission of the IWW, the union also pursued an important cultural project: namely, mobilizing the hobo identity and subculture for the purposes of larger social and political transformation. Specifically, Wobblies considered the hobo as on the vanguard of social change and as representing broader constituencies apart from merely those on the main stem. "Nowhere else can a section of the working class be found so admirably fitted to serve as the scouts and advance guards of the labor army," wrote one Wobbly in 1914. "Rather, [hoboes] may become the guerillas of the revolution—the franc-tireurs of the class struggle" (Kornbluh 66-7).

The endeavor to reshape the politics and cultural meanings of the hobo community informed the pages of the IWW's numerous newspapers, pamphlets, and especially its famous "Little Red Songbook." Issued first as a thin flyer by the Spokane local in 1908, the Little Red Songbook eventually went through twenty-nine editions and included over 175 songs under the title, *Songs of the Workers, On the Road, In the Jungles, and In the Shops—Songs to Fan the Flames of Discontent*. Although the editions changed significantly over time, they all bore the heavy imprint of hobo subculture. Specifically, these songs provided a community that lacked clear boundaries with a powerful set of myths to enhance group definition and continuity. These myths also effectively composed a folklore which endowed the hobo with new authority as a bearer of authentic proletarian consciousness. The impact of this new folklore on the hobo community was swift and far reaching. "Where a group of hoboes sit around a fire under a railroad bridge," noted Parker in 1914, "many of them can sing I.W.W. songs without a book" (190).

IWW folklore, especially the selections from the Little Red Songbook, depicted the hobo's detachment from the feminine sphere of home and the bonds of settled society as providing a freedom to discover an authentic proletarian identity. "The Mysteries of the Hobo's Life," written by Matt Valentine Huhta, alias T-Bone Slim, for the songbook's 1916 edition, represents initiation into hobo subculture simultaneously as an exile from civilization and an induction into manhood and class consciousness:

> The boss put me driving spikes
> > And the sweat was enough to blind me
> He didn't seem to like my pace,
> > So I left the job behind me.
> I grabbed a hold of an old freight train

And around the country traveled
The mysteries of a hobo's life
To me were soon unraveled. . . .
I ran across a bunch of 'stiffs'
Who were known as Industrial Workers.
They taught me how to be a man—
And how to fight the shirkers.
I kicked right in and joined the bunch
And now in the ranks you'll find me,
Hurrah for the cause—To hell with the boss!
And the job I left behind me (*IWW* 7).

Invoking hobohemia's gendered rituals of solidarity, reciprocity, anti-acquistiveness, and autonomy, "The Mysteries of the Hobo's Life" constructs migratory labor as a community of authentic masculinity which also signified the larger collective.

Not surprisingly, jungle life provided a particularly popular trope in this folklore of the hobo, for it was in the absence of domesticity, civilization, and workplace subordination where the IWW's imagined community of masculinity flourished. In the Wobbly anthem, "Meet Me in the Jungles, Louie" (composed to the tune of the popular song, "Meet Me in St. Louis, Louie"), a worker "out of a job" and "dead on the hog" departs conventional society to join a host of jungle-dwelling hoboes:

Louie went out of his shack,
He swore he would never come back;
He said, "I will wait, and take the first freight,
My friends in the jungles to see;
For me there is waiting out there,
Of a mulligan stew a big share.
So away I will go and be a hobo,
For the song in the jungles I hear." (Kornbluh 72)

Constrasting "the song in the jungles" heard by Louie was the siren song of domestic life which carried "scissor-bills," "sissies," and other "homeguard" workers to the embrace of feminine civilization. In a cartoon drawn by Joe Hill and published in a 1913 issue of the *Industrial Worker*, for example, a "migratory worker" chases a female apparition whose graceful and diaphanous body encodes the settled existence of civilized society as distinctly feminine (Figure 1). With a crown atop her head reading "job," the female form speeds along on a unicyle tied to one foot while holding a pork chop just of the migratory worker's reach. Also beckoning the migratory is a "homeguard" man in a rocking chair perched on the front porch of a grocery store who calls upon the hobo to "stay in one place and vote the Socialist ticket." Joe Hill's cartoon suggests that the promises of capitalist civilization, represented by the female apparition and housed worker, are illusory and deceptive, diverting the migratory from his true path and authentic identity in the masculine community of the hobo.

In its conflation of class consciousness with virile masculinity and the rejection of feminine "civilization," the IWW's hobo folklore also deployed the dominant myth of the frontier West and its "savage" Native American inhabitants. As the work of such diverse men and organizations as Theodore Roosevelt, Frederic Remington, and the Boy Scouts of America testifies, frontier mythology enjoyed broad currency among a

Figure 1. Joe Hill. Industrial Worker *24 (April 1913). Reproduced in Joyce L. Kornbluh, ed.* Rebel Voices: An IWW Anthology, *129.*

turn-of-the-century bourgeoisie beset by overdetermined crises of masculinity and "overcivilization." These crises arose from an array of challenges and uncertainties confronting middle-class men in this period: powerful urban immigrant political machines, the expansion of public sphere activities among women, and the diminishing economic independence and bodily vigor among a sedentary corporate salariat. Fostering key qualities that modern industrial society supposedly suppressed—rugged individualism, manly self-reliance, and physical strength and endurance—the mythic frontier West offered an ideal site for regenerating "morally flabby" white middle-class men.

Wobbly folklore both reconfigured and reinforced this frontier myth by invoking the West time and again as the mythic space of the hobo community, a crucible of vigorously masculine and revolutionary activity standing in contrast to the settled domesticity and docility of the East. "[The hobo] is the leaven of the revolutionary industrial union movement in the West," announced the *Industrial Union Bulletin* in 1908, "and his absence . . . from the East, accounts in large measure for the slowness of the Eastern workers to awaken from their lethargy" (Dubofsky 140). While the bourgeois West offered individual escape and regeneration from an East plagued by immigration, feminism, and corporate domination, the West of hobo folklore provided a uniquely masculine environment for the collective expression of revolutionary class power. An illustration submitted by a contributor to an October 1916 edition of *Solidarity*, for example, represents militant working-class manhood as specifically western. Entitled "Now for the Eastern Invasion!" this drawing depicts the "Harvest Spirit" as a brawny hobo with a black cat and wooden *sabots*, heading off to organize "eastern factories" (Figure 2).

Whereas fiercely oppositional Indians had once contested the dominant claims made by whites on the West, radical hoboes like the "Harvest Spirit" now roamed the plains and forests, offering their own opposition. Former hobo and editor of the *Industrial Worker*, Fred Thompson described the "process of selection" through which he believed western hoboes evolved: "those who least tolerated the ways of the east, went west. There most of them did not become settled or tied in a specific location—there weren't enough females to tie them. They were footloose" (Dubofsky 25). This explanation of the West's masculinity combined Frederick Jackson Turner's frontier thesis with the natural selection principles of Social Darwinism. As an environment free of women and the influences of civilized domesticity, the West, according to this myth, renewed men's primitive freedoms of movement and habits of collective association. By cutting male workers loose from enslaving feminine regimes, the "wageworker's frontier" created "natural" revolutionaries. Hobo folklore encoded this revolutionary environment entirely as masculine. "The nomadic worker of the West embodies the very spirit of the I.W.W.," wrote one contributor to *Solidarity* in 1914:

> His cheerful cynicism, his frank and outspoken contempt for most of the conventions of bourgeois society, including the more stringent conventions which masquerade under the name of morality, make him an admirable exemplar of the iconoclastic doctrine of revolutionary unionism. . . . His anomolous position, half industrial slave, half vagabond adventurer, leaves

Now For the Eastern Invasion!

Solidarity. October 14, 1916.

Figure 2. "Bingo." Solidarity (14 October 1916). Reproduced in Joyce L. Kornbluh, ed. Rebel Voices: An I.W.W. Anthology, 242.

him infinitely less servile than his fellow worker in the
East. Unlike the factory slave of the Atlantic seaboard
and the Central States, he is most emphatically not
'afraid of his job.'

His mobility is amazing. . . . No wife or family encum-
ber him. The workman of the East, oppressed by the
fear of want for wife and babies, dares not venture
much. He has perforce the tameness of the domesticated animals (Kornbluh 66-67).

Encapsulating the folklore of the hobo, this passage reflects
and reproduces dominant constructions of masculinity, domesticity, civilization, and even race by linking the hobo's
revolutionary freedom with the "savage" characteristics of the
frontier. Meanwhile, the servility of family-encumbered eastern workers is inscribed on their very bodies through the
metaphor of tamed domestic animals.

Another prominent contribution to the hobo frontier myth
was Ashleigh's essay on "The Floater," published in the *International Socialist Review* in 1914. Ashleigh's essay similarly
inscribes the attributes of western "savagery"—masculine
strength, virility, and fearlessness—on the hobo's body while
depicting the eastern working-class as feminized and ane-
mic. Recapitulating hobo folklore's Darwinian environmentalism, Ashleigh described the East's "permanence of industry" as encouraging "marriage, the procreation of children and
some amount of stability." The region's monotonous and im-
prisoning factory labor, however, engendered a "loss of ner-
vous and physical vitality and the creation of bodily weak-
lings" among the eastern working-class. In the West, by contrast, where manufacturing had not yet dominated, extractive sectors like lumbering, mining, and agriculture created
"a man's country" characterized by bunkhouses and lodging
houses. Western workers were "[s]un-tanned, brawny men,
most of them in early manhood or in the prime of life," and
animated by a "growing spirit of passionate rebellion." Subli-
mating the well-known homosocial eroticism of hobo subculture into a discourse of revolution, Ashleigh freights the very
bodies of these workers with class power:

[T]he arduous physical toil in the open air does not
have the same deteriorating effect as does the mechani-

cal, confined work of the eastern slave. The constant
matching of wits and daring needed for the long trips
across country have developed a species of rough self-
reliance in the wandering proletarian of the West. In
health and in physical courage he is undoubtedly the
superior of his eastern brother. (Kornbluh 82-83)

As Ashleigh's references to "daring," "rough self-reliance," and
"physical courage" suggest, the IWW's folklore of the hobo
was susceptible to immediate appropriation by a dominant
culture already invested in myths of frontier individualism
and virile masculinity. The shifting of hobo folklore from the
IWW to the mainstream occurred especially as the hobo
community's power and prominence declined in the 1920s
and 1930s.

According to Anderson, the hobo was clearly "on his way
out" by the time of his investigations of the subculture in
1922. This decline resulted from multiple interventions in
labor, transportation, and housing markets on the part of
state reformers, who increasingly defined the hobo as "homeless," and business persons, who considered the hobo a problem of labor discipline. Selective applications of new tech-
nologies, such as the harvest combine in the Great Plains,
diminished the need for migratory workers in logging, mining, agriculture, and other key sectors of the West. Strategic
changes in management practices also reduced dependence
on the hobo. Owners of mines, farms, lumber companies, and
railroads followed advice from state and federal officials and
increased wages, improved housing, and recruited more
settled and vulnerable family groups, often unnaturalized
Mexicans, as laborers. The automobile, in turn, made family
migration possible, privatizing travel and allowing workers to
commute from towns and cities to nearby worksites. All of
these changes drastically reduced the need for urban hobo
commercial services like the lodging house, which also suffered from zoning ordinances and housing regulations designed to reclaim downtown space for higher uses. Finally,
these social and economic vicissitudes, as well as official state
repression, crippled the IWW during and after World War I.
By the mid-1920s, the hobo's once premier organization stood
on the verge of collapse.

The fall of the IWW and its hobo base precipitated the
production of a new folklore which bowdlerized the hobo's

subculture and frequently celebrated the hobo as an exemplar of possessive individualism. "Hoboes of America, Incorporated," a group organized in the 1930s to preserve hobo lore, called upon members:

> to do all in their power to aid and assist all those willing to aid and assist themselves, to aid all runaway boys to return to their homes and parents, never to be unjust to others, never to take advantage of their fellow men, and to do all in their power for the betterment of themselves, their organization and America, so help them God. ("Hoboes" 2).

While "Hoboes of America" promoted mainstream patriotic values, "Hobo King" Ben Benson extolled "the road" as a proving ground for traditional American self-reliance. Having won his crown at a folk festival in the 1940s, Benson explained that hoboing had once provided adventure for "men and boys who had the right stuff—sometimes called the American Rugged Individualism" (Allsop 45). Hoboes also attracted the attention of academic folklorists such as George Milburn who in 1930 published the first collection of hobo songs, poems, and slang for the public at large. As was typical among these new popularizers and folklorists, Milburn limned the hobo as an individualist "who does not seek society" and whose songs "narrate the feats and adventures common to the vagrant life" (xi, xiv). While some Depression-era artists, such as Woody Guthrie, revived old IWW themes of proletarian collectivism to address the period's dislocations, most folklore after 1930 domesticated hobo life through stories of individual freedom, adventure, and reverie.

Thus the mythic hobo, debunked by Stegner as a grasping and pillaging western "boomer," was of recent vintage, the product of a new tamer folklore constructed in the wake of the hobo community's collapse. Stegner, in effect, had uncovered the wrong "underside" of hobo life in his critique of the twentieth-century West. Beneath both the hobo myth and Stegner's critique lay the story of an erotically-charged masculine subculture which had mobilized itself against "wage slavery" and capitalism in general. It is ironic that in his travels among the boomers and pillagers of the West, Stegner might have found, but did not, a countervailing source of community in the American hobo.

ACKNOWLEDGEMENTS

Figures 1 and 2 are from *Rebel Voices: An I.W.W. Anthology,* originally from the Labadie Collection, Special Collections Library, University of Michigan and are reprinted by permission of Edward C. Weber, Curator, Labadie Collection.

Those illustrations as well as the lyrics from *The Little Red Songbook* and *Industrial Worker* appear in the revised and expanded edition of Kornbluh's *Rebel Voices* and are reprinted by permission of the publisher, Charles H. Kerr Publishing Company.

REFERENCES

Allsop, Kenneth. *Hard Travellin': The Hobo and His History.* New York: The New American Library, 1967.
Anderson, Nels. "The Juvenile and the Tramp." *Journal of Criminology and Criminal Law* 14 (August 1922): 290-312.
———. *The Hobo: The Sociology of the Homeless Man.* 1923. Reprint. Chicago: Phoenix Books, 1965.
Ashleigh, Charles. *Rambling Kid.* London: Faber, 1930.
Bailey, E. Lamar. "Tramps and Hoboes." *The Forum* 26 (October 1898): 217-220.
Chauncey, George. *Gay New York: Gender, Urban Culture, and the Making of the Gay Male World, 1890-1940.* New York: Basic Books, 1994.
"Chicago: Hobo Captial of America." *Survey* 50 (1 June 1923): 287-290, 303- 305.
DeCaux, Len. *Labor Radical: From Wobblies to CIO: A Personal History.* Boston: Beacon Press, 1970.
Dubofsky, Melvyn. *We Shall Be All: A History of the Industrial Workers of the World.* Chicago: Quadrangle Books, 1969.
Edge, William. *The Main Stem.* New York: Vanguard, 1927.
Flynn, Elizabeth Gurley. *Rebel Girl.* New York: International Publishers, 1973.
Flynt, Josiah [Josiah Flynt Willard]. "Homosexuality Among Tramps." *Studies in the Psychologuy of Sex.* Vol. 2. Ed. Havelock Ellis. 1910. Reprint. New York: Random House, 1936.
Greenway, John, ed. *American Folksongs of Protest.* New York: Octagon Books, 1970.
Hapgood, Powers. Journal. Powers Hapgood Papers. Minnesota Historical Society. St. Paul, Minn.
"Hoboes of America, Incorporated." *1939 Year Book, Encyclopedia, and Reference Manual.* vol. 1. n.p.: Printed by the Executive Board, 1938.
Industrial Workers of the World. *Songs of the Workers: On the Road, in the Jungles, and in the Shops.* Cleveland: I.W.W. Publishing Bureau, 1916.

Kemp, Harry. "The Lure of the Tramp." *Independent* 70 (8 June 1911): 1270-1271.

Kornbluh, Joyce L., ed. *Rebel Voices: An I.W.W. Anthology.* Ann Arbor: University of Michigan Press, 1965. Revised and expanded edition. Chicago: Charles H. Kerr Publishing Company, 1988.

London, Jack. *Jack London on the Road: The Tramp Diary and Other Hobo Writings.* Ed. Richard W. Etulain. Logan: Utah State University Press, 1979.

Milburn, George. *The Hobo's Hornbook: A Repetory for a Gutter Jongleur.* New York: Ives Washburn, 1930.

Nylander, Towne. "Tramps and Hoboes." *Forum* 74 (August 1925): 227-237.

Park, Robert E. "The Mind of the Hobo: Reflections Upon the Relation between Mentality and Locomotion." *The City.* Eds. Robert E. Park, Ernest W. Burgess, Roderick D. McKenzie. Chicago: University of Chicago Press, 1925.

Parker, Carleton H. *The Casual Laborer and Other Essays.* New York: Harcourt, Brace, and Hose, 1920.

Quirke, Will J. "A Hobo Deluxe Cruise." "Hobo."*News* (May 1919): 4.

Rosenzweig, Roy. *Eight Hours for What We Will: Workers and Leisure in an Industrial City, 1870-1920.* New York: Cambridge University Press, 1983.

Rotundo, E. Anthony. *American Manhood: Transformations in Masculinity from the Revolution to the Modern Era.* New York: Basic Books, 1993.

Schwantes, Carlos A. *The Pacific Northwest: An Interpretive History.* Lincoln: University of Nebraska Press, 1989.

Slotkin, Richard. *Fatal Environment: The Myth of the Frontier in the Age of Industrialization, 1800-1890.* New York: Atheneum, 1985.

Spence, Clarke C. "Knights of the Tie and Rail—Tramps and Hoboes in the West." *Western Historical Quarterly* 2 (January 1971): 5-17.

———."Knights of the Fast Freight." *American Heritage* 27 (August 1976): 50-57 , 92-97.

Stegner, Wallace. *Where the Bluebird Sings to the Lemonade Springs: Living and Writing in the West.* New York: Penguin, 1992.

Vincent, Henry. *The Story of the Commonweal.* 1894. Reprint. New York: Arno Press, 1969.

Woirol, Gregory R. *In the Floating Army: F.C. Mills on Itinerant Life in California, 1914.* Urbana: U of Illinois P, 1992.

Las Vegas
Community as Real Life
Virtual Reality

FELICIA FLORINE CAMPBELL

"We are what we think," said the Buddha, "what we are arises out of our thoughts. With our thoughts we make the world." If this is true, perhaps we all created the Strip, a dreamlike melange of times and places designed to lift its viewers from the ordinary by confronting them with the extraordinary. This is, perhaps, what joins Las Vegans, both old and new, in community.

The extraordinary was certainly what I was looking for in 1962 when I took the train to Las Vegas for a year's sojourn at what is now UNLV before writing my dissertation on Melville at the University of Wisconsin, Madison, then called "the Athens of the midwest." Young academics were in short supply, so I applied to only two universities, one the University of Ife in Ibidan, Nigeria, the other in Las Vegas, either of which I felt sure would provide me with a year out of the ordinary.

After the offer came from Las Vegas, I found myself, on a hot August evening, walking for the first time through a Las Vegas Casino, the Sahara. My train had arrived after midnight and Jim Dickinson, after whom UNLV's library was subsequently named, had picked me up and taken me to his neighborhood bar, the Sahara. My first reaction was disappointment. Women weren't wearing glamorous gowns and men weren't tuxedoed. In fact, the early morning crowd looked decidedly scruffy. This didn't fit the fantasy.

Felicia F. Campbell, is Professor of English at the University of Nevada, Las Vegas. Founder and Executive Director of the Far West Popular and American Culture Associations and editor of The Popular Culture Review, *she is also book critic for KNPR, Nevada Public Radio.*

After a quick drink, Jim drove me along dark, empty roads to Longacres Park, an apartment complex, he assured me, that was across from the University. He'd rented me a single room and bath, part of another apartment, but with a separate entrance. This was the only place that I could live, he explained, because I didn't drive. When I said that I would take buses, he smiled and left without disillusioning me. Early the next morning, I was blasted out of bed by enraged bellows coming from the apartment next door where the tenant was threatening to shoot his wife. Fearing stray bullets, I bolted outside to be met by the wife who said, "Don't pay no attention to him, honey. He never really shoots anybody." Far from convinced, I knew that the adventure had begun.

Feeling a little as though I had suddenly been conscripted by the French Foreign Legion, I dressed and trudged to the road looking for a restaurant, a bus stop or anything that smacked of what I thought of as civilization. Across Maryland Parkway was a complex of five unprepossessing, low slung buildings. Another woman stood at the curb dispiritedly looking across the road at the campus. Her first words were: "My god, it's a gas station." She too had arrived the previous night to teach at the University of Nevada, Southern Regional Division. Neither of us had been informed that we were coming to a non-degree granting institution.

Certainly the buildings were created on the gas station motel model, easily reached by car, with classroom doors facing outside corridors. Raw desert (how I'd love to see that now), stretched for three miles in all directions around this small enclave of apartments and university buildings. We were marooned. There were no bus stops or restaurants, no shops, nothing but heat. Fortunately she had a car and we soon repaired to the Stardust for breakfast, where we sat one table over from Jimmy Durante and considered our options, the first of which was to buy a gallon of wine.

In 1962, without shopping malls, with few restaurants outside hotels, no public radio or public TV, the Strip hotels became an integral part of our lives in a way that they are unlikely to for new residents today. We ate our meals next to celebrities and gangsters at the Tropicana, the Stardust, the Riviera, the Silver Slipper and the Desert Inn, where we waved at our students as they dealt craps and twenty-one or schlepped cocktails. We shopped for clothes in the hotel shops, because our only other choice was a Sears downtown. We often debated the schizophrenic nature of the community which greeted tourists with a sign that said welcome to ninety-three or ninety-seven, or some odd number, of churches, and discussed the ironies involved in the conservatism of both gamblers and the professional classes brought here by the test site and related activities. No matter what, like Dorothy in Oz, we definitely weren't in Kansas, or in my case Wisconsin, anymore. Of course, we complained incessantly. "Las Vegas has all the disadvantages of both a city and a small town and none of the advantages," we would moan. Still living here was, and still is, rather like being in a movie or wandering a virtual world.

This was particularly true for me as I had gone into culture shock when I got here, almost immediately marrying and later divorcing a man who was both a gambler and a dealer, and found myself veering between the worlds of academe and the Strip. This trapped me in Las Vegas. Although I had left Wisconsin lacking only the dissertation for completion of my doctorate, my marriage, children and finances intervened, and my course work ran out. I had to start over. Rather than relearning everything I had already learned, I decided to pursue a wholly new interdisciplinary degree and set out to a ninety thousand mile commute, in which for almost three years, I drove my little Toyota to San Diego early in the morning to attend classes, and returned to Las Vegas that same evening so that I could teach at UNLV the next day, and, of course, take care of the kids.

When the time came to do my dissertation, I decided to study the local gambling scene, and wrote a humanistic study and typology of normal gamblers who make up about 98 percent of the normal gambling population, people for whom I believe gambling serves some positive purpose. In the process, I hoped to destroy a number of myths about gamblers. I was successful and my thesis on *The Gambling Mystique: Mythologies and Typologies* was picked up by the wire services and major news magazines, giving me my fifteen minutes of fame. Examining casino regulars among the population, I came to a number of conclusions about community in the casinos. Certainly many of the retired elderly have carved out new worlds for themselves in casinos which cater to locals. Here they create communities in which they socialize with other regulars and the staff, finding respite from boredom in the altered state of consciousness that gambling creates for many people. As gambling itself is a kind of metaphor for life, it's little wonder that those shut out on other levels find satisfaction in intense involvement with casino games. Even the intensity of a small win can be meaningful for those excluded from life on a number of levels.

During the sixties and seventies, locals often referred to Las Vegas as "an old people's town." Older out-of-town gamblers were the ones with the money to spend and themes designed to lure them were appropriately old west or Hollywood glamorous. Places like the Silver Slipper and the Frontier reproduced the Old West theme while the first El Rancho hardly missed a beat as it burned, as gaming tables were carried outside while patrons ran along side refusing to stop playing. Hotels like the Sahara, the Desert Inn, the Dunes and the Riviera played to the idea of international glamour as portrayed in the movies. Here the visitor from Dubuque didn't need a virtual reality helmet to experience safe sin, but could ogle high rollers, entertainers, mobsters and sports figures, and return home infused with reflected glory to tell about it.

Times change, however, and a new generation became the prime market for Las Vegas, a generation that grew up on ersatz adventure in Disneyland and Magic Mountain and on the tube, a generation that wanted adult versions of the theme parks that they had enjoyed as children, and Las Vegas rose to the challenge.

Of course this is too simplistic to explain the evolution of Las Vegas into a themed virtual realty setting. For that we must look deeper.

Inconvenient as it may be for reductionists and those devoted to simple causality, we do not live a predictable, logical and linear universe, but in a turbulent world of complexities, intersecting realities and non-linearities so that we, like Chuang-Tsu are not certain whether we are butterflies dreaming we are people or people dreaming we are butterflies, and in either case find ourselves flapping over some strange terrain. Obviously we need new maps both to chart our courses and understand where we have been.

Of course, as philosopher/physicist F. W. Peat explains in *The Philosopher's Stone*, the old maps provided by individual disciplines such as psychology and sociology are useful. Road maps too are certainly useful to the traveler, but they and similar maps are only very restricted examples from the world of maps, a world which includes native American sand paintings and mandalas, maps which like fractal mathematics map infinity extending both inward and outward. Only these non-linear maps can help define my position in this discussion.

Peat defines a map as a true synchronicity, symbolic of the connection between actual events in the tangible outer world and the inner lives of those with whom it is connected. As he explains, the maps of indigenous people, which represent the cosmos, are drawn on materials from sand to skins; scientific maps, which reflect our views about ourselves and nature, are created on paper out of numbers and abstract mathematics. Naming scientific maps "maps of alienation," he calls for their reanimation (9-14). In turn I wonder whether theming in general and the Las Vegas Strip in particular could map elements of the collective psyche. Could they in some sense be inevitable?

We learn from science that the same patterns recur time and again, the same, yet always different. Searching makes the patterns appear. What appears as chaos is really a subtle form of order or perhaps many subtle forms of order. Systems within systems show self-similarity. Briggs and Peat tell us "that randomness is interleaved with order, that simplicity enfolds complexity, complexity harbors simplicity, and that orders can be repeated at smaller and smaller scales—phenomena the scientists of chaos have dubbed 'fractal'" (43).

What follows is an illustration from my own experience of one such pattern reflected in systems seemingly as diverse as memory, cable television and the growth and theming of the Las Vegas Strip, and what that pattern means to community.

A visiting professorship in Bozeman, Montana, several years ago, not only showed me that the legend that those who move away from Las Vegas will always return may well be true, but uncovered a set of patterns combining memory, the programming on cable television, and the theming of the Las Vegas Strip.

The communities of Las Vegas and Bozeman, Montana, have more in common than might be obvious on the surface. Bozeman itself displays an uncanny resemblance to the small

Wisconsin town in which I grew up. It also displays an incredible resistance to surface change. This resistance to physical change has created an atmosphere as themed and artificial as that of Las Vegas. Each community defines itself in romantic images, Bozeman's that of the past and Las Vegas' that of the past and future, with all stops between. This is, of course, iteration, or feedback, which involves continual reabsorption of what has gone before, and applies not only to weather systems and artificial intelligence, but to our communities as well.

Every year Las Vegas suffers, and I use the term advisedly, a population growth of about thirty-thousand people, roughly equal to the entire population of Bozeman. Vibrant, showy and glitzy, Las Vegas, which may be the ultimate postmodern city, is pushing its way into the twenty-first century as aggressively as Bozeman attempts to retreat into the nineteenth. Romantically, Bozeman wants to see itself as somehow virginal and unspoiled, untouched by time, while Las Vegas sees itself as sort of a time machine that will take the travelers either backward or forward to a high-tech version of whatever fantasy they choose.

Drawing on the principles of chaos theory, we can see that the environments of two such seemingly different communities may reflect the same pattern on different scales. To map that pattern, we must avoid a linear approach and look at it as though we were looking at a Native American sand painting in which each element is of equal importance and the role of the observer is minimized. This is in contrast to looking at a painting that makes traditional use of perspective, putting nature on a grid as it were, to create an illusion of reality through distortions, such as foreshortening, of the objects in it to reproduce the painter's vision; thus, for good or ill, condemning the viewer to share the painter's vision. In a traditional painting using perspective the viewer's eye is constantly drawn to the focal point created by a painter, a rather linear exercise; while the viewer of a sand painting where all objects are depicted as roughly the same size, whether man or tree, is not condemned to the single vision, but can begin or end anywhere (Peat 15-18).

By and large, Bozeman resists surface change, clinging to the last century. There seems to be a moral imperative of some sort operating here, a self-righteousness, a political correctness that attempts to freeze yesterday, which not only leads to the preservation of houses that even the original tenants must have hated, but to a denial that the only constant is change. This has the effect of turning the town into a rather linear, themed, old west tourist attraction. It was also, for an old Las Vegas resident like myself, incredibly boring, the only excitement coming from attempting to drive through icy, unmarked four way stops. This is in contrast to the giddy veering of Las Vegas' from century to century, which makes every commute an adventure of sorts, a foray into often unknown and ever changing territory and is probably an integral part of what forms our community.

The Bozeman experience did, however, offer me a paradigm shift. On my return visits, I saw Las Vegas from a tourist perspective. I'd check into a hotel, pretending to be a first time tourist so that I could exchange comments with my fellow travelers. Suddenly, I was no longer offended by the glitz that I had fled, the Strip seeming to glitter with the promise offered by other exotic cities that I had visited all over the world. I was, once more, enchanted.

When I moved back from Bozeman for good, the Luxor, one of my favorite buildings, was under construction and I risked life and limb every morning as I tried to simultaneously drive and gawk at the construction of the giant, peculiarly western looking sphinx that guards the gates. Not for centuries had anyone viewed such construction. More recently, my stop light stops were made interesting as the skyline of New York, New York rose before my eyes. I am addicted to the change and give a silent cheer when an old structure such as the Dunes makes way for the new, for Las Vegas is about creating new versions of the past, not creating history by preserving outworn hotels. I would guess that many in our community are as addicted to this change as I am.

In Bozeman, where only the seasons are allowed to change, I became desperate enough to, for the first time, subscribe to cable television and found myself glued to the set seeking stimulus. It's a truism that searching makes the pattern appear and as I surfed channels, a pattern appeared.

Suddenly the range of popular culture images from the films that had formed so many of my attitudes in rural Wisconsin and are now firmly lodged in my memory were present again, juxtaposed with the present. With a click of the remote, Claudette Colbert as Cleopatra gloried in her milk bath; another click brought the Rodney King beating, another George Raft as a mob hero, another the Gulf War, another Charleton Heston in a chariot race, another a basketball game. Each click unites past and present in an absolute equality, providing the same general effect as viewing a painting done without perspective in which all elements are weighted equally.

Captured on the screen was the world of the forties, where a dime and a trip to the local movie house opened the way to what I thought was the real world. Suddenly in middle age, I was viewing all the films that had made such an impression on me as a child, and living in a house the same vintage as the one I grew up in Wisconsin. Time had lost its linearity, as the popular culture images of my childhood passed before my eyes. Claudette flirted and died as Cleopatra; Busby Berkeley dancers pranced through art deco sets; Rome fell; knights jousted; cowboys cowboyed; pirate ships battled and sank; volcanoes erupted on tropical islands; and golly gee, it was just like home—Las Vegas that is.

That same non-linearity that exists in memory and cable TV is present in the configuration of the Las Vegas Strip. Wandering it is like flipping channels. The Luxor with its laser-eyed sphinx welcomes the tourist to a version of ancient Egypt that Egypt's early residents would probably have loved. Next door the Excalibur, that wonderfully goofy castle, which has been compared to something by Disney on acid, welcomes the tourist with a chance to pull the sword from the stone (remember King Arthur), although in this case the stone is a slot machine, or to watch a jousting match while partaking of a medieval banquet, and later take the elevator to the medieval village. When that palls, one can move to Caesar's Palace where a robot Bacchus in Caesar's Forum welcomes visitors under a glitter of laser lightning, while other ancient gods revolve and lift their cups in tribute to the tourist. Mirroring ancient Rome and perhaps one of C. B. DeMille's epics, the Forum's marble floors reflect the ceiling, a seemingly ceaselessly changing blue sky which moves from morning to evening. In the Forum, dwarfed by massive columns surmounted by even more statues, tourists are sprayed by fountains as they sample the expensive shops or dine at Spagos. Downstairs is an arcade where among other things one can sample virtual reality, if the Strip isn't virtual reality enough.

Inside the casino Megabucks stands at several million dollars. Rome may have fallen, but it's been recycled here in all of its corrupt glory, and you get the feeling that the original Forum's crowds would be right at home here.

Emerging from ancient Rome, one hears the toot of Harrah's nineteenth-century riverboat moored in the sand across the Strip next to the Oriental splendors of the Imperial Palace. Elvi, flying or otherwise, appear in many guises, another example of iteration. Back across the street, the volcano goes off outside Steve Wynn's Mirage, while inside Seigfried and Roy's bored white tigers ignore gaping visitors, while waiting for the next show. At Bally's, Busby Berkeley dancers go through their routines. Walk or drive a little further and a Spanish galleon and a pirate ship duel at regular intervals, one of them listing and sinking after a colorful battle outside Treasure Island, shades of swashbucklers such as Tyrone Power and Errol Flynn. New York, New York is completed, and the Sands has been demolished to make way for another exercise in imagination, or another iteration, depending on how you see it.

So here it is, my community, more blatantly than many others, an example of iteration and feedback, the continual reabsorption or enfolding of past occurrences. Whether in rolling storm systems, in the constant retelling of events through historians' ever-changing eyes, in the fictionalization of times and events in films, novels, and television, in the vagaries of memory, the recycling replacement of our bodily cells, or in the creation of the Las Vegas Strip, the past recycles into the present in an altered form. Contrary to popular belief, even those who study history are doomed to relive it.

What has this to do with community? Probably more than is readily perceived. For those of us in Las Vegas, even those of us who seldom venture into casinos unless escorting visiting relatives, the ceaseless evolution of the Strip is the basis of community and camaraderie. Whether we discuss the good old days when the mob ruled and some feel the place was safer, or argue the merits of leveling the Dunes or the Sands, whether we watch the building of the sphinx or the addition of a compressed New York to our skyline, we are all drawn together in one heck of a ride.

In Las Vegas, old timers don't gather around a cracker barrel, but in casino lounges to regale each other with tales of "Bugsy" and the "Good Fellas," swapping critiques as to the accuracy of the films, while current residents debate the accuracy of such films as "Leaving Las Vegas" and delight in the realization that they aren't in Kansas anymore. Old fellas, good fellas, newcomers and I always find community, and a bit of glamour, in discussing Las Vegas, our home town.

REFERENCES

Briggs, John and David F. Peat. *Turbulent Mirror: An Illustrated Guide to Chaos and the Science of Wholeness.* New York: Harper and Row, 1989.

Peat, F. David, *The Philosopher's Stone: Chaos, Synchronicity, and the Hidden Order of the World.* New York: Bantam, 1991.

At the Enchanted Palace

STEPHEN LIU

Las Vegas, ah Las Vegas,
entertaining me with naked girls,
charging me $3.50 for a soft drink,
in the jittery jazz, in the agitating sparkles.

Through my Roentgen-ray eyeglasses,
I see a galaxy of skeletons tumbling
on the moonlit floor: they spur my flesh,
they kick out dust into my face.

In a few hours I've idiotically hurled away
more dollars than my father gleaned for a
month down the Nevada gold mines . . .
I can hear him flipping over in his sand bed,

and as I drain my last cup and stagger out
that sepulchre-dim cabaret, my hair and my hand
smell nitric acid. The afternoon sun blinds me.
Over my Puritan conscience I nauseously vomit.

*"An old, old desert rat," as he often describes himself, Steve S.
N. Liu teaches at the Community College of Southen Nevada.
His translations and poems have appeared in a number of
literary magazines and high school and college texts in China
as well as the United States.*

Sim(ulacrum) City

SHAUNANNE TANGNEY

Coming west across the blasted earth of the Nevada desert, my companion asleep in the seat beside me, I temporarily forget the desert's precariousness, the brief range of mountains we have to climb, and all of this intensified, traveling as we are in a 1973 Volkswagen bus that is missing more parts than it is running on, and my mind fixes on that place beyond that awaits us. Eventually, we turn off the two-lane blacktop that serves as highway 447 and onto I-80; we pick up the Truckee River in a few miles and travel with its slender silver thread weaving up close and then darting away again from the freeway, its own ontology evident. The mountains fade into hills, a scrub of suburbia, and then you see it: Reno, Nevada. It seems right, after such a mental forty days and forty nights in the desert, to come upon such a Cibola. It's faith that drives us across the desert, just as it's faith that leads us to build churches and cathedrals, temples and synagogues and pagodas. Again it's faith that leads us to fill them with crucifixes and menorahs, candles and censers and oranges. Representations, signifiers—but faith is always a wager, and ours is the bet that the icons we build, and even more so that the rituals we perform at their feet, mean something. That something is God, and the biggest bet we make is ultimately that God guarantees the meaning of its own images. So after such a mythic and treacherous journey—even

Having recently completed her dissertation on postmodern apocalyptic American literature at the University of Nevada, Reno, ShaunAnne Tangney now teaches American literature, literary criticism, and creative writing at Minot State University in Minot, N.D. She is a published poet and a long time desert rat. She misses Nevada very much.

just returning from a weekend of camping, crossing the desert always feels mythic and treacherous—it seems fitting indeed to come upon Reno. And no matter that its churches are instant-wedding chapels, its cathedrals casinos; no matter that its temples are censered by cigarette smoke, its synagogues echoing with the chant of "C'mon, baby, c'mon!" and its pagodas dedicated with oranges-oranges-oranges, or lemons-lemons-lemons, cherries-cherries-cherries. Arising as if by magic in the arid desert of the wild west, Reno is a glittering jewel set in a ring of dusty purple mountains, an oasis, certainly God's last known address.

But what if God itself can be simulated, reduced to the signs which attest to its existence? That is, what if we've lost the bet? If in America our God is life, liberty, and the pursuit of happiness, is Reno the embodiment of the American Dream gone bust? Is it a buzzard of a city, feeding on the carrion of the American Dream? What if Reno, the neon city at the end of the road, is the end of the road? I worry about this. Like a postmodern Diogenes, I find myself walking the streets of Reno, at all hours of the day, looking for some representation of truth. Walking through Reno, morning or night, I can smell the cigarette smoke, hear the jingle of change, the jangle of bells. At night the neon is blinding; early morning, the smell of "Ham and .99" is overwhelming; noon in August and the amazing cool rushes out the always-open casino doors; noon in December, and I stop for a moment to warm myself in the equally amazing heat coming out of those same always open doors. But even all this sensory overload can't quite convince me that Reno is real. Reno seems to betoken life, liberty, and the pursuit of happiness, but what if all we have is the token? Do we trot it upstairs at Circus Circus and plunk it into the "Deathrace 2000" game? Are we caught in an uninterrupted circuit of exchange, never exchanging for what is real, but exchanging for exchange's sake? Is Reno Simulacrum City?

Reno is the reflection of a basic reality: There are real people here doing real-people things. When I walk Virginia Street at sunset, for example, I see a street filled with middle-aged, middle Americans. Baptists from Iowa and high school principals from Arkansas, they are not dressed for the heat and they clutch at their wallets and pocketbooks with a delighted fear. But once they decide on a casino and settle in at a Quartermania machine, they get the most wonderful blissed-out look on their faces, and I know that they have realized some kind of nirvana. In the early evening I also see a younger, rowdier crowd. College kids in shorts and T-shirts. Young men disappointed to discover that prostitution is illegal in Washoe County; their female counterparts secretly glad that it is. Cowboys in tight Wranglers and painfully pointed boots; young—but not naive—ladies in spandex and leather and incredibly big hair, all come to Reno to celebrate their very youth. Maybe they aren't twenty-one, but they get away with at night a blackjack table, and all the beer they can down. Maybe they've driven over from California and the thrill of what was unavailable only twenty miles ago is enough. Whatever it is, and whichever group of people you examine, they're all here to participate in the sacrament of taking a chance. They are all here at the beckoning of the giant Circus Circus clown (oh, that smiling face, that mask, that masque), who bids us drop our Puritanism, our work ethic, our ceaseless pursuit of a morality we believe inherent in conspicuous consumption, and invites us to live for the moment, spend an hour, spend a dollar. It asks us to actually participate in what we hold dear and precious: life, liberty and the pursuit of happiness.

The sacrament of taking a chance is embedded in another ritual, in one of our most sacred rites: marriage. That same walk down Virginia Street at sunset avails to me a parade of the young and in love. It is doubtless that they have just gotten married in one of *those* chapels. But it doesn't matter, for they invariably cling to one another, kiss one another sloppily, share a single can of Budwieser—they are in love—and in Reno *those* chapels seem the perfect place whereat to celebrate love. Outsiders hold an image in their minds that Reno weddings are tawdry and unreal, but that is not entirely so. I have seen, on the curb outside a wedding chapel, full wedding parties, five or six bridesmaids in pastels and hats, groomsmen in tuxedoes with tails, and friends and family galore. I have seen conservatively suited men and handsomely dressed women, uniformed men, and women in satin and frills. Whether at the Silver Bells Wedding Chapel or at the Adventure Inn, these are still weddings and they still precede marriages: they are on the order of sacrament. The bride and the groom say "I do," and make the promises of love, fidelity, and forever. Regardless of their seemingly impromptu manner, they do exchange for what we perceive as real love; they are not merely image. And after the ceremony, the bride and groom, arm-in-arm, wander off down Virginia Street, in search of their all-night honeymoon.

In the morning, Virginia Street takes on a decidedly different appearance. It is clean, for one thing. I cannot imagine when, but sometime between when I left it at sunset and my return in the morning, the street has been swept, the trash cans emptied, the windows washed, the dead light bulbs replaced. In the morning I notice Reno's working side. Dealers and cocktail waitresses, still in their hideous costumes, wait at bus stops; delivery trucks line the streets; janitors push vacuum cleaners in the open entry ways of the casinos—folks facing the reality of making a living, at minimum wage behind a craps table or at the wheel of the linen supply truck. But the gambling and debauchery continue. In the morning, you see the truly hard core—gamblers who are just going home, or just starting up, both equally gray-faced, Camel straights parting their lips. The partiers are also still about, just stumbling home, or into the next bar for the Bloody Mary that will help them survive the daylight, make it until dusk comes for them again. The daylight brings the tour busses—"Frontier Lines," "Lucky Tours"—and the tour busses bring the day trippers. The L.O.L.s (little-old-ladies) with their fanny-packs bulging with nickels, quarters, silver dollars, their timid and frighteningly thin husbands in tow. The Asians, who truly do seem to gamble with a unique abandon. At night they stop me and ask me to take pictures of them with all the lights blinking in the background; in the morning, they wearily climb the steps into the tour busses that daily deposit and pick them up at the casino front doors. It is in the daylight that I realize that these day trippers represent someone's paycheck. This seems like a good and a true (or at least truthful) image, and I like thinking of work on the order of sacrament. I make sure to smile at the exhausted dealers and cocktail waitresses, trudging out to the parking garage, and to the day trippers; I feel in this I, too, participate, in my own small, individual way, in the sacrament.

But daylight foreshadows the malefice that lurks behind what we perceive as sacramental about Reno. During the day I am acutely aware of the homeless, sleeping in the parkway along the Truckee, in the doorway of the defunct Mapes, along the railroad tracks. The city is pretty good about keeping the homeless off the streets at night—at night the neon becomes its own attraction, and folks will actually wander from casino to casino so that they can partake in the festival of lights, and the city feels that bums or beggars about spoil the scenery. I realize an irony: neither I nor the homeless have any intention of participating in the economy, the ritual, the worship that is the ceaseless business of downtown Reno. But because I am clean, well-enough attired, and even my walking gives me the look of purpose, it is OK for me to be here. The homeless, however, cannot shower or purchase new clothes; they have nothing to be busy with and therefore they are unwelcome, unwanted. It must be a supreme irony to be homeless in Reno—a town of glitz and possibility, the holy shrine of taking a chance. Here, the homeless embody the perversion of taking a chance.

The homeless make me think about the concept of Reno as home. For some 250,000 of us, Reno is indeed home. We pay rent or mortgages here, we work here, vote here, do our grocery shopping here, have our cars fixed here. We participate in co-op daycare and curbside recycling and charity auctions for our churches. We worry about which school district we're in and we wish they'd hurry up and fix the South Virginia off-ramp from highway 395. These are the kinds of things that make a place a home—a certain amount of participation, a certain amount of hope and fear attached to a place changes it to a home. But downtown Reno, really, is home to no one. In downtown, all of us are transients, but some of us have money enough to sleep inside, rather than on the streets. And, really, if downtown weren't there, would there be the car repair shops and grocery stores, churches and day-care centers that allow the rest of us to feel that participatory feeling of home? Really, Reno is a city of hotels. Big, snazzy ones with room service and valet parking, a wet bar and mints on the pillows; medium-sized, pull the car in and park it ones with a Denny's with a lounge next door; small, cheap ones with thin sheets and plastic glasses in the bathroom, hourly rates and no TV. Oftentimes on my walks, I look longingly at the Holiday Casino, the El Dorado, the Sundowner, and even though I live here, I want to spend a night or two there—swim in the pool, order cocktails on the balcony, have sex with a stranger between the often-slept-in sheets on the always-too-small bed. Like the gamblers in the Silver Legacy who sit beneath the revolving, simulated sky, I am convinced—tricked—by the sorcery that Reno unabashedly performs. My own transience is perversely celebrated by Reno's mocking "homes" that ignore their own temporariness as well as mine. Again I turn, warily, and see that which ever watches over Reno: the Circus Circus clown. That evil, grinning, neon thing actually convinces us that we can continue the moment, continue the ever-present, can catch the Dream, make Cibola our permanent address.

And I think to myself, so we are back to signs. Signs are the way we make meaning. Languages are sign systems that we learn to read, analyze and synthesize in order to make meaning. Deer tracks in the dirt are signs that make meaning. The international no—the red circle and slash—is a sign that makes meaning. We read the return of the swallows to Capistrano as a sign of impending spring; we sniff meaning out of the tracks of words that make up novels. But the signs that make up Reno—do they make meaning? "Certified loose slots." "97% payback." "American Superstars." One of my favorites runs beneath the giant mural that adorns the now-defunct Harold's Club. The mural depicts a wagon train of white pioneers being pursued by a gang of scantily clad Indians, who hide behind a huge rock out-cropping, over which tumbles a neon waterfall. The caption reads: "Dedicated In All Humility To Those Who Blazed The Trail." All of this would be ironic, and funny, if there was anything of substance that these signs satirized or parodied. But the Circus Circus clown, said to be the largest neon sign of its kind in the world—what does it mean? A sign in the image of a clown, made of glass that is neither transparent nor reflective, filled with neon, that calls us not to a circus, but an imitation circus. This circus flies over a gambling hall, which represents not a real economy, a real exchange of tokens for value (labor, material, emotional investment), but an image of an economy, an image of exchange. The Circus Circus clown wants to imagine—and wants us to imagine—a day at the circus, a day of fun and family, of laughter and thrills, of wild animals and magic. But does a gambling hall really fulfill that image? Indeed, does a circus? The very concept of magic is one of chicanery, of deceit, of sleight-of hand and connivance. I never liked the circus as a little kid. I thought it was a sham, as lacking in substance as cotton candy, which I never liked either. As an adult, I want to like Reno. I want to join in, dance around the burning bush that is Reno, but I hesitate, a bit frightened, because the burning bush does not seem to speak, but only to emit a constant stream of white noise, a hypnotic hiss that we are all too willing to accept as—meaningful.

Our weekend in the burning desert has been one largely of silence, and it has seemed meaningful. Not only the silence but also the preciousness of water, the insistence of the sun, our cars circled against what might lurk out there in the vast emptiness have all resonated meaning. Leaving that behind we have been chasing the sun all afternoon. It is dusk now, and even though I know he needs the sleep after a long weekend of camping, I nudge my companion awake. "Look," I say, as we round the last curve and Reno, warding off the gloaming with its gaudy glimmer, presents itself out in front of us. He stares at it, hesitates his answer. It's as if we don't want Reno to compare with the austere grander and silent echoing spirituality of the desert we have just spent two days in, and yet we realize that we are drawn to it, like moths to a flame. From this distance the possibility of Reno being a mirage seems acceptable, and I suppose I'd like to maintain this distance, that possibility—a mirage is, after all, the one thing we are satisfied to have exist as an image of an image. But mile by rattling mile, we pull ever closer to its seductive presence. The sun finally drops behind the Sierra, and the desert night air takes on a full measure of cool. We pull on sweatshirts, roll up windows, and rattle on into town. Into the shameless glitter that is Reno, nestled on this high desert plateau, always more poignant at night, seemingly built of neon, and like neon, that noble gas which is actually rather stable, seems always to shiver.